"十二五"重点图书规划项目：电信法系列丛书

电信法原理（中英文对照）

The Theory of Telecommunications Law

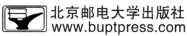

北京邮电大学出版社
www.buptpress.com

图书在版编目（CIP）

电信法原理 = The Theory of Telecommunications Law：中文、英文 / 娄耀雄著．-- 北京：北京邮电大学出版社，2016.3

　　ISBN 978-7-5635-4505-6

　　Ⅰ．①电… Ⅱ．①娄… Ⅲ．①电信－法律－研究－中国－汉、英 Ⅳ．① D922.296.4

中国版本图书馆 CIP 数据核字（2015）第 199144 号

书　　　　名	：电信法原理（中英文对照）
著作责任者	：娄耀雄　著
责任编辑	：王丹丹　刘佳
出版发行	：北京邮电大学出版社
社　　　　址	：北京市海淀区西土城路 10 号（邮编：100876）
发　行　部	：电话：010-62282185　传真：010-62283578
E-mail	：publish@bupt.edu.cn
经　　　销	：各地新华书店
印　　　刷	：北京鑫丰华彩印有限公司
开　　　本	：720 mm×1 000 mm　1/16
印　　　张	：12.25
字　　　数	：240 千字
印　　　数	：1—1 000 册
版　　　次	：2016 年 3 月第 1 版　2016 年 3 月第 1 次印刷

ISBN 978-7-5635-4505-6　　　　　　　　　　　　　　　　　　　定价：30.00 元

·如有印装质量问题，请与北京邮电大学出版社发行部联系·

序

人类的发展离不开对稀缺资源的依赖。当科技把人从对一种稀缺资源的依赖中解放出来后，人类就会陷入对另一种稀缺资源的依赖。于是，一个哲学问题出现了：科技真的能带给人自由吗？我们看到的满眼都是科技带来的资源依赖症！我们已经离不开石油、空气清洁器、高楼大厦、瓶装饮用水了。如果说，摆脱对人的依赖的代价是对自然资源的依赖，那么，面对资源有限、欲望无穷的现实，争抢无法避免。这时，法律就要出场了，它可以被看作是对稀缺资源的一种权威性分配技术，受到公平、平等、效率等价值目标（统称为正义）的约束。

以电信法为例，当有线电话依赖于电信管网资源时，分配这种资源的法律表现为共建共享、地理唯一通道的强制开放、接入和互联互通的制度设计；当无线通信技术把人类从对管网资源的依赖中解放出来后，如何分配稀缺的频谱带宽和卫星轨道又成为了法律不得不面对的难题，于是频谱和卫星轨道分配制度应运而生。面对管网有限、频谱带宽和卫星轨道稀缺的现实，电信从诞生之日起就无法摆脱自然垄断的特征，法律能做的只是通过制度设计——通常表现为将规制经济学的研究成果固化为电信管制规则，在自然垄断的环境下最大限度地模仿竞争的效果。

在技术的推动下，法律从来就不缺少话题。技术可以改变人类所依赖的资源，但无法改变人类对资源的依赖。于是，面对科技刺激出来的更大的欲望和资源日益稀缺的矛盾，作为分配、流转、利用资源和协调利益的工具，法律必须日日新、又日新。

相对于传统法学的"问题推动"，科技法学往往是"技术推动"的。如果说传统法学格局已定、能研究的话题已被无数人咀嚼过，那么，科技法通常表现为科技发展引发的前沿问题的预防性研究，它只有雏形、没有定势，往往实验室的一个新动向，就会引发制度的前瞻性探讨，为科技发展可能引发的问题留下制度变革的空间。比如，3D打印技术带来的知识产权问题在这项技术尚未成熟之时就被广泛探讨；而十几年前"三网融合"刚一提出，法律课题已经跟进。

规制经济学喜欢使用"激励"一词，它也是电信法学发展的动力。电信法在两条路径下被"激励"着：既定法律关系在新技术挑战下面对问题的迫切性激励，以及技术发展可能引发的法律问题的前瞻性激励。前者是现实的法律问题，后者是建构的法律问题。从技术发展引起的主体关系变化中发现"法律问题"，既是电信法研究的客体，也是研究的起点。

在人类的发展史中，人们追求速度和远方的努力，既靠电信来实现，又靠电信来记录，电信技术的历史是人类近代史的缩影。然而，在技术话题层出不穷的大背景下，如何选择电信法的研究客体是需要斟酌的。并不是每一项电信"大事"，都值得电信法研究。面对市场驱动下的新技术炒作，电信法必须清醒地认识到有所为、有所不为的边界，以免侵入经济学或管理学的领地。浮躁是面向市场的技术盈利的特点，保守却是面对问题的制度变革的基调。无论多炫，或者从技术本身看多么"飞跃"，技术如果带不来法律关系的变化——引起法律问题，就不值得电信法关注。比如，去年热炒的"量子通信"的概念，以及我国正在布局开展的5G技术，并不会引起权利义务的变化——量子通信只是利用量子的纠缠态进行加密，不是传输，更不是超光速通信；5G也只是传输速率和带宽的增加，不会引起既有电信法律关系的变化。相反，能引起法律关系变化的技术应用是电信法研究的兴趣点。比如，微信增加的免费视频聊天和语音聊天功能，引起了权利义务关系的变化：当数据和语音的差别变模糊后，法律关系随之改变，一方面，监管机构行政许可的标准会调整，甚至推倒重来；另一方面，消费者与OTT (over-to-top) 之间的电信服务合同的客体，又增加了一项IP电话服务。又如，Uber等O2O（online-to-offline）电子居间的兴起，直接引发了电信居间是否应承担超越传统居间的担保责任，即与其居间业务相关的连带责任的法律问题。

本书是中英双语的电信法教材，适用对象为法学研究生。其中中文内容曾经在2010年以《电信法问题研究》为名，由北京邮电大学出版社出版，其英文翻译是我在给外国研究生用英语讲授电信法的基础上翻译的。

娄耀雄

2016年3月5日于纽约曼哈顿

目 录

第一章　电信法的概念和研究方法 1
 第一节　电信法的概念 2
 第二节　电信法的研究方法 9

第二章　面向问题的研究实例——微信中的法律问题 20
 第一节　技术引发的电信法律问题 20
 第二节　面向问题的电信法研究实例——微信中的法律问题 22

第三章　电信管制 40
 第一节　电信管制及其边界 40
 第二节　不对称管制 50

第四章　电信市场准入 67
 第一节　我国电信企业市场准入的行政许可类型 68
 第二节　传统电信特许理论及其面临的挑战 74
 第三节　欧盟和美国的电信准入立法实例 81

第五章　接入和互联互通 91

第六章　普遍服务 107
 第一节　电信普遍服务 107
 第二节　普遍服务制度中的信息披露义务 112

第七章　无线电频率管制 122
 第一节　无线电频谱的特征及管制 123
 第二节　技术发展对频谱法律性质的影响 126
 第三节　频谱使用权制度构建 130

第八章　电信资费 138
 第一节　我国当前电话资费模式及法理依据 138
 第二节　电信技术发展引发的电信网络使用权的准物权特征 140

第三节　电信网络使用权的准物权特征及用户的电信网络接入权‥144
　　　第四节　确立用户的电信网络接入权及电话资费改革……………147
第九章　电信转售……………………………………………………………154
第十章　电信建设和通路权…………………………………………………167
　　　第一节　电信建设争议………………………………………………168
　　　第二节　电信通路权…………………………………………………169
　　　第三节　各国立法……………………………………………………173
第十一章　电信设施共享……………………………………………………178

Content

Chapter 1 The Concept of Telecommunications Law and The Research Method 1

    Section 1 The Concept of Telecommunications Law ································ 2

    Section 2 The Approach of Telecommunications Law Reserch ·················· 9

Chapter 2 An Example of The Research Method Orientating to Question:
The Legal Problems in WeChat 20

    Section 1 Legal Problems Caused by Developing of Technology ············· 20

    Section 2 Cases Research in Telecommunications Law—The Legal Problems in Wechat ·· 22

Chapter 3 Telecom Regulation and Asymmetric Regulation 40

    Section 1 Telecom Regulation and its Boundary ································· 40

    Section 2 Asymmetric Regulation ·· 50

Chapter 4 Telecom Market Access 67

    Section 1 The Classifications of Telecom Market Access in China ·········· 68

    Section 2 The Concept and Challenges of Traditional Telecom Special Pormission ·· 74

    Section 3 The Specific Legislation Cases in EU and USA ···················· 81

Chapter 5 Access Network and Interconnection 91

Chapter 6 Universal Service 107

    Section 1 Telecom Universal Service ··· 107

    Section 2 The Information Disclosure Duty in The Universal Service Institution ·· 112

Chapter 7 Radio-frequency Control 122

    Section 1 The Characteristics and Regulations of Radio-frequency Spectrum ·· 123

Section 2 The Development of Technology Effects The Legal Characteristic of Radio-frequency Spectrum ·················· 126

Section 3 The Structure of Spectrum Right ······································ 130

Chapter 8 Telecom Service Price 138

Section 1 Our Country's Current Telecom Tariff Mode and Legal Basis ··· 138

Section 2 The Quasi-right Characteristic of Telecommunications Network Caused by the Development of Technology ················ 140

Section 3 The Attribution of Quasi-right in Rem of Telecom Network and Users' Access Right to Telecom Network ··················· 144

Section 4 Establishing Users' Right of Access to Telecom Network and Phone Tariff Reform ································· 147

Chapter 9 Telecom Service Resale 154

Chapter 10 Telecom Construction and Right of Way 167

Section 1 Dispute of Telecom Construction ································· 168

Section 2 Telecom Access Right ··· 169

Section 3 Legislation of Other Countries ··································· 173

Chapter 11 Telecom Infrastructure Sharing ··· 178

第一章
Chapter 1

电信法的概念和研究方法
The Concept of Telecommunications Law and The Research Method

[电信法是指对以电、磁手段传递信息过程中形成的社会关系进行调整的规范总和。当人类文明进入到工业社会，通过电、磁手段传递信息越来越便捷、即时、保真、低成本，围绕着这种信息传递方式，形成了广泛的社会关系，对其规范的总和即电信法。]

[在烽烟、信鸽、驿站传递信息的时代，并没有相应的烽烟法、信鸽法、驿站法，为什么到了电磁传播信息的时代，就要建立电信法？这涉及技术与法律的关系，如果技术引起的社会关系变革超越了原有规范的框架，就要修改规范，或者建立新的规范，如果技术只是单纯地提升了生活的方便性，并未引发新的社会关系，或者改变已有的社会关系，就不会产生法律问题。法律问题的产生是旧有社会规范无法规制技术引发的新社会关系或对已有社会关系的改变引起的。]

电信，虽然只是一种信息传播手段，

批注：Telecommunication law refers to the assemble of rules adjusting all of the relations formed in the process of transmission of information by electromagnetic way. After mankind entering industry society, the way of information transmission in electromagnetic form is more and more convenient, instant, high fidelity, cheap, so around this kind of information transmission, extensive society relationship is formed. The sum of rules adjusting the above relationship is referred to as telecommunication law.

批注：In the era of transmitting information by the way of beacon fire, pigeon and courier station, there were no beacon fire law, pigeon law, or courier station law, however when it is in the era of transmitting information by electromagnetic way, we legislate telecom law. Why? The reason hides behind the relation between technology and law. If the relation incurred by technology goes beyond the frame of old law, we should modify the old law or establish a new law. If the consequence of new technology is only to make our life convenient, and does not incur new relation or alter the existing relation, there is no law

但却引发了广泛的社会关系的变革，因此需要建立专门规范以规制这种信息传播方式，这些规范统称为"电信法"。非法律专业人士经常问的一个问题就是，[我国没有"电信法"，为何要研究"电信法"，还要写一部《电信法》的书？我们讲的电信法渊源，是散见于行政法规、部门规章、地方规章等多层次的有关电信法律关系的全部规范，而不仅仅指哪部"电信法"法典，正如，我国没有一部法律叫作"民法"，也没有一部法律叫作"行政法"，但却有《民法》和《行政法》。中国的"电信法"的立法已经开始了三十多年了，起草始于1980年，但命运多舛，至今没有结果，但对"电信法"的研究一直没有中断。]在此，我们从其调整对象、价值目标、与相邻学科的研究客体区别、随技术发展的变化等方面来理解电信法。

problem occurred. The law problem is caused by the inability of old law, which cannot regulate the new relation, or the modification of old relation, triggered by technology.

批注：China has no telecom law, why should we research telecom law and write a book named telecom law? The origin of telecom law includes not only the law named Telecom Law, but also all of other rules adjusting telecom relation and passed by a diversity of legislation hierarchy, which are scatted in administrative law, ministry regulation and local regulation. This phenomenon likes that, China has no the law named Civil Law or Administrative Law, however it has civil law and administrative law research and books. China has been on the process of establishing the law named "telecom law" for over 30 years, starting from 1980, but it suffers from many mishaps and no outcome until now. However, the research about telecom law has never stopped.

第一节　电信法的概念

Section 1　The Concept of Telecommunications Law

1. 电信法的调整对象

[人们在利用电信技术传播信息过程中形成的特定关系即电信关系，这种关系是在电信管制者、电信服务提供者、电信服务消费者之间发生的，主要涉及电信管制、电信经营、电信竞争、电信消费及消费者保护、信息安全。]电信法是调整电信法律关系的规范，其调整对

批注：The specific relationship, formed in the process of information transmission by means of telecom technology, is telecom relation, formed among subjects as telecom regulator. Telecom relation is between telecom service provider and telecom service consumer, which mainly involves telecom regulation, management, competition, consuming, consumer protection, information security.

象是电信管制机构、电信企业与电信用户三者之间的关系[1]。

概括起来，[电信法律关系包括四个方面：电信管理部门之间的关系、电信管理部门与电信企业和用户之间的关系、电信企业之间的关系、电信企业与用户之间的关系[2]。]其中电信管理部门之间的关系之所以成为电信法调整的对象是因为随着"三网融合"的出现，[电信管制机构出现了多个部门联合监管的趋势，明确各部门之间的权力界限成为必须；电信管理部门与电信企业和用户之间的关系属于行政监管关系，是电信法的重点研究领域，包括入门许可、价格管制、普遍服务、信息安全、电信标准和设备入网等内容；电信企业之间的关系围绕竞争和互联互通展开；电信企业与电信用户之间的关系属于平等主体间的服务合同关系。]可以看出，电信法具有平权型法律关系与隶属型法律关系共存的特征，兼具公法与私法的属性[3]。

2. 电信法的价值

在现代法经济学影响下，大量经济学研究成果需要定格为制度，这是经济法律规范的起因。[大量电信法律规范源于规制经济学的研究成果，电信法较多地呈现出对效率和利润的关注。然而，这种关注只是作为电信制度对规制经济学的回应，是电信权利义务关系产生的经济原因。作为一种具有内在价值的规

> **批注**：The telecom legal relation involves 4 aspects, relation among or between regulators, relation between telecom regulator and enterprise, relation among or between enterprises and relation between enterprise and consumer.

> **批注**：It's a trend for telecom regulators to be organized to jointly supervise. Therefore, one of them should demarcate its obligation from others'. The relationship between regulators and enterprises, as well as the relationship between regulators and users, belonging to administrative supervision relation, and being the focus research area in telecom law, includes the following direction: access permission, price regulation, universal service, information security, telecom standards and network access license for device. The relationship among telecom enterprises is concerning competition and interconnection. The relationship between telecom enterprise and consumer belongs to service contract relation between equal parties.

> **批注**：A lot of telecom legal norm derive from research achievements of regulation economics, so telecom law demonstrates concerns to effectiveness and profits. However, this kind of concern is as the consequence of telecom legal system's responding to regulation economics, and being the economic reason for the generation of telecom rights and obligations. As a kind of norms with intrinsic value, in the meanwhile of caring of effectiveness, telecom law should not neglect other values as fairness and justice, as well as the connection with other legal branch, such as reference to or restatement of concept, rule and principle from other legal branch.

---

[1] 何晓行，王剑虹．论加入 WTO 后的中国电信立法 [J]．重庆邮电学院学报（社会科学版），2004（2）：60．
[2] 王敏．论电信法的概念与特征 [J]．北京邮电大学学报（社会科学版），2005，7（1）：67．
[3] 陈新焱．论我国电信市场竞争中的新型法律关系 [J]．市场周刊·商务，2004（7）：71．

范，电信法在关注效率的同时，不应当忽略了公平、正义等其他法律价值，以及与其他法学部门的联系，包括对其他法学部门的概念、规则、原则的借鉴和重新解释。]

批注：The institution stemming from economic requirement faces a general problem, not only in telecom law, but also in any other branch of economic law, which acquires the balance between effectiveness value of economy and justice value of rules.

其实，[起源于经济需要的制度，一直面临着经济的效率价值和规则的正义价值的平衡问题，这不仅是电信法的问题，也是经济法的一个普遍问题。]任何源于经济要求的利益分配，在规范化过程中，即在立法层面，必须考虑超越效率价值之外的其他价值。利益分配或权利配置必须兼顾公平、正义的要求而不仅仅是效率或经济分析[4]。

法的规范价值在于其从形式上确立了实现公平、正义等价值的规则体系，没有规范的内在价值就无法实现法律关系主体间的公平、正义乃至效率[5]。电信法律规范中的很多制度设计都直接反映了对公平、正义等其他价值的关注：普遍服务、价格管制制度源于公平价值；信息内容管制制度源于国家利益和公共利益；不对称管制制度追求的虽然是公平竞争的效益价值，但其方式却反映了杀富济贫的正义价值。还有一些电信制度设计，似乎完全出于经济需要，但规则本身的内在价值一样应受到关注：比如，出于竞争需要的接入制度和以方便用户为出发点的互联互通制度，其中包含的接入义务的设定、互联规程的制定、互联争议的解决，都体现了对弱者保护和对强者限制的正义价值观；再比如，出于总量控制需要的入门资格许可、稀缺资源使用权许可，在许可程序、招标程序中必须关注程序自身的合理性；又如，关注电信建设效率的电信建设制度，必须考虑土地和建筑物所有人的物权，其制度设计必须平衡电信建设效率和公民私权利等多元价值，在利益平衡过程中，利益分配规则不能局限于效率本身。从这个意义上讲，[电信法律制度的价值体系超越了经济学，而带有了效率以外的多重价值。]

批注：The telecom legal value system extends beyond economy and possesses diversity values, as well as effectiveness.

3. 与相邻学科研究客体的区别

由于"电信"的技术外延不同，电信法的研究客体存在广义和狭义之分。[广义的电信指以电磁方式传递或接收信

批注：The telecommunication, in generally, refers to communication by means of transmission and reception information with electromagnetic way.

---

[4] 王压非，张剑军.法律经济学效率理念缺陷分析[J].商场现代化，2009，2（5）：272.
[5] 张文显.法理学[M].3版.北京：法律出版社，2007：293-350.

号的通信方式,包括广播、电视、电话、互联网等各种使用电磁方式的通信手段,]而不论传播路径是由发信者选择收信者(如电话、电子邮件),还是由收信者选择发信者(如广播、电视、互联网网页浏览);不论传输路径是单向的(如传呼),还是双向的(如电话);不论传输介质是双绞线、五类线,还是光纤;也不论传输内容是语音(如电话),还是数据(如计算机通信)。[广义的电信也称为通信,包括狭义电信、广播、电视、网络。狭义的电信,是指由发信者选择收信人和信息内容的电磁传输,比如电话(固话、移动电话、卫星通信)和电子邮件,而排除了发信者向不特定公众传输、由收信者选择接受的信息传播方式,如广播、电视、互联网网页浏览[6]。]需要特别说明的是,电子邮件属于狭义电信范畴,因为收信人由发信人指定;但互联网网页浏览不属于狭义电信,因为其路径不是由发信者选定,而是由收信者选择,其类似于广播,是向不特定的人发送并由接收者选择路径或内容接收的。

[各国电信法律规范一般采纳"电信"广义外延,比如我国《电信条例》[7]以及美国1996年电信法。以后者为例,其定义的"电信(telecommunications)""是指在使用人(user)指定的两点或多点之

> 批注:The general telecommunication concept, also called communication, includes narrowly defined telecommunication, as well as broadcast, television and internet. The narrowly defined telecommunication refers to the electromagnetic communication, in which sender designates the recipient and transmission content, such as telephone (line phone, mobile phone and satellite phone) and E-mail, excludes the way of the sender broadcasting to non-specific public and the recipient choosing the transmitted content, such as broadcasting, television and internet web browsing.

> 批注:Telecom law of various countries applies the concept of Telecommunication as its general denotation, such as Chinese Telecommunication Regulations and the Act of Telecommunications (1996) of USA. We use the latter as an example. In Act of Telecommunications, "The term 'telecommunications' means the transmission, between or among points specified by the user, of information of the user's choosing, without change in the form or content of the information as sent and received."(47 USC sec 3(a)(2)(48))
>
> In the definition above, 'User' includes not only sender, but also recipient. This definition show us 3 characteristics about general definition of Telecommunication as following, (1) the transmission route is designated by users, either sender or recipient; (2) the transmission content is designated by users, either sender or recipient; (3) the form and content of the information is not changed before transmission and after receipt.

---

[6] Charles H, Kennedy. An Introduction to U.S. Telecommunications Law. 2nd ed. Massachusetts: Artech House, Inc., 2001.

[7] 我国《电信条例》第二条"本条例所称电信,是指利用有线、无线的电磁系统或者光电系统,传送、发射或者接收语音、文字、数据、图像以及其他任何形式信息的活动。"

间传输由使用人（user）选定的信息，发送和接受的信息在形式上或内容没有改变[8]。"其中使用人（user）既包括发信者也包括收信者。上述定义表明了广义电信的三个特征：其一，发送路径为使用人（发信者或收信者）指定的两点或多点之间；其二，发送的信息内容由使用人（发信者或收信者）选定；其三，发送和接受的信息在形式上或内容没有改变[9]。]在"电信"做广义解释的语境中，"电信服务"自然也有了广义的外延，如美国1996年电信法将"电信服务（telecommunications service）"定义为："无论使用何种设备，直接向公众，或者如同直接向公众一样可以被有效获得地向某用户群体，有偿提供电信[10]。"其具有三个特征：有偿、向公众提供、无论使用何种设备[11]。

> 批注：Taiwan researchers tend to separate telecom apart from broadcast according to the following criterion: telecom is bi-directional (two-way) and one-to-one transmission, and broadcast is unidirectional (one-way) and one-to-many transmission. In the traditional regulation framework, which makes dual separation between telecom and broadcast. Any form of one-way and one-to-many transmission is classified into broadcast domain, and accepted the jurisdiction of Radio Television Law, Cable Television Law, Satellite Television Law, according to its transmission mode. Any form of two-way and one-to-one transmission is classified into Telecom domain, and accept the jurisdiction of Telecom Law.

[台湾学者倾向于根据传输是"双向、一对一"还是"单向、一对多"来区分电信和广播，将后一种传输模式归类为传播、前一种传输模式归类为电信，"在传统的电信/传播二元化的管制框架下，凡是属于单向、一对多的通信媒介均被归类为传播的范畴，并且照其所使用平台的性质分别接受无线广播电视法、有线广播电视法、卫星广播电视法的管制。而凡是属于双向、一对一的通信媒介则被归类为电信的范畴，须接受电信法的管制[12]。"]

---

[8] 47USC sec 3(a)(2)(48) "TELECOMMUNICATIONS- The term 'telecommunications' means the transmission, between or among points specified by the user, of information of the user's choosing, without change in the form or content of the information as sent and received."

[9] Sharon K, Black. Telecommunications Law in the Internet Age. San Francisco: Morgan Kaufmann Publishers, 2002: 62.

[10] 47USC sec 3(a)(2)(51) "TELECOMMUNICATIONS SERVICE- The term telecommunications service' means the offering of telecommunications for a fee directly to the public, or to such classes of users as to be effectively available directly to the public, regardless of the facilities used.'"

[11] Sharon K, Black. Telecommunications Law in the Internet Age San Francisco: Morgan Kaufmann Publishers, 2002: 62.

[12] 黄宗乐. 数位汇流趋势下之竞争法与竞争政策[M]//范建得. 电信法制新纪元——全国资讯通信法律研讨会论文集. 台湾：台湾元照出版公司，2003: 82-83.

[电信法教材一般采纳电信的狭义解释，故其不包括广播法、有线电视法、网络法内容。广播法、有线电视法属于传播法或媒体法研究的客体，而网络法的研究客体独立出来由专门的网络法研究。然而，这种界限在三网融合的背景下面临模糊化的趋势。在传统上，通信业是按照不同的技术平台、不同的产业部门而建立相应的法律秩序的[13]。三网融合后，广义电信（通信）和狭义电信的区分变得模糊，技术的发展对以传播平台为基础的归类管理提出了挑战。]

另外需要说明的是，虽然电信服务和信息服务都属于电信法律规范的客体，但二者具有独立的范畴[14]，区别在于：[电信服务指提供电信网络硬件的物理接入服务；而信息服务，按照美国1996年电信法的解释[15]，是有关信息本身的生产、获取、存储、改变（存储形式和代码方式）、处理、检索、使用的服务。电信法学仅将电信服务纳入其研究客体，而将信息服务留给信息法或大众传播法学研究[16]。]

4. 电信法随技术发展的变化

电信规范应当与电信技术变革产生

> 批注：Most of telecom textbooks adopt the narrow definition of Telecom concept. So they might not involve the content of Broadcast Law, Cable TV Law, Cyber Law. Broadcast Law and Cable TV Law is the research object of broadcast law or media law, meanwhile, the research object of cyber law is owing by a separate branch--cyber law. However, this kind of demarcation is becoming increasingly blurred, in the background of three networks convergence, which means integration of telecom network, cable TV network and internet network. Traditionally, the communication business establishes corresponding legal order according to the different technology platform and transmission sector. After the convergence of three networks, the demarcation between broad and narrow Telecom concept would became blurred. The development of technology challenges the system of classified management based on transmission platform.

> 批注：Telecom service refers to physical access service to telecom network hardware, meanwhile, according to Telecommunication Act of USA (1996), "The term 'information service' means the offering of a capability for generating, acquiring, storing, transforming, processing, retrieving, utilizing, or making available information via telecommunications, and includes electronic publishing, but does not include any use of any such capability for the management, control, or operation of a telecommunications system

---

[13] 荀爱华. 论我国反垄断法在三网融合中的适用 [J]. 南京财经大学学报，2009（1）:5-8.

[14] Charles H, Kennedy. An Introduction to U.S. Telecommunications Law [M]. 2nd ed. Massachusetts: Artech House, Inc., 2001: 118.

[15] 47USC sec 3(a)(2)(41) INFORMATION SERVICE- The term 'information service' means the offering of a capability for generating, acquiring, storing, transforming, processing, retrieving, utilizing, or making available information via telecommunications, and includes electronic publishing, but does not include any use of any such capability for the management, control, or operation of a telecommunications system or the management of a telecommunications service.

[16] Charles H, Kennedy. An Introduction to U.S. Telecommunications Law [M]. 2nd ed. Massachusetts: Artech House, Inc., 2001: 139.

良性互动，发挥制度对技术和市场的促进作用[17]。[电信法，作为调整电信技术引发的社会关系的规范，必须对电信技术的发展变化做出回应。]电信法律关系的基本结构是稳定的，但具体的制度规则又是随技术发展而变化的。监管者和运营商之间以管制为基础的行政法律关系、运营商之间的受到政府管制的竞争法律关系、运营商和消费者之间的合同法律关系是稳定的，这是电信法的基础法律关系。另一方面，具体的电信法律规范又是变化的。[电信技术的发展可能产生新的电信法律关系，比如无线通信引发了频率使用权许可的法律关系、互联网技术催生了网络法律关系，需要建立专门制度（如频率使用权拍卖、网络侵权归责原则）用以规范之；电信技术的发展也可能改变了原有的电信法律关系，需要修正原有规范以应对技术发展，比如，波分复用技术的出现使得电信网络资源不再稀缺，甚至严重过剩，原有的电信资费模式所依据的租赁权理论不再适用新技术条件下的电信网络环境，电信网络使用权表现出准物权属性，建立于准物权理论之上的电信网络使用权许可制度，即包月制，是制度对技术发展的回应。]

特别是进入 21 世纪后，电信技术的飞速发展不仅使得电信传输效率剧增，也使得电信产业的边界进一步模糊。脉冲编码（PCM）技术可以实现在一对电线中同时传送多路呼叫。网络的出现模

or the management of a telecommunications service." (47USC sec 3(a)(2)(41))
Telecom law includes telecom service in its research field, and excludes information service, which Information Law or Mass Communication Law takes in as their object.

批注：As a kind of norm, adjusting social relationship initiated by telecom technology, telecom law should response to the telecom technology development.

批注：The development of telecom technology could generate new telecom legal relationship, such as radio communication incurring legal relation concerning permission of the right to use of frequency, internet giving birth to cyber law relation, which requires as to establish specific system, such as selling the right to use frequency in auction, the principal of liability attribution for internet tort. The development of telecom technology could alter the existing telecom legal relationship, which requires modifying the existing norm to response to the technology development. For example, the technology of wavelength-division multiplexing (WDM) makes the telecom network resource no longer scarce, and even badly surplus, which causes that, the leasehold (rental right, right of lease) theory, based by telecom service price mode, is no longer fit for the telecom network environment created by new technology. The right of use of telecom network has the nature of quasi-property (similar to jus ad rem, or real rights). The system of permission to apply (access permission) to using the telecom networks, i.e. flat-rate system (fixed rate plan), based on the theory of quasi-property, is the system's response to technology development.

---

[17] 陈新淼. 论我国电信市场竞争中的新型法律关系 [J]. 市场周刊·商务，2004（7）：69.

糊了语音和数字的概念；综合业务数字网（ISDN）可以用同一网络传送语音、数字、视频；调制解调器（Modem）使得语音网传送数字信号；网络电视（IPTV）使得数字网传输视频；网络电话(VoIP)使得数字网(互联网)传送语音。最为典型的是[三网融合的出现、移动业务替代固话、数据业务替代语音成为趋势。技术与产业的发展对立法也产生了深刻的影响[18]。]如果既有的电信法律规范不能靠扩大法律概念的内涵或者法律解释来应对技术变革，比如3G技术的出现对电信运营商的管道商归责原则提出了挑战[19]，就需要修改法律或者制定新法，否则电信法律制度不仅对电信监管带来困难，而且会影响到未来电信业的发展[20]，违背了法律促进社会进步的初衷。

批注：It's a trend, that tri-networks convergence will be realized, mobile phone will replace fix-line phone, and digital business will replace voice service. The development of technology and business has made a far-reaching impact to legislation.

第二节　电信法的研究方法

Section 2　The Approach of Telecommunications Law Research

[虽然电信法的大量规范起源于经济学研究成果，但电信法不能局限于在法律语境下重复经济学命题，]它必须发现特有的研究内容。电信法既要关注电信法律关系背后的多元价值，通过精确的制度设计平衡多元利益，[又要以权利义务关系为主要研究内容，]避免过多论述经济学、电信管制史、电信技术、信息

批注：Although a lot of rules of telecom law derived from the achievements of economy research, telecom law should not confine itself to repeating economy proposition in law context.

批注：Telecom law should assume rights and obligations as its main research content, avoiding to talking about non-legal topic excessively, such as economy, history of

---

[18] 续俊旗.法律法规研究领域深度观察[J].现代电信科技，2009，39（3）：22.
[19] 美国通过判例确立了电话运营商的管道商归责原则，电话运营商仅提供信道，不对里面的信息内容承担任何责任，就如同污水管道商仅维护管道的物理连接畅通，对里面的污水不承担责任一样。这种归责原则形成于有线电话时代，有线电话侵权范围小、扩散面窄，而3G时代，手机的技术定位已经远远超过了电话接收器，向数据终端趋近，类似于计算机终端，不仅仅是语音终端，因此，应给电话运营商适用网络运营商的归责原则——安全岛责任，或更加严格的归责原则，而不再维持管道商的归责原则。这种归责原则在我国治理手机传播的垃圾短信、病毒、黄色信息过程中，对手机运营商归责时，已经开始适用。
[20] 曾剑秋，钟伏初.从《电信法》到《通信法》—英国电信立法给中国的启示[J].当代通信，2006，13（9）：117.

传播学等非法学内容。电信法研究进路的起点是发掘法律问题。]

1. 关注电信法律关系背后的多元价值

[电信法的价值在于规范电信市场秩序、保护公平交易、保护平等竞争、保障电信网络和信息安全[21]。]电信规范体系的制定不仅要兼顾行业管理，而且要促进电信技术发展和电信市场繁荣，保护电信用户的合法权益[22]。电信法律规范的评价体系中，规范的内在价值应当占有相当的比重，立法者不能仅以经济学视角关注制度效益，即法律实施后投入产出比是否最大，还应当关注由法律内在逻辑确定的规则质量，即法律体系结构的严谨性、权利义务关系的详尽程度、法律责任的公平合理等规范的内在价值指标。评价电信法律规范，不仅需要从多维的利益视角考察各主体的诉求，而且还应当在制度效益之外探讨规范的内在价值。例如，美国1996年电信法，虽然从经济学视角看，其实施效果是失败的[23]，但该法却体现了规范的内在价值，比如其逻辑严谨、反映了电信权利义务关系的所有方面，从各利益群体的多元价值目标来看，该部电信法对于资源集中的限制、对于公共利益和意见多样性的保护又是成功的[24]。

telecom regulation, telecom technology, information propagation. The starting point of telecom law research is to find legal problem thereof.

批注：The value of telecom law is to standardize telecom market order, protect fair trade, safeguard equal competition, guarantee security of telecom network and information therein.

2. 以权利义务关系为主要研究对象

电信法是以电信法律制度及其发展规律为研究对象的法学学科，电信法学具有其自身的独立性，无法为其他法学学科所替代，因而电信法属于一个新兴

批注：2. assume rights and obligations as main object of research

---

[21] 刘德良.WTO与中国电信立法的完善[J].北京市政法管理干部学院学报，2003（1）：9.
[22] 秦成德.试论我国电信法学的框架体系[J].西安邮电学院学报，1999，4（1）：63-64.
[23] [美]罗伯特·W·克兰德尔.竞争与混沌——1996年电信法出台以来的美国电信业[M].匡斌，译.北京：北京邮电大学出版社，2006：4.之所以说美国电信法从经济学视角看是失败的，在于立法者寄予厚望的语音市场并未达到充分竞争的立法初衷，电信法重点规制的本地电话接入远未产生竞争的效果，虽然本地运营商必须以受规制的价格提供非捆绑元素给竞争对手，但是，本地或长途的竞争并不像预想的充分，本地电话资费居高不下，而且更重要的是，强制接入的法定义务和过低的以成本为基础的接入费，削弱了本地运营商大规模投资网络建设和科技研发的动机；而在法律规范明显少于本地网的无线市场和有线电视市场，自发的竞争获得了管制者意想不到的效果：资费降低，服务提高、抢占了原固话的客户。由于大量客户被无线网抢走，即使自己有网络的本地和长途运营商的收入也呈下降趋势，他们盈利的主要方式是利用自有网提供宽带业务。
[24] 戴元初.1996电信法与电子传媒管制的制度演进[J].国际新闻界，2007（5）：36-37.

的法学独立学科[25]。作为法学学科，[电信法应当以权利义务关系为主要研究内容，而不是电信效益、管制历史和电信技术；应当充满法理的思考和价值分析，而不是经济学推导、电信技术解释和各国制度罗列。]

[（1）电信法应当与经济学和管理学保持适当的距离

我国的电信法论文过多地论述了制度的经济学起因，并大段地引用经济分析来论证制度的正当性，而较少涉及权利、义务、责任的法理分析。这些电信法论文更像出自经济学或管理学专业，而非法学。有法学同行认为，电信法不成其为一个独立的学科，故不存在作为独立法律部门的电信法。造成这种误解的原因在于电信法研究者没有在研究内容、研究方法、叙述语境上将电信法从经济学和管理学中区分出来。]电信法应以权利义务关系为主要研究对象，否则就会混淆电信法和规制经济学、电信管理学的学科差异，这也是导致目前我国电信法学研究偏离法学方向的症结所在。

[（2）电信管制史不应当成为电信法的主要内容

翻开美国电信法教材，大量内容是在讲电信管制的历史，尤其是对 AT＆T 的管制史，这是因为判例法国家的规则产生于判例，对判例的阐释离不开形成判例的背景。]一个国家现有的管制制度形成于漫长的管制历史中，由各时期的

> 批注：Telecom law should assume rights and obligations as its main object, rather than business profit, regulation history, telecom technology. Telecom law should regularly use jurisprudential reasoning and value analysis, rather than economic deduce, technology explanation and list out systems of various countries.

> 批注：(1) Telecom law should maintain a good distance (appropriate distance) from economy and management
>
> Chinese telecom law thesis excessively discuss telecom system's origination from economy, and extraordinary cite economic analysis to argue the system's legitimacy (justification), however, jurisprudence analysis for rights, obligations and liabilities are less involved. This kind of thesis seems coming from economy or management, instead of law. Some law researchers suppose that telecom law were not an independent discipline, therefore telecom law, as an independent legal branch, does not exist. The reason for the above misunderstanding is that, telecom law researcher have not distinguished telecom law from economy and management on the aspect of research content, methodology, and describing context (language environment).

> 批注：(2) The regulation history should not be the main content of telecom law
>
> If we browse through telecom textbooks of USA, we would find most of the content narrating regulation history, especially the history of regulating to AT＆T. The reason is that case law countries' rules are derived from case, so it's impossible to describe the rules without telling about the case background.

---

[25] 孙占利．电信法学探略[J]．河北经贸大学学报（综合版），2004，4（1）：35-38．

管制措施进化而来。因而，完整评价现有管制制度，不能回避形成其的历史条件，以及被其淘汰的其他管制制度的社会和技术背景。这似乎给人一种错觉，电信管制史应是电信法的主要内容。然而，[作为法学学科，电信法应从程序和实体的角度研究权利、义务，避免过多论述电信管制史。]即使电信规制和特定历史环境无法分开，历史研究的方法是电信法研究的方法之一[26]，历史分析也不是法学的主要研究方法，[历史只能作为背景介绍，不应成为重点内容。电信法应以逻辑分析和价值分析的研究方法，从法学的视角重点论述电信法律关系。]

（3）电信法也不应过多涉及电信技术本身

电信制度不仅受到规制经济学理论的影响，还必须对电信技术变革做出回应。然而，[电信法对技术回应的阐释语境应是法学的，而非技术本身。有些电信法论文较多地涉及电信技术细节，似乎没有学过无线电技术、通信理论就不能学习电信法。这是技术法研究中的技术夸大论。]诚然，对于所有技术法，了解技术对理解制度不无裨益，但并非精通技术才可以研究技术法。纵然电信技术属于电信生产关系要素之一，是电信法律制度的基础[27]，技术的进步产生了新型的社会关系，或者改变了原有的社会关系，进而引起了电信法律制度的变革，但是，[电信法仍应以权利义务关

批注：As a law branch, telecom law should research mainly rights and obligations from prospective of procedure and substantive law, instead of discussing regulation history excessively.

批注：History should only be regarded as background introduction, rather than critical content. Telecom law should pay attention to analyzing telecom legal relationship from legal perspective, with the method of logic and value analyzing.

批注：The explanation context, in which telecom law response to technology, should be juristic other than technology itself. Some of the thesis explain unnecessarily technology detail, which seems that, the people could not understand telecom law unless studying radio technology and communication theory first. This judgment is technology exaggerating suppose in researching technology law.

批注：Telecom law should assume rights and obligations as its research object, while the introduction of telecom technology should not beyond the extent of making clear of the reason for legal relationship generation or modification. Telecom technology is not a part of telecom law's content.

---

[26] 孙占利. 电信法学探略. 河北经贸大学学报（综合版），2004，4（1）：38.

系为研究对象，对电信技术的介绍以说清法律关系发生或变革的原因为限，电信技术本身不是电信法的内容。]

[（4）电信法不应沉湎于电信制度比较法]

电信法也不应将重点放在各国电信规范的罗列，纠缠于不同国家的制度细节，而忽略了作为各国电信管制共性的电信法律关系。[法学的研究重点应是多元价值取向下的法律关系，而不应沉湎于各国具体而烦琐的制度细节比对。]电信法应重在分析电信法律关系，以说明权利义务产生之必要、划分之合理、处分之公允。举例而言：有关监管机构对互联争议的调处规则之研究，不应罗列各国互联裁决委员会的产生办法、表决机制等，而应重点分析裁决机构的权力来源、裁决的执行力、裁决的司法审查，以及将裁决作为司法前置程序的必要性[28]。

批注：Telecom law should not indulge into comparing telecom system of various countries.

批注：Legal research should focus on legal relationship with value diversity, other than indulge into comparing concreted and complicated system details of various countries.

批注：To research telecom law by the way of jurisprudence, we should not restrict us from legally response and justification for the achievement of economic. Even though telecom law might apply with the achievement of regulation economy and refer to its research method, telecom should research legal question by the way of legal paradigm and route, and illustrate the research achievement in legal context. It is critical for telecom law researcher to find legal question, which is the start point of research route.

3. 发掘法律问题是电信法研究进路的起点

[以法学的研究方法推进电信法研究，就不能局限于对经济学的研究成果作出制度回应和正当性解释。固然电信法可以借鉴规制经济学的研究成果、参考其研究方法，但是电信法学应当以法学范式和进路研究法学问题，以法学语境阐述研究成果。电信法研究的关键是发掘法学问题，这是研究进路的起点。]目前我国电信法研究中大量重述规制经济学的内容、使用规制经济学的研究方法，根本原因在于没有发掘出法学问题。以下举三个例子，说明什么是电信法律问题。

以电信通路权为例：为保证电信建设效率需要设立电信通路权，赋予电信建设者穿越或使用他人土地或房屋的权利。电信法面对的不仅是在不动产物权和电信通路权之间的利益平衡，还应深入探讨电信通路权的法律属性属于地役权，还是租赁

---

[27] 陈新淼. 论我国电信市场竞争中的新型法律关系 [J]. 市场周刊·商务，2004（7）：69.
[28] 对于专业性较强的电信互联争议，在司法介入之前增加行政调处置程序，可以减少司法资源过多用于专业审查，这类似于作为劳动诉讼前置程序的劳动仲裁制度。

权。如果属于地役权，是否具备从属性？需役地又在哪里？穿越"供役地"的电信管线如果可以绕道或者架空，是否说明其不属于定着物？其与"供役地"本身使用的电信管线的法律差异在哪儿？

再 [以不对称管制为例：监管机构根据特定区分标准，对不同电信运营商区别对待的所有管制手段都可以归为不对称管制，其目的是扶持新兴电信运营企业，防止主导运营商滥用优势资源妨碍竞争。] 比如，曾在天津试点过的中国移动用户可以携带码号转入其他运营商，而其他运营商的用户无法携带码号转入中国移动。[这项被经济学论证为有效促进竞争的管制措施潜伏着多个法律问题：区别对待是否涉及反向歧视？法人是否有权要求平等对待？法人平等权是否为一项宪法权利？如果说，可以对不同法人区别对待，谁有权制定这样的规则？是管制机构、政府还是立法机构？] 从法学的角度研究不对称管制，就不必将研究重点放在介绍不对称管制的产生及发展历史、不对称管制的经济和社会效益等，也不应当过于细节性地罗列各国的具体制度[29]。

[最后以电信网络使用权为例：现有的电话资费模式以用户的通话时间和距离为计费标准，其法理依据是电信网络的租赁物权。随着电信技术的发展，电信网络传输能力大幅提升，传输距离和

批注：Take asymmetric regulation for example, all of the regulation methods, adopted by the regulator to differently treat telecom operators according to a given distinguish criteria (classification standard), could be ascribed to asymmetric regulation methods, the aim of which is to support the new comer in order to prevent incumbent operator from abusing of dominant resources for impediment to effective competition.

批注：This regulation method, demonstrated by economy to promote effective competition, conceals many legal problems, such as, does different treatment incur reverse discrimination? Does the legal person have the right to require equal treatment? Is right of equality for legal person a constitutional right? If different legal person could be treated differently (unequally), which level of legislation has the right to establish the discrimination rule, regulation agent or legislative body?

批注：At last, take the right of use of telecom networks for example, the existing price mode of telecom service is according to call time and communication distance. This kind of charge mode is based on the legal theory of lease rights for telecom networks. However, with the development of telecom technology, the transmission capability of telecom networks has improved greatly, which caused that, the influence of communication distance and time to telecom service cost could be neglected (ignorable cheap).

---

[29] 比如美国1996年电信法中规定的不对称管制措施为：①地区贝尔经营长途业务和电子出版、家庭电子安保、通信设备制造等业务被附加了特殊条件（美国电信法271~275条），而这些条件其他公司是不要求的，原因在于地区贝尔具有本地网资源，为防止其利用本地网进行妨碍竞争性行为，而增加了这些条件。②为有线电视业者进入通信领域和通信业者进入有线电视领域设定的条件不同（美国电信法651，571，572，541），前者的限制较少，原因在于通信业者的竞争实力远大于有线电视从业者。

时间对电信成本的影响可以忽略不计。]这种技术变革催生了大量法律问题,有待电信法回答:[同一电信网络同时传输几乎无限路电话而互不干扰的技术背景,是否意味着,同一电信网络可以同时设定无限多使用权?是否可以断言电信网络基于实物占有和有形控制的物权特征已经消失,而具有了基于使用许可的准物权特征?如果这种断言为真,是否应当修正用户与网络所有者之间的租赁合同关系,变更为使用权许可关系?是否应当确立基于使用许可法律关系的用户接入权,在其缴纳了接入费后,可以不限次数、不计时长和距离地使用电信网络(包月制)?]从法理上讲,电信技术变革带来的福祉是应当分享于全社会,还是由运营商——技术变革的直接推动者独享?

批注:Does the fact of simultaneous transmitting of almost unlimited phone on a single telecom network without interference mean we could establish infinite amount of rights of use on that network simultaneously (synchronously)? Could we affirm that, the telecom networks' characteristic, the right of property based on that networks' physical occupation and tangible control, has been disappeared, meanwhile it possesses the characteristic of quasi-property based on access permission? If the above affirm is right, should the lease contract relationship between consumer and the network's owner, be altered into access permission relationship? Should we establish the consumer's right of access, based on access permission relationship, that entitles consumers the right of access to the network unlimited times, time and distance, in case of paying access fee(flat rate system, fixed rate plan)?

生词和词组

第一章

1. 电信法 telecom law, telecommunications law
2. 电信管制 telecom regulation
3. 不对称管制 asymmetric regulation
4. 市场准入 market access
5. 市场准入障碍 market access barriers
6. 接入 access network

7. 互联互通 interconnection

8. 普遍服务 universal service

9. 无线电管制 radio control

10. 电信资费 telecom service price

11. 转售 resale

12. 通路权（路权）right of way

13. 设施共享 infrastructure sharing

14. 电磁 electromagnetic

15. 社会关系 social relationship, social relation

16. 规范总和 the assemble of rules

17. 技术引发的法律关系 legal relation incurred by technology

18. 改变已有的法律关系 alter the existing legal relations

19. 法律渊源 legal source

20. 立法层级 legislation hierarchy

21. 用电信技术传输信息 transmit information by means of telecom technology

22. 电信服务提供者 telecom service provider

23. 联合监管 jointly supervise

24. 分清职责 demarcate its obligation from others'

25. 行政监管 administrative supervision

26. 设备的入网许可 network access license for device

27. 平等主体之间的合同关系 contract relation between equal parties

28. 电信法律规范 telecom legal norm

29. 起源于规制经济学的研究成果 derived from research achievements of regulation economics

30. 效率和效益 effectiveness and profits

31. 具有内在价值的规范 norms with intrinsic value

32. 公平正义 fairness and justice

33. 借鉴和重新解释 reference to and restatement of

34. 法律部门 legal branch

35. 起源于经济需求的制度 the institution initiated from economic requirement
36. 取得经济的效率价值和规则的正义价值的平衡 acquire the balance between effectiveness value of economy and justice value of rules
37. 价值系统 value system
38. 多重价值 diversity values
39. 通过电磁方式传递和接收信息 transmission and reception information by electromagnetic way
40. 广义 in generally, broad definition, general denotation
41. 狭义 narrow definition
42. 发送者 sender
43. 接受者 recipient
44. 有线电话 line phone, fix-line phone
45. 无线电话 mobile phone
46. 卫星电话 satellite phone
47. 网页浏览 web browsing
48. 传输路径 transmission route
49. 双向一对一传输 bi-directional (two-way) and one-to-one transmission
50. 单项一对多传输 unidirectional (one-way) and one-to-many transmission
51. 接受无线电视法的管辖 accepted the jurisdiction of Radio Television Law
52. 三网融合 tri-networks convergence
53. 根据传输平台的分类管理 classified management based on transmission platform
54. 物理接入 physical access
55. 频率使用权许可 permission of the right to use of frequency
56. 拍卖频率使用权 sell the right to use frequency in auction
57. 归责原则 the principal of liability attribution
58. 网络侵权 internet tort
59. 电信网络资源 telecom networks resource
60. 在法律语境下重复经济学命题 repeat economy proposition in law context
61. 规范电信市场秩序 standardize telecom market order

62. 公平交易 fair trade

63. 以权利义务为主要研究对象 assume rights and obligations as main object of research

64. 制度合法性 legitimacy of system, justification

65. 研究内容、方法和叙述 语境 research content, methodology, and describing context (language environment)

66. 从程序和实体法视角 from prospective of procedure and substantive law

67. 法学的 juristic, legal

68. 技术法研究过程中的技术夸大论 technology exaggerating suppose in researching technology law

69. 价值多样化 value diversity

70. 法学范式和进路 legal paradigm and route

71. 沉湎于具体且复杂的各国制度细节对比 indulge into comparing of concreted and complicated system details of various countries

72. 在法学语境下阐明研究成果 illustrate the research achievement in legal context

73. 主导运营商 incumbent operator

74. 监管机构 regulator

75. 电信运营商 telecom operator

76. 妨碍有效竞争 impediment to effective competition

77. 滥用优势资源 abuse dominant resources

78. 法人 legal person

79. 区别对待 differently treat

80. 给定的区分标准 a given distinguish criteria (classification standard)

81. 反向歧视 reverse discrimination

82. 平等权 right of equality

83. 租赁权 The right of lease, lease rights, leasehold, rental right

84. 物权 jus ad rem, the right of property, real rights,

85. 电信网络 telecom networks

86. 传输能力 transmission capability

87. 同时传输 simultaneous transmission

88. 占有权 rights of possession, occupation

89. 所有权 ownership, title

90. 准物权 quasi-property

91. 接入权 right of access

92. 使用权 right of use

93. 使用许可，接入许可 access permission, using permission, using authorization

94. 包月制 flat rate system, fixed rate plan

95. 对立法的深刻影响 a far-reaching impact to legislation

96. 通话时间 call time

97. 传输能力 transmission capability

98. 可以忽略不计 could be neglected (ignorable cheap)

第二章 Chapter 2

面向问题的研究实例
——微信中的法律问题

An Example of The Research Method Orientating to Question: The Legal Problems in Wechat

［实证主义下的电信法研究是问题导向的，它摒弃了空谈法律架构和理论体系的形而上倾向，以发掘电信实务中的法律问题为研究的起点。只要电信技术没有停止前进的脚步，电信法律问题就会出现。正是这些问题把电信法学带向更广阔的领域。］

批注: Under the positivism, the telecom law research should be question oriented, which should get rid of the tendency of talking in vain about legal frame and theoretical metaphysics, and devote to finding legal question in telecom practice as start point of research. Only if telecom technology does not stop its forward step, telecom legal questions would not stop appearing. It is these questions that bring telecom law into a more broad area.

第一节 技术引发的电信法律问题

Section 1　Legal Problems Caused by Developing of Technology

在电信技术的推动下，电信法问题层出不穷，为了回应这些问题，［电信法沿着"技术—问题—应对—制度"的方向不断推进。电信技术通过建构信息空间、改变传统概念和规范，以及对原有管制政策提出挑战等形式，引发了法律问题。］

批注: Telecom law develops continually along the rotation of "technology-question-response-institution". Telecom incurs legal questions in the following three aspects: (1) constructing information space (cyberspace); (2) going beyond traditional concept and norm; (3) challenging existing regulation police.

[其一，电信技术建构了信息空间，这是一个不同于现实空间的新时空，一方面，现实空间的规范不能当然适用于信息空间。比如，无法用"签名"识别身份、"原件"的证据效力需要重新定义、"书面"的证据资格需要重新确认。另一方面，信息空间存在现实空间已经解决的，或者根本不存在的新问题。比如，原创作品的作者难以确定、发言者的身份模糊、追寻责任人困难、自媒体的不当言论后果异常严重等。因此，我们需要为信息空间专门建立规范，或者修订现实空间的规范，使之适用于信息空间。下面这些例子都涉及电信技术建构的信息空间中存在的法律问题：信息空间实名制是否侵犯言论自由？现实空间可以匿名发言，信息空间为何要实名制？即时通信软件是否应该为国家安全机关预留"后门"，并将密码规则向政府备案，以利于国家监控犯罪？国家的管制权与公民的隐私权如何平衡？]

[其二，电信技术在从语音到数据、从模拟到数字的发展过程中，不断向基于先前技术建立起来的概念、规范和原则提出挑战。比如，为适应4G的外部竞争环境，中国电信推出了"流量宝"、中国联通推出了"流量银行"，那么，"流量"在法律上属于什么？是无形物，还是服务？流量转让制度应当仿照无形物所有权的转让制度，还是服务合同的权利义务概括性转让？]

批注：First, telecom technology constructs the information space, which is a new space-time differing from physical space-time. On one hand, norms in physical space could not be used in the information space rightly, for example,(1) in the cyberspace, we could not use signature to identify a person; (2)the effectiveness (validity) of "original" should be redefined; (3)the "written"form is required by evidence qualification (competency of evidence) should be recognized. On the other hand, in cyberspace, there are new questions, which have been resolved or never exist in physical space. For example, (1) it's difficult to confirm identification of the author of original works; (2) the cyberspace speaker's identification is hard to verify; (3) it's hard to investigate and charge the responsible person; (4) the result of inappropriate remarks in We-Media (user-operated-media) is extraordinarily severe. Therefore, we should either establish specific norms for cyber space, or modify the exiting norms of physical space to suit for cyber space. The following examples are relate legal questions in information space constructed by telecom technology: (1) Is the real-name registration system infringes (violates) citizens' right of free speech? (2) In physical space, citizen has the right of anonymous speech, why not in cyber space? (3) Does the instant messaging software programmer have obligation to reserve a backdoor, and register its password rule to national security department for crime supervision and investigation? (4) How to remain the balance between the right of government regulation and the citizens' right of privacy?

批注：In the development process, which is from voice to data, from analog to digital, telecom technology constantly challenges the exiting concept, rule and principal based on previous technology. For example, to adapt to the external competition environment of 4G, China Telecom introduced "data flow (data traffic) treasure" and China Unicom introduced "data flow bank", then, what is the legal attribution of data flow? Is it intangible property or service? When the data flow legal

[其三，电信技术的发展向原有电信管制方法提出了挑战，]其在改变人和人、人和环境关系的过程中，也改变着竞争环境，使得原来关注某一价值目标的管制政策必须考虑多元化的价值目标。[伴随技术发展，电信管制手段要经常变化，这种变化对原有电信法律关系势必造成影响。于是，法律问题就在管制手段变还是不变、变化方案的优劣之间出现了。比如，在与OTT应用与服务提供商的竞争中，主导运营商担心自己沦为管道商，开始推广融合通信，而融合通信将带来数据与语音的混同。于是，传统电信业务分类中对语音和数据的区分管制已无意义，新的管制手段还要做这种区分吗？]

[以下以微信中的法律问题为实例，详细说明如何从发掘法律问题入手研究电信法。]

批注：system being devised, does it copy ownership transfer system used for intangible property, or integrity transfer system used for rights and obligation in service contract?

批注：The third, the development of telecom technology challenges telecom regulation method.

批注：Accompanied by technology development, telecom regulation method should be changeable constantly, that must have impacted the existing telecom legal relationship. As a result, legal questions appear, when regulator considering whether the regulation method should be changed or not, and which is better among different methods. For example, in the competition with OTT (over the top) application and service provider, incumbent operators are afraid of becoming duct provider, consequently they promote convergence communication, which would confuse data and voice. Therefore, the distinction between voice and data, that had ever been a kind of classification of traditional telecom business, is meaningless. Should the new regulation method remain this kind of classification?

批注：The following is an example to illustrate in detail about how to research telecom law staring from finding legal question.

第二节　面向问题的电信法研究实例——微信中的法律问题

Section 2　Cases Research in Telecommunications Law--The Legal Problems in Wechat

一、微信中的法律问题

微信是腾讯公司于2011年1月21日推出的一款集文字、音频、视频、图片、表情等多种媒介为一体的手机聊天软件[1]。微信建构了一个信息空间，其主要功能包括聊天（发送文字、语音短信）、朋友圈（文字、照片分享）、漂流瓶（匿名交友）、查看附近的人（LBS功能）等。在发布后的2年内，其注册用户突破3亿人[2]。

[微信的出现给语音（尤其是长途）和短信业务造成了巨大冲击，其OTT式的运营对现有法律规制体系提出了挑战，]其快速发展给我们带来便利的同时，诸多问题也凸显了出来，[其中包括：微信实名制、微信对于位置隐私的泄漏、微信收费、微信捆绑嘀嘀打车软件是否涉嫌垄断或不正当竞争（如当年微软捆绑IE销售被起诉）、微信电话本运营资质、抢注微信公众号是否侵犯在先权利（如有人抢注了"北京大学"的微信号，是否侵犯了北京大学的权利）等问题。]

批注：The emerging of WeChat has caused great impact on voice business (especially long distance call) and SMS (short message service), whose OTT mode operation challenges the existing legal regulation system.

批注：That includes, real name registration in WeChat, WeChat leaking privacy of user's position, WeChat charging, whether WeChat bundling of DD taxi calling software, being suspected of monopoly or unfair competition(the same as the sale of Microsoft bundled with IE being prosecuted), operation qualification of WeChat Phone_ Book business, squatting (scrambling register) public account name infringing prior right (for example, does someone, who squatting "Peking University" account name in WeChat, violate the right of Peking University)

二、现存观点及缺陷

有关微信实名制，2013年2月，微信公众平台推出实名认证，不经认证的公众账号将不能继续使用，腾讯官方发布公告称此举的目的是为了"打造真实、合法、有效的品牌推广平台"[3]。微信强行推行实名制，遭到很多用户的抵制，不少用户选择离开微信平台[4]。反对微信实名制的主要观点包括：（1）微信公众平台上有很多个人用户，通过微信平台和朋友分享自己的见闻，没有必要实名制[5]；（2）微信实名制是对言论自由的约束，会压缩言论空间。同时，也有许多人表示赞同微信实名制，

---

[1] 曹进，吕佐娜. 大众文化视角下的"新新"媒介探析——以腾讯微信为研究对象[J]. 东南传播. 2012（9）：36.
[2] 廖丰. 微信用户数量大增腾讯盈利122亿同比增58%[EB/OL]. （2014-08-15）http://media.people.com.cn/BIG5/n/2014/0815/c40606-25470311.html
[3] 网易科技. 微信公众平台全面开启实名认证[EB/OL]. （2013-02-06）http://tech.163.com/13/0206/15/8N1PVUIG000915BF.html
[4] 蒋薇. 再见，微信[EB/OL]. http://www.hothk.com/thread-5348-1-1.html
[5] 知乎. 如何看待微信公众平台实行实名制[EB/OL]. http://www.zhihu.com/question/20765980

主要理由有：(1) 腾讯作为私营企业，对于微信有自己服务的要求，只要这些要求无歧视性、无欺诈，就是合理的，如果用户不接受，可以选择其他竞争对手的服务[5]；(2) 微信公众账号享有比普通账号更大的权利，执行实名制也无可厚非；(3) 实名制是对企业进行微信营销的保驾护航，它能有效保护企业的品牌和产品的利益，在打击冒名顶替方面也有一定的作用[6]；(4) 微信具有点对多的传播方式，通过微信传播违法内容，其影响力和破坏力较大；(5) 早期微信公众平台注册门槛低，运营无序，此次实名使得这种无序的状态收紧，同时实名也可当作规避内容风险的一种手段[7]。

有关微信对于位置隐私的泄露，一直遭人诟病。2012年11月，随着一条微博信息"亲，别让你的位置'裸奔'啦！"的走红，微信对于基于"查看附近的人"功能产生的位置信息的泄露引起了更多人的关注。微信在定位功能中"只要变换三个位置进行定位，就能找到对方的准确位置……"[8]。微信对于个人位置信息的泄露令用户担忧，很多网站也发文告诉用户如何关闭位置服务以保护自己的隐私，但是，尚未有人从法律的视角探讨位置信息是否应囊括个人隐私、腾讯公司以及微信用户在使用该功能时是否侵犯了他人的隐私权等相关问题。

有关微信收费问题引发了自微信发布以来最广泛的争论。反对微信收费的观点从财经作家崔林的微博中基本能得到总结："第一，微信已收流量费，再收费属于重复收费，没有任何法律依据支撑。第二，微信收费无疑对创新产品进行毁灭性打击，在当前移动应用层出不穷的形势下，几天时间，微信的客户便会呈断崖式下降。第三，在互联网免费为主流趋势的前提下，微信收费是逆势而行[9]。"同时，反对微信收费的声音往往伴随着对国内三大运营商垄断基础网络的指责[10]，腾讯扮演了悲情的免费互联网卫道士角色。另一方面，赞成微信收费的声音也有充分的理由：(1) 微信占用了过多的信令[11,12]，可能会造成网络的拥堵甚至瘫痪；(2) OTT企业已经逐渐壮大，付一点点网络使用费不会成为其负担；(3) 海外同行先

---

[6] 程小永，李国建. 微信营销解密：移动互联网时代的营销革命 [M]. 北京：机械工业出版社，2013.
[7] 宋宣. 微信公共平台推实名制内容管理收紧 [EB/OL]. (2013-02-06)
 http://it.sohu.com/20130206/n365697910.shtml
[8] 人民网. 网传微信"三点定位法"可准确知悉对方位置 [EB/OL]. (2012-11-06)
 http://society.people.com.cn/n/2012/1106/c1008-19511754.html
[9] 百度百科. 微信收费事件.
 http://baike.baidu.com/link?url=sgBqhR0UlWLEGGDl039JZceJp37qSpzWF7pfHcRl4fYVrojxTwjMGOlBNMCSONI4vebdo3ce-f2BfQKpK6oERa
[10] 叶愚. 微信收费的事实与常识追问 [J]. 财政监督, 2013, 12:74-75.
[11] 关于信令，摘自百度百科信令词条："通信设备之间任何实际应用信息的传送总是伴随着一些控制信息的传递，它们按照既定的通信协议工作，将应用信息安全、可靠、高效地传送到目的地。这些信息在计算机网络中叫作协议控制信息，而在电信网中叫作信令(Signal)。英文资料还经常使用"Signalling"(信令过程) 一词，但大部分中文技术资料只使用"信令"一词，即"信令"既包括"Signal"又包括"Signalling"两重含义。"
[12] 蔡恩泽. 一场垄断与创新的较量——微信到底会不会被收费 [J]. 微电脑世界, 2013, 05:96-98.

行实践也证明，对 OTT 业务提供商收费是可行的；（4）既然短信收费，微信也应该收费[13]。

对于微信引发的各种问题，许多人都提出了自己的见解，但是许多观点并未将基本法律关系理清，以微信泄露用户位置信息为例，我国法律并没有规定个人位置信息是否属于隐私的范畴，是否应纳入法律保护的范围，断言微信泄露了用户隐私、侵犯了用户权利、用户该如何保护自己不受侵害等，缺乏了论证的根基。更有甚者提出腾讯应为隐私泄露承担一定的责任[14]。另外，有的观点并未站在法学的视角进行分析，以微信收费问题来说，赞成者认为，既然短信收费，微信也应该收费，这一点忽视了微信和短信之间存在的根本性技术差异，只有短信收费的大前提成立，却没有微信和短信同质的小前提存在，结论并不能令人信服。再例如，反对者提出在互联网免费为主流趋势的前提下，微信收费是逆势而行，微信收费会导致用户数量的急剧下降；赞成者提出 OTT 企业已壮大，收费不会对其造成很大影响等，这其中没有法理分析，甚至无任何逻辑可言，只是作者从主观出发的判断。

三、微信法律问题分析

1. 微信号实名制

> 批注：Concerning WeChat account's real name registration

微信用户大致可以分为两种：普通用户和公共平台用户（包括服务号和订阅号）。对于不同的用户群，微信有着不同的功能和吸引力，那么，对于这两类微信用户，是否都应进行实名制？

对于普通用户，其获取微信号的途径有两种：手机号注册或者 QQ 号直接登录。开通微信后所添加好友大多也源自原 QQ 好友和手机通讯录[15]。这种模式说明微信对于普通用户是一个较为私密的圈子，其信息传播，无论是通过点对点的语音、短信，还是点对多的群聊、朋友圈，影响力相对较小。这一点微信和短信、imessage、飞信等通信工具并无根本区别。对于这样的一个用户群体，并无实名制必要。同时，从追究网络虚假信息传播责任人的角度讲，后台实名制是一个很好的办法。微信建立的是对手机号、QQ 号的对应，而目前我国手机已经实行实名制，QQ 号通过腾讯公司对大量数据的分析也已基本做到后台实名[16]，如果发生侵权或者更严重的犯

---

[13] 新华网. 发改委专家：既然短信收费 微信就应该收费 [EB/OL].（2013-03-27）http://finance.ifeng.com/news/tech/20130327/7832950.shtml
[14] cnBeta. 微信助强奸 律师：腾讯担责任 [EB/OL].（2012-07-15）http://www.cnbeta.com/articles/197080.htm
[15] 通过附近的人、漂流瓶等功能也可以添加陌生人，但用户可以清晰地知晓这种方式所添加的为陌生人。
[16] 使用 QQ 校友等服务时，发现虽未自己提供真实姓名，但却可将自己的真实姓名、好友真实姓名等显示出来，那么，通过对大量数据的分析，其实 QQ 已能实现后台实名制。

罪行为，侦查机关要掌握从微信到具体个人的映射关系并不困难，那么，[对普通用户实名制的做法则更无必要。]

> 批注：It's unnecessary for ordinary users to register in real name.

对于公众平台账号，微信 5.0 推出后将公众平台账号分为了订阅号、服务号。不管是订阅号、服务号，其特点都是能向大量用户推送信息，这种模式和普通用户使用微信的模式完全不同，相比之下，更类似于微博中的大 V 和企业号[17]。微信公众账号发展速度很快，已有很多公共平台账号积攒了数万的订阅量[18]，随着更多企业[19]的入驻，微信公共平台的影响力将不断扩大，那么，如何建立信息空间的匿名自由和责任追究的方便之间的平衡呢？笔者认为，可以通过建立"政府映射式实名制"实现[20]。政府映射式实名制旨在建立一个由政府主导的实名制数据库，映射数据库的建立、维护、使用人都是政府，而非任何商业主体。各商业主体只有对数据库传入数据的义务，除非征得国家同意，并无使用数据的权利。类似微博现行的实名制度，用户在前台有很大的任意性，可以自行选择是否实名；在后台，只有政府掌握其实名信息。这样，在保证信息空间主体和现实主体之间映射方便、快捷、低成本的同时，很好地保护了用户的隐私信息不被非法利用。同时，在 2014 年 8 月 7 日，国家互联网信息办公室发布了《即时通信工具公众信息服务发展管理暂行规定》，其中第七条规定：即时通信工具服务使用者为从事公众信息服务活动开设公众账号，应当经即时通信工具服务提供者审核，由即时通信工具服务提供者向互联网信息内容主管部门分类备案。这一规定和笔者所建议的方式一样，[采取对普通用户不做要求，对公众账号后台实名（读者查不到账号真名，但监管者或其他政府机构可以）的办法进行管理。只有被授权机关才可以看到真名和虚拟名的映射关系图。]

> 批注：The real name registration system should be carried out in a way that ordinary user is not required, and public account is required to register in background, that means the message reader could not find the real name, but the regulator and other government agent could. Only the authorized organization could see the mapping relation graph, which connects accounts name with real name.

同时，微信在 2013 年底开始了对公众账号的认证收费，收取 300 元 / 年的认证费用[21]。那么，微信在收取认证费

---

[17] 一些较有影响力的人物实名认证后的拥有较多粉丝的微博账号俗称大 V。
[18] 例如微信法律类公众号"法律读库"订阅量已达 3.5 万。
[19] 例如招商银行已经开通了微信官方账号。
[20] 娄耀雄.论信息空间责任人的追踪机制[J].北京邮电大学学报（社会科学版），2010,01:12-15.
[21] 北京商报，微信公众号实行收费认证，2013-12-25：继"服务号"认证收费后，昨日，微信也开始对公众账号体系中的"订阅号"收取 300 元认证年费，认证成功后将自动免费获得微信公众平台新开放的所有技术接口，如果现有 200 万公众账号全部收费，则可为腾讯每年带来 6 亿元收入。

用后，如果发生由于公众账号信息虚假、错误而导致的用户损失，微信是否也应该承担一定的责任。笔者认为，微信应该承担一定的责任。微信从认证行为中收取了一定的费用，产生了盈利。收取费用后，微信有责任对公众账号所提供的认证材料进行实质性审查。通过微信认证后的公众账号，其公信力得到很大的提高。首先，从公众号运营商的角度讲，收取一定的认证费用后，带给公众号的是用户认可度、信任度的提升。在进行推送类似内容的公众号之间，用户更倾向于选择经过认证的公众号，这对公众号的运营有着正面的促进作用，有利于公众号吸引更多的用户。其次，从用户的角度讲，用户在选择不同的公众号接收消息时，对于来自于经过认证的公众号的消息的可信度自然高于非认证的公众号。从用户的角度看，同样来自微信的信息，相对于没有认证的信息，从认证后的公众号发出的信息，至少还有一层腾讯公司对公众号身份认定的保证。

那么，[如果用户由于该公众号发出的错误信息导致利益损失，而这其中该公众号的运营者身份在认证过程中存在着瑕疵，腾讯（身份注册人）就应该承担相应责任。]

批注：If the readers suffer losses caused by wrong message published by a public account, and the identification of that account has something wrong, Tencent (ID registrant organization) should take corresponding liability.

2."附近的人"功能中的位置隐私权

批注：The right of position privacy in the function of "Look Around"

"附近的人"（海外版的"Look Around"）是微信重点推荐的一个产品亮点，即通过 LBS 服务[22]搜索并添加附近的微信用户。很多用户担心这项功能会泄露自己的位置隐私[23]。要回答"附近的人"功能中是否存在侵犯他人位置隐私的问题，我们首先须探讨个人位置信息是否属于个人隐私的范畴。

就个人的位置是否属于隐私的问题，我国法律体系中并无对隐私边界的具体界定，张新宝教授认为"隐私权是公民享有的私生活安宁与私人信息依法受到保护，不被他人非法侵扰、知悉、搜集、利用和公开等的一种人格权[24]"。王利明教授认为"凡是私人支配的空间场所，无论是有形的，还是虚拟的，都属

---

[22] 维基百科，位基服务（Location-Based Service，LBS）又称适地性服务、移动定位服务、位置服务、置于位置的服务，它是通过移动运营商的无线电通信网络（如 GSM 网、CDMA 网）或外部定位方式（如 GPS）获取移动终端用户的位置信息（地理坐标）。网址 http://zh.wikipedia.org/wiki/地理位置服务

[23] 新华网．微信"附近的人"：使用手机地理位置服务存在隐私暴露风险 [EB/OL].（2013-07-05）http://news.xinhuanet.com/legal/2013/07/05/c_124963881.htm

[24] 张新宝．隐私权的法律保护 [M]．北京：群众出版社，2004：21，8，9，299．

个人隐私的范围[25]",同时我国已有的判例也支持这种观点[26]。那么,原则上任何私人不愿意对外公开且与公共利益无关的信息都可构成私人的秘密信息,只要个人隐匿这些秘密信息不违反法律和社会公共道德,都构成受法律保护的隐私[27]。用户在使用微信时的位置信息符合上述概念,应属于法律保护的隐私范畴。

有关"附近的人"功能是否侵犯隐私权问题,可以具体化为:用户在使用微信"附近的人"功能看到别人信息的时候也同时将自己的信息透露给别人,这样的情况是否涉及侵权?在第一次使用此功能时,微信会弹出提示框"请注意:你可以在此看到附近使用此功能的人和他(她)的照片相册(最多10张),同样你也会被他们看到。你的地理位置信息会被自动保存一定时间,你也可以随时手动清除。"用户同意此条款后开始使用"附近的人"功能,那么,此时就可视为用户同意公开自己的位置信息。并且[微信设置了"清除位置信息并退出"的选项,赋予用户对自己的位置信息的充分控制权,在使用此项功能时,不会存在腾讯公司或者别的用户侵犯自己隐私权的情形。]

> 批注:WeChat prepared with an option of "eliminate position information and exit", empowered users the right of fully control of position information thereof. That function guarantees the users private right from being infringed by Tencent or other users.

3. 微信收费的正当性问题

> 批注:The justification of WeChat charge

微信是否该收费成了当下热炒的问题[28],针对微信的收费,运营商和腾讯各执一词,笔者认为,对微信增加收费

---

[25] 王利明.隐私权内容探讨[J].浙江社会科学,2007,03:57-63,79:"第三,空间隐私从有形的物理空间转向无形的虚拟空间。私人空间传统上大都认为是物理上的特定空间,属于物权法中不动产的保护范畴,而现代社会随着互联网络的发展,出现了虚拟的空间,从而产生了虚拟空间中隐私权的法律保护问题。其实,凡是私人支配的空间场所,无论是有形的,还是虚拟的,都属于个人隐私的范围。空间隐私除了物理空间之外,还应当扩及电子空间等虚拟空间,如侵入他人电脑系统,即使不盗取信息,也构成对公民隐私权的侵犯。正如有学者所言,互联网络的开放性、交互性、虚拟性、技术性、数字化、无纸化、高效率等诸多特征已经对传统民法学的许多领域产生了重要影响,这些影响涉及民法的诸多方面,在隐私权领域尤其如此。"

[26] 张礼洪.隐私权的中国命运——司法判例和法律文化的分析[J].法学论坛,2014,01:11-19."针对一妇女因怀疑其丈夫和女同事之间有非正常男女关系而实施窥视后者住所的行为,福建省厦门市思明区人民法院(2000)思民初字第281号判决认定了其构成对隐私权的侵犯。判决原写到:'公民的隐私权是公民所享有的个人的、与公共利益、群体利益无关的个人信息、私人活动和私有领域进行支配的具体人格权。'"

[27] 同注25.

[28] 微信收费事件在2013年上半年中国电信界引起极大的关注。微信收费的起源在于中国移动公司声称微信APP过多地占用了信令资源。在其中,固然2G网络承载能力的限制是原因之一,更重要的在于APP的开发者经验的欠缺和对形式估计的不准。微信收费事件的结局是腾讯微信团队启动2.5G网络优化计划,和运营商运维部门共同探讨信令解决方案,以缓解微信占用通信网络信令资源过多的问题。同时,中国联通联合微信推出了微信沃卡,包含10元300M的微信专属流量,给微信和运营商的合作做出了一个示范。不管运营商是否最后收取了微信的费用,解决网络拥堵、实现更好的用户体验才是微信、运营商共同追求的目标。

是应该的。在微信出现之前,作为话音、数据业务的支撑服务之一——信令服务,一直保持着和上层业务的协调。但是,微信的出现打破了这种平衡,作为一款[即时通信工具,为了保持其信息的即时性,需要以很高的频率发送信令[29],同时,随着微信用户数量的不断增多,微信逐步占据了大量的信令资源,使原有的通信网络无力承受,并有可能造成网络阻塞,影响到其他正常的电信服务。]同时,

> **批注**: In order to maintain its message's instantaneity, instant messaging tool needs to send signaling with very high frequency, meanwhile, with the number of users escalating, WeChat gradually occupies too much signaling resource for the existing communication network to endure, which would cause the network congestion, and influence other normal telecommunication serives.

从技术的角度,微信占用过多的信令资源,类似病毒攻击[30]时占用了大量的网络资源,使得网络无法提供其他的正常通信服务。当然,我们并不能把通信APP和病毒画等号,但任由心跳信令无序增长的话,就算是把所有的业务信道变成信令信道都于事无补,而没有了业务信道又如何提供电信服务?信令风暴的根本原因在于APP设计者为了实现自身利益,或者由于设计经验不足而造成网络承载过重,在这一点上,微信存在一定过错。同时,无线网络技术是当今发展最快的技术之一,[运营商在制定接入费的时候无法预见微信等软件对信令资源的过量占用而产生对其他基础业务的影响,当时运营商以为,收取最终用户的流量费和腾讯的网络资源占用费(接入费)足以弥补网络资源成本,然而,现在的情况是微信占用了中国移动60%的信令资源,但仅带来10%的客户流量[31],这样对运营商来说是显失公平的。]

> **批注**: When setting the access price, incumbent operators cannot anticipate that the overuse of signaling resource by software such as WeChat, would influence other basic telecom business. At that time, incumbent operators supposed that it is enough to charge end users' network traffic fee and Tencent network resource occupation fee (access fee) to cover the network cost. However, at present, WeChat occupies 60% signaling resource of China Mobile, but brings 10% end-users' data traffic. It's unconscionability (obvious unfairness, apparently unjust) to incumbent operators.

那么,就[有必要重新制定将信令使

---

[29] Oasis Feng. 微信收费事件背后被广泛忽略的技术细节[EB/OL].(2013-04-14)[2013-09-29] http://blog.oasisfeng.com/2013/04/14.

[30] 比如在09、10年期间给互联网带来很深影响的ARP攻击,ARP等众多以太网协议与通信网各类信令协议起到类似的作用,在网络节点/通信设备之间传递控制信号,当信令风暴发生、信令信道被占满时,造成其他用户的通讯异常,这种情况就类似于ARP病毒占用网络通道造成用户连接断时续,而这种情况对于其他用户是很不公平的。

[31] 搜狐IT. 微信占用中移动60%信令资源 但仅带来10%的流量[EB/OL].(2013-03-22) http://it.sohu.com/20130322/n369832465.shtml

用频率考虑在内的收费标准,或者针对信令的过度使用收取专门费用,]或者促使 APP 的设计者优化程序设计、主动减少信令使用。运营商有两种方式可供选择。[其一,增加收取腾讯的接入费,以弥补信令资源的过分付出。]由于当时运营商与腾讯签订协议确定接入费时,无法估计微信发展的速度如此之快,其占用的信令资源急剧增加。运营商可在现行合同结束后,在新的合同中提高接入费用以弥补其损失。同时,在极端的情况下[32],运营商可以援引民法上的情势变更原则,或者合同法上的显失公平条款,主张增加接入费,弥补当初无法预见的微信对信令资源的过分使用。[其二,通过增加收取最终用户的流量费来弥补微信对信令资源的过分占用。运营商调整最终用户流量费的一个可行做法是区分流量[33],对于不同应用或者不同类型的应用产生的流量进行区别定价[34]。]区别定价的根据在于不同应用产生的流量对于支撑其正常传输的信令的需求不同,从而产生了数据传输中的成本差别。对于上网浏览等即时性较弱的应用,其信令成本较低;另一方面,微信应用程序消耗相同流量时所耗费的信令资源却是数倍于即时性较弱的软件。目前只以流量来定价而忽略信令资源占用,显然对于即时性较弱的软件是不公平的,会激励其在升级版中滥用信令资源。那么,[对于占用信令资源较少的应用采取低价,占用信令资源较多的应用采取高价,这种定价策略是比较公允的。]

在传统的市场经济中,价格应由市场主体自行决定,充分的竞争使价格能够回到一个合理的水平。可是,对于垄

批注:It is necessary to redesign the charge criteria concerning the signaling frequency, or charge special fee for overusing of signaling.

批注:The first way is to increase the charge of Tencent access fee, to cover the loss of overusing signaling resource.

批注:The second way is to increase charge of end users' data traffic fee to cover the occupation of signaling resource. A feasible method for telecom operator to adjust end users' data traffic fee is to classify different kinds of data traffic, and set price discriminations for different applications or different types of application.

批注:It's a fair price policy to charge lower for less using signaling resource and charge higher for overusing signaling resource.

---

[32] 例如信令风暴造成类似 2012 年日本运营商 NTT DOCOMO 东京地区网络障碍导致 252 万用户 4 小时内通信障碍、2009 年 AT&T 纽约地区 iphone 掉话率高达 30% 等情况。但情势变更原则应用的条件较为苛刻,在诉讼中并不会被轻易采用。

[33] 区分流量的方法有两种,第一种可在终端用户处直接区分,另一种是在特定应用程序的流量包汇集到增值服务商机房时进行区分。两种方式目前在技术上都已实现。

[34] 由于手机应用程序众多,按应用的类型进行区别定价更具有可操作性。

断市场，应当进行价格管制[35]。在国内电信业相对缺乏竞争的环境下，放任市场定价会导致电信运营商利用自己的垄断地位制定过高的价格，损害用户和增值电信服务商的利益。然而，国家干预应该是双向的，对于明显损害电信运营商利益显失公平的合同，也应当进行干预。对微信的电信资费可以考虑分为两类计费方法：第一，对于不占用过多信令资源的应用，如心跳周期在 15 分钟以上的应用，仍采用现行的流量计费标准。现有应用程序大多属于这一类型，它们只有在需要时才发出信令请求建立连接，对于这一类应用，并不会产生信令风暴的风险，故适用现行的计价方式并无不妥。第二，对于以即时通信软件为主的心跳周期在 15 分钟以下的应用，由于该类应用对网络即时性要求较高，会产生额外的信令成本，需区别定价。区别定价的方式有两种。第一，可以继续使用原有流量包，但从心跳频繁的应用软件中产生的流量需要提高计价标准；第二，可以借鉴国外电信公司对 VoIP 业务的定价方式，采取制定专门的定向流量包[36]，类似微信这样的应用程序的流量只能购买专门的流量包。

4. 微信捆绑滴滴打车涉嫌滥用市场支配地位

> 批注：WeChat bundling DD taxi calling application software is suspected of being involved abuse of market dominate position

滴滴打车是一款免费打车软件，是目前覆盖最广、用户最多的召唤出租车类的应用，入选"App Store2013 年度精选"[37]。滴滴打车于 2012 年上线，2014 年 1 月 4 日，滴滴打车正式与微信达成合作，开启了线上预约、线下支付的模式[38]，滴滴打车功能正式嵌入微信中。滴滴打车的崛起与微信的入主有着极大的关系。打车软件市场原本呈现充分竞争的状态，存在着数家不同的公司运营类似的软件。在腾讯公司入主后，滴滴打车得到了来自微信的用户流量、微信的快捷支付帮助[39]，例如，滴滴打车仅在嵌入微信后的 3 日内就得到微信带来的超过 10 万单的流量[40]。根据最新数

---

[35] 我国电信网络设备由 3 家电信运营商掌握，电信市场属于自然垄断市场。根据《中华人民共和国价格法》第 18 条："下列商品和服务价格，政府在必要时可以实行政府指导价或者政府定价：… （三）自然垄断经营的商品价格；"规定，若是电信运营商向腾讯收取费用，应由政府制定指导价或者政府定价。

[36] 以中国联通为例，2013 年 8 月广东联通和腾讯合作推出的微信沃卡，10 元包 300M 微信定向流量。微信沃卡得到了极大的关注，2013 年 8 月 8 日开始发售，而在 8 月 5 日首日预售中销售量突破 70 万张。同时在 2013 年 9 月，联通将此项优惠推广到所有联通用户都可以享有。

[37] 百度百科.滴滴打车.
http://baike.baidu.com/view/9487618.htm?fromtitle=%E5%98%80%E5%98%80%E6%89%93%E8%BD%A6&fromid=6853265&type=search

[38] 褚伟 2012. 连接一切之后的微信，下一步打算怎么走？[EB/OL].（2014-10-20）.
http://www.tmtpost.com/161367.html

[39] 同时，腾讯入主后滴滴打车用高额补贴拉拢消费者的行为，涉嫌交叉补贴，在此并不展开讨论。

[40] 企鹅生态.滴滴打车：微信三天带来十万单[EB/OL].（2014-01-13）
http://it.sohu.com/20140113/n393396501.shtml

据显示，滴滴打车以 60.2% 的高比例占据了市场支配地位[41]。

[借助对滴滴打车的投资，打车软件市场的后入者腾讯公司，利用自己在微信上的垄断地位，实现了对打车软件市场的垄断。这不禁使我们想起 20 世纪末，微软因 Windows 操作系统捆绑 IE 浏览器涉嫌垄断而引发的一系列诉讼案例[42]。] 微信捆绑滴滴打车，是否涉嫌类似于微软垄断案中滥用市场支配地位呢？笔者认为两者之间有类似之处，[从我国反垄断法角度分析，腾讯捆绑滴滴打车的行为同样属于滥用市场支配地位。]

批注：By means of investment in DD, as a new entrant of taxi calling application software, Tencent established the monopoly position in that market with the help of WeChat monopolization. This phenomenon reminds us the case occurred in the end of 20th century, Microsoft was sued in a series of litigations for being suspect of monopolization because one of its products, Windows operation system was bundled with IE browser.

批注：In the perspective of anti-monopoly law, the behavior of Tencent bundling DD taxi calling application software belongs to abusing of market dominant position.

首先，微信在手机端即时通信市场中占有无人能及的市场支配地位。早在 2014 年 2 月，微信每月活跃用户数就达到 2.31 亿，市场占有率达到 57%[43]。依据《中华人民共和国反垄断法》第十九条规定，有下列情形之一的，可以推定经营者具有市场支配地位：一个经营者在相关市场的市场份额达到二分之一的。微信在移动即时通信市场占有市场支配地位应无异议。

其次，滴滴打车利用微信强大的市场占有率进行了推广，极大地提高了自身的市场占有率和装机量。打车软件和即时通信软件分属两个不同的市场，在融入微信之前，滴滴打车是一个独立的 APP。在该市场中，还有快的打车等类似的竞争对手。在融入微信后，滴滴打车得到了来自微信平台的巨额流量，极大地提升了自身的用户数量[44]。2014 年 4 月 2 日，速途发布《2014 年 Q1 打车软件市场分析报告》，其中显示，滴滴打车市场份额达 60.2%，其中 2014 年第 1 季度打车软件活跃用户分布，滴滴打车以 88.4% 遥遥领先于其他打车软件。这其中，微信带来的巨大装机量和使

---

[41] 冀静. 速途研究院：2014 年 Q1 打车软件市场分析报告 [R].（2014-04-02）
http://www.sootoo.com/content/487342.shtml

[42] 维基百科. 合众国诉微软案.
http://zh.wikipedia.org/zh/%E5%90%88%E4%BC%97%E5%9B%BD%E8%AF%89%E5%BE%AE%E8%BD%AF%E6%A1%88

[43] 同时，市场占有率第二的手机 QQ 达到 39.3%，微信及手机 QQ 在内地即时通信的市场占有率（以月度时间计算）合共 96%，两者同样来源于腾讯公司。腾讯完成了对移动即时通信市场的绝对垄断。而 2014 年 3 月 28 日，滴滴打车宣布入驻手机 QQ。数据来源大行报告，截止 2014.04.03。

[44] 数据显示，从 2014 年 1 月 10 日滴滴刚接入微信至 2014 年 3 月末，3 个月内滴滴打车的用户从 2200 万增加至 1 亿，日均订单量从 35 万增长至 521.83 万，取得绝对领先优势。

用上的便捷性无疑是滴滴打车取得成功的关键所在。在合众国诉微软案中，IE 浏览器预装在 Windows 操作系统中，而其他公司浏览器需要下载使用，预装行为带来的巨大装机量和便捷性使得 IE 浏览器获得了极大的成功，但是微软公司为此付出的反垄断和解费用也是巨额的。同样，微信成了移动互联网用户日常使用频率最高的软件之一，嵌入微信，首先给滴滴打车带来了极大的装机量。所有微信用户都默认安装了滴滴打车应用，意味着滴滴打车共享了微信所有的用户，这是其他打车软件不能望其项背的。另外，绑定带来了使用上的便捷，用户无须额外再下载一个单独的 APP，只需打开微信便可接通滴滴打车的业务。

第三，用户并不享有选择的自由。能够看到在微信相应的位置，并没有选择其他打车软件的自由。进入微信钱包的打车功能，便自动进入了滴滴打车服务，用户无法从这一渠道接入其他打车软件。这一做法对其他的打车应用来说形成了不公平的竞争。

综上，[微信在绑定滴滴打车、对滴滴打车进行推广的过程中，利用自身在即时通信软件领域的优势，排他性地预装滴滴打车软件，形成了不公平的竞争优势，涉嫌滥用市场支配地位。微信在推广滴滴打车的同时，至少应在相应的位置留给用户选择的权利，预留接口可以接入其他的打车应用。]

批注：In the process of bundling and promoting DD taxi calling application software, WeChat is suspected of being involved abuse of market dominate position, because it obtained the unfair competition, using its advantage in the market of instant messaging software to preload DD software exclusively. In the meantime of promoting DD taxi calling application software, WeChat should at least give users options at the corresponding position thereof, to access others' taxi calling software from reserved interface.

5. 微信电话本的运营资质

2014 年 11 月 11 日，微信推出微信电话本 3.0，使得微信进入从文本信息、语音信息后的高清免费通话时代。此服务一经推出，便受到极大关注，截至 12 日 21 时，在短短一天内，微信电话本在苹果应用商店（App Store）"工具"类下载榜单中排名第一，在"应用宝"安卓商店中下载量共 2 268 万[45]。

批注：Concerning the operational qualification for WeChat Phone List

回想 20 世纪 90 年代，电信业还处于垄断经营的时代，IP 电话尚不能由私人运营，典型的如福州 IP 电话案中，福州公安局以涉嫌非法经营罪对 IP 电话经营者立案[46]。

---

[45] 百度百科. 微信电话本. http://baike.baidu.com/view/10847151.htm?fr=aladdin
[46] 老榕 IP 电话，曾经说案（一）．（2007-02-24）http://blog.sina.com.cn/s/blog_59179f44010006s0.html

微信电话本的发布其实是另一个技术进步引起运营资质混淆的案例。[在语音和数据业务混同的互联网时代，二者的界限越来越模糊，是否需要对微信电话本进行专门许可，是技术长足发展后的今天，监管部门应该考虑的问题。]

批注：In the era of Internet, whose feature is a convergence of voice business and data business, the distinction of which is more and more vague, the regulator should consider whether WeChat Phone List is obliged to obtain specific license, after the technology developing rapidly.

这个问题的实质是，其是否属于第一类基础电信业务中的 VoIP 业务[47]？微信电话本的实现原理在于：如果有 Wi-Fi 存在，就通过互联网用数据通信实现实时语音通信[48]，而并不使用公共交换电话网（Public Switched Telephone Network，PSTN）[49]；如果没有 Wi-Fi，则手机通过 3G 或 4G 网络，使用 PSTN 传输数据（使用电话网传输数据，类似于 ISDN 或早前的双绞线拨号上网）。对于后一种情况，没有 Wi-Fi 必须使用 PSTN 的 IP 电话，属于使用电话网络的 Phone-Phone 的 VoIP 业务，应当取得第一类基础电信业务许可证；对于前一种情况，在 Wi-Fi 环境下不使用 PSTN 完成的 IP 电话，属于互联网提供的 IP 电话，即使是通过手机拨打，仍属于 PC-PC 的网络通信（手机只是互联网终端，而非电话，类似于 Skype 或者 QQ 聊天）。

就 PC-PC 的 IP 电话是否属于第一类基础电信业务，监管者在法律规定和实际操作中态度暧昧、政策摇摆。第一，[在《电信业务分类目录（2003 版）》中，国际、国内的 PC-PC IP 电话业务都不属于受管制对象，第一类基础电信业务管理的仅限于 Phone-Phone 以及 PC-Phone，]IP 电话的定义是："IP 电话业务泛指利用 IP 网络协议，通过 IP 网络

批注：In the "Catalogs of telecom business (2003 version)", both international and domestic PC-PC IP phones do not belong to the scope of those being regulated. Concerning IP phone, the first class of basic telecom business exclusively includes Phone-Phone and PC-Phone.

---

[47] VoIP 是指互联网协议电话，即网络电话（Voice over Internet Protocol），其原理是将模拟的声音讯号经过压缩与封包之后，以数据封包的形式在 IP 网络进行语音讯号的传输，通俗来说也就是互联网电话或 IP 电话。
[48] 微信电话本的免费通话功能实际上是基于 VoIP 技术，就是将双方的语音数据打包，通过 Wi-Fi 无线网络或 3G、4G 移动数据进行传输。从原理上讲，微信电话本和 QQ 语音聊天无本质的却别。
[49] PSTN 是一种用于全球语音通信的电路交换网络，是目前世界上最大的网络，包括电话线（双绞线）、光纤电缆、微波传输链路、蜂窝网络、通信卫星与海底电话电缆，从而允许在世界上的任何电话与任何其他终端通信，依功能属性分为端局、长途电话中心局、主中心局及国际电话交换中心等，主要由交换系统和传输系统两大部分组成，其中，交换系统中的设备主要是电话交换机，传输系统主要由传输设备和线缆组成。为了适应业务的发展，PSTN 目前正处于满足语音、数据、图像等传送需求的转型时期，正在向 NGN（Next Generation Network）、移动与固定融合的方向发展。

提供或通过电话网络和 IP 网络共同提供的电话业务。IP 电话业务在此特指由电话网络和 IP 网络共同提供的 Phone-Phone 以及 PC-Phone 的电话业务，其业务范围包括国内长途 IP 电话业务和国际长途 IP 电话业务。IP 电话业务在整个信息传递过程中，中间传输段采用 IP 包方式。"第二，在执法层面，国际、国内的 PC-PC 都受到规制，未取得第一类基础电信业务许可，不得经营。2010 年 12 月工信部《关于公布打击非法 VoIP 社会举报电话的通知》中所禁止的 VoIP 电话并不排除仅使用本地网（包括 ISDN 网）的 IP 电话，也就是说，PC-PC 的电话也被禁止。第三，[在《电信业务分类目录（2013 版）》（征求意见稿）中，区分了国内 PC-PC 和国际 PC-PC，前者不受到管制，后者必须取得第一类基础电信业务许可。]该目录中的 A15-1（国内 IP 电话业务）的定义是，"国内 IP 电话业务的业务范围仅限于国内电话网络和互联网共同提供的 IP 电话业务。"而国际 IP 电话业务则不要求一定使用本地网，即使是全部通过互联网的国际 PC-PC 模式也受到规制，该目录 A15-2（国际 IP 电话业务）的定义不同于国内 IP 电话业务，"国际 IP 电话业务的业务范围包括一端经过国际电话网或国际互联网提供的 IP 电话业务。"

[在放松管制、将技术进步的福祉还与公众的大背景下，可以考虑，对于 IP 电话的监管，是否可以全面放开。]其实微信电话本并不是一个最新的技术突破，原有的 Skype、苹果公司的 Facetime 等也都基于类似的原理，实现了跨平台的即时通信。在国家逐步放开行政审批的背景下，单纯运营此类业务并无监管的必要，其是否收费、收费多少的问题也应该由市场决定。国家应该管控的是此类业务带来的流量费用的高低，因为这属于自然垄断定价。监管政策更应该保证的是在数据业务经营中，消费者如何得到一个合理的价格。

批注： In the "Catalogs of telecom business (2013 version)" (draft for comment), there is a distinction between domestic PC-PC and international PC-PC, the former is not regulated, the letter's provider is obliged to obtain license for the first basic telecom business.

批注： In the background of deregulation and assignment to public of the welfare brought by science and technology development, the plan of fully opening the market of IP phone should be considered.

6. 微信公众号名称的保护问题

2014 年 12 月 25 日，腾讯公司旗下微信公众账号"微信派"发布《公众号认证看过来，命名松绑啦》一文，公布了新的微信公众号命名规则，其中包括一条：[新注册公众账号名称将不能与取得微信认证的账号重名。]

批注：The new registered name of public account should not clash with the existed name of public account, which has been authenticated by WeChat.

这条新规的发布本意在于对已认证的公众账号的保护，但是却引发了[一些订阅量小的公众账号对于未认证的较为有名的大号名称的恶意抢注。]新规出台后，一些未来得及认证的微信大号，如"一条"等公众账号遭到恶意抢注，部分未认证的大号也人人自危。

批注：Some of the less subscribed public account maliciously register of the name of well-known public account, not being authenticated.

微信公众号名称的保护随着微信的普及、公众号带来利益的增长，已变成摆在微信公众号运营者面前的一道难题。但是，我国现行法律条文中，并无相应的处理办法。类似情况的解决可以参考美国商标注册的过程。美国商标的[注册采取使用在先原则，]即按使用商标的先后来确定商标的归属，谁最先使用该商标，谁就享有商标专用权。[微信公众号名称可采取类似的措施，谁先使用该账号名谁便享有专用权，别的号不可使用，这样有利于比较有名的大号的保护。同时，微信可以开设一个申诉渠道，对于被抢注的号，可以有申诉的机会。对于被抢注的大号，可以申请申诉，表明自己于该名称的使用以及推广较早，主张相应的权利[50]。]

批注：Registration should apply the "prior-user priority" principle.

批注：WeChat public account registration could adopt the similar measure, which is the prior user has the exclusive right of use, others are prohibited from using thereof. It's in favor of famous public account's protection. Meanwhile, WeChat could open a complain channel for the account name squatted. The owner of the famous account name squatted, has the right to complain to illustrate that he has already used and promoted that account prior to the registrant, and consequently claims for the corresponding right.

微信的新规类似我国对商号权的使用规定。商号权是指商业主体对其注册取得的商业名称依法享有的专有使用权。我国有关商号权的法律中采取登记生效主义。《企业名称登记管理规定》第三条规定，企业名称经核准登记后方可使用，在规定的范围内享有专用权。第二十六条规定，如果使用未经核准登记注册的企业名称从事生产经营活动的，将受到相应的处罚。微信公众号也可采取类似的政策，对于已经认

---

[50] 微信运营团队之后又发布名为《关于公众号认证新规，我们想谈谈心》的文章表示，永远支持高质量的自创内容，不欢迎任何"吸血虫"行为，如果有用户认为微信公众平台上已认证的公众号名称侵犯其合法权益，可进行投诉。经核实后会对侵权账号进行强制改名或封号等处理。

证的微信公众号名称，给予一定的专用权，其余公众号不能与之重名。比如北京大学公众号已经经过认证，其他公众号便不能再以北京大学为名，无法经过认证或者无法注册，能够有效地避免山寨公众号的出现。

四、结论

微信作为中国大陆用户群激增的应用程序，一直受到多方的关注。围绕微信所产生的几个问题，笔者认为：（1）微信实名制问题应区别对待，对于普通用户，并无实名制必要，对于公共平台账号，则有必要进行实名认证。实名认证的方式可以是政府映射式实名制，即由政府主导的实名制数据库，政府负责数据库的建立、维护等，商家使用数据库的资料须经过申请。（2）基于"附近的人"产生的位置信息也属于个人隐私的范畴。但是，在使用该功能时，腾讯公司已经给予用户充分的提示和选择的权利，并不存在侵犯用户隐私权的情形。（3）微信庞大的用户群和其即时在线的特点，使得其占用了大量的信令资源，造成了通信成本的差异，这其中有很大一部分原因在于应用程序设计者的经验不足。运营商可以收取腾讯额外的接入费或者调整对最终用户的收费。运营商对最终用户的收费可以通过信令用量区别不同类型流量的方式进行。同时，应用程序自身做出调整后，减少对信令资源的占用，才是解决问题的最根本方法。（4）微信捆绑滴滴打车的行为可以认定为微信滥用市场支配地位为滴滴打车提供了不公平的竞争优势，微信应在嵌入滴滴打车相同的位置提供用户可选项，使得用户能够在相同的条件下接入别的打车软件。（5）技术的发展使得运营商的资质变得模糊，监管应该及时作出变革以适应技术的快速发展。在现行的电信业务分类目录中，微信电话本可以划入基础电信业务的范畴，但在现行的技术背景下，简单地区分电话、计算机已无意义，应尽快出台可行的电信业务分类标准，避免监管政策阻挠的技术的发展。（6）微信公众号名称的保护可以参考美国商标注册过程中采取的使用在先原则，即按使用的先后来确定名称的归属，谁最先使用该名称，谁就享有名称专用权。此项也类似我国对商号权的使用规定。

生词和词组

第二章

1. 实证主义 positivism
2. 证据资格 qualification of evidence, competency of evidence
3. 确认身份 verify (confirm) identification
4. 原创作品的作者 the author of original works
5. 承担责任 be held accountable (take liability)
6. 自媒体 we media, user-operated media
7. 实名制 real-name registration system
8. 侵犯言论自由权 infringe (violate) citizens' right of free speech
9. 即时通信 instant messaging
10. 预留后门 reserve a backdoor
11. 密码规则 password rule
12. 备案 register to authority
13. 从语音到数据 from voice to data
14. 从模拟到数字 from analog to digital
15. 为适应外部竞争环境 to adapt to the external competition environment
16. 数据流量 data traffic, data flow
17. 网络流量 network traffic, network flow
18. 无形物 intangible property
19. 所有权转让制度 transfer of ownership system
20. 权利义务的概括性转让 integrity transfer of rights and obligation
21. OTT over the top
22. 长途电话 long distance call
23. 短信 SMS (short message service)
24. 公众号抢注 public account squatting

25. 在先权利 prior right

26. 优先权 priority right

27. 后台注册 register in background

28. 身份注册人 ID registrant organization

29. 位置隐私权 the right of position privacy

30. 附近的人（微信的一个功能）Look Around（a function of WeChat）

31. 信令 signaling

32. 网络阻塞 network congestion

33. 基础电信业务 basic telecom business

34. 增值电信业务 value-added telecom business

35. 最终用户 end user

36. 网络资源占用费 network resource occupation fee

37. 显失公平 unconscionability, obvious unfairness, apparently unjust

38. 区别定价 setting price discrimination

39. 滥用市场支配地位 abuse of market dominant position

40. 涉嫌 be suspected of being involved

41. 借助 In virtue of , with the help of , by means of, have the aid of

42. 后进入者 new entrant, late-comer

43. 即时通信软件 instant messaging software

44. 预留接口 reserved interface

45. 运营资质 operational qualification

46. 获得许可 obtain license

47. 属于受管制范围 fall within the scope of regulated

48. 电信业务分类目录 catalogs of telecom business

49. 征求意见稿 draft for comment

50. 放松管制 deregulation

51. 认证 authentication

52. 恶意抢注 malicious register, squat, scrambling registration

53. 使用在先原则 prior-user priority

54. 专用权 exclusive right

第三章 Chapter 3

电信管制
Telecom Regulation and Asymmetric Regulation

第一节　电信管制及其边界
Section 1　Telecom Regulation and its Boundary

[电信管制的主要目的是在不充分竞争的市场（自然垄断）最大限度地模拟竞争的效果，]这是一个经济学问题，法学作为支撑，不是制度的起因，但为制度提供了强制力。[基础电信领域是一个自然垄断行业，没有网络资源的竞争者必须从其竞争对手——本地运营商处租用基础电信资源，或者转售其从本地运营商趸购的服务，才能开展与本地运营商的竞争业务。本地运营商有很多手段在提供给竞争对手网络资源时，掐住竞争者的喉咙，比如，提供低质量的接入网络、拒绝互联互通、通过交叉补贴或征收高昂的接入费，使其同类服务的价格具有垄断性优势，而将竞争者赶出市场。这些行为成为电信管制的重点。当然，电信管制还有另外一些与其他行业管制

批注：The aim of telecom regulation is to simulate the competition consequence to the maximum extent in an incomplete competition market (natural monopoly).

批注：The basic telecom business is a natural monopoly field. Consequently, if one intending to run competing business with local operators, the competitor, who has no network resource, has no choice but to lease basic telecom resource from its competitor or resale services bought in whole from the latter. Local operators have a lot of methods to restrict their competitors service ability in the process of offering network resource to them. The above methods, include offering low quality access network, refusing the application for interconnection, setting so low retail price for the similar service, by cross subsidization or imposing very high access fee, that make their service fee having monopoly advantage to expel their competitor out of the market. All of the above behavior should be regulated

相同的目的，比如，促进科技创新[1]和维护公共利益等，但这些不是电信管制的特色，本节不做阐述。]

随着技术的提高和市场的开放，电信管制表现出两个趋势。

其一，管制对象表现为从管制主体到管制行为，比如，美国电信法对 BELL 公司专设一章（第三章有关贝尔运营公司的特别条款，SEC.271-276），日本有专门的《日本电报电话公司法》（NTT 法）。电信垄断时代需要对垄断主体专门立法，而当市场开放后，竞争环境下的规制重点是对大量电信运营商的行为进行统一规制，这要管制的对象势必从主体过渡为行为。然而，鉴于电信自然垄断的特点，对特定控制电信资源的企业的不对称管制（主体管制）仍然存在。

其二，管制者的角色，从以行政命令调控的指挥者，变为公共利益的公权力代言人。原来管制者主要管市场准入、行政审批，随着市场的开放，放松了这方面的管制；而另一方面，比如环境、消费者权益保护、公共健康和安全、劳动者保护方面，亟须政府作为公共利益或弱者的代言人，这时的电信管制开始转向信息安全、国家利益和公共利益。

1. 放松管制和反垄断

[随着自 20 世纪后期开始的发达国家的电信市场开放，促进竞争成为各国电信规制的主题。以美国为例，美国 1996 年《电信法》完全开放了电信市场，除本地网络建设（美国电信法 Sec. 214）、有线电视（美国电信法 Sec. 621）和频率分配（美国电信法 Sec. 301、307）涉及特许权例外，其他市场

批注：mainly. Certainly, telecom regulation has the same aim as other business regulation, such as promoting science and technology innovation, safeguarding public interest etc. which are not the feature of telecom law and deserve illustrating.

批注：With the telecom market opening of developed countries since late 20th century, promoting competition became the theme of various countries' telecom regulation. Taking USA for example, through the Act of Telecommunications (1996), USA completely opened the telecom market, all of the market other than what relates to privilege, such as network construction (SEC.214), cable TV (SEC.621) and frequency allocation(SEC.301 and SEC.307), was completely opened (SEC.257), especially SEC.253(a) has deprived any state from legislating to prohibit

---

[1] 促进科技创新是电信管制的一个重要目标。由于电信技术的提高可能威胁到基于已有技术确定的盈利模式，使用新技术将破坏性地动摇以后技术的生产线，电信企业并非一定具有主动投放新技术的动力，因此，各国电信法都将推广新技术作为立法目的。比如美国电信法 SEC. 7. [47 U.S.C. 157] NEW TECHNOLOGIES AND SERVICES. (a) It shall be the policy of the United States to encourage the provision of new technologies and services to the public. Any person or party (other than the Commission) who opposes a new technology or service proposed to be permitted under this Act shall have the burden to demonstrate that such proposal is inconsistent with the public interest. (b) The Commission shall determine whether any new technology or service proposed in a petition or application is in the public interest within one year after such petition or application is filed. If the Commission initiates its own proceeding for a new technology or service, such proceeding shall be completed within 12 months after it is initiated.

完全开放（美国电信法 Sec. 257），尤其是美国电信法 Sec. 253（a）规定的"各州和地方政府不得限制任何实体提供州内或长途电信服务的权利"，被认为是完全开放市场的标志。]

telecom market entering, which is deemed as the stigma of completely opening market.

[对上述经审批才能准入的项目，都有严格的法律规定，相关条文在美国电信法中被一一列明。]

批注：There are strict regulations for what should get permission before starting operation, which are stipulated in details in Act of Telecommunications of USA as following:

Network construction 【SEC. 214. [47 U.S.C. 214] EXTENSION OF LINES. (a) No carrier shall undertake the construction of a new line or of an extension of any line, or shall acquire or operate any line, or extension thereof, or shall engage in transmission over or by means of such additional or extended line, unless and until there shall first have been obtained from the Commission a certificate that the present or future public convenience and necessity require or will require the construction, or operation, or construction and operation, of such additional or extended line】

Cable TV 【SEC. 621. [47 U.S.C. 541] GENERAL FRANCHISE REQUIREMENTS. (a)(1) A franchising authority may award, in accordance with the provisions of this title, 1 or more franchises within its jurisdiction; except that a franchising authority may not grant an exclusive franchise and may not unreasonably refuse to award an additional competitive franchise. Any applicant whose application for a second franchise has been denied by a final decision of the franchising authority may appeal such final decision pursuant to the provisions of section 635 for failure to comply with this subsection. (2) Any franchise shall be construed to authorize the construction of a cable system over public rights-of-way, and through easements, which is within the area to be served by the cable system and which have been dedicated for compatible uses,】

Frequency allocation 【SEC. 301. [47 U.S.C. 301] LICENSE FOR RADIO COMMUNICATION OR TRANSMISSION OF ENERGY It is the purpose of this Act, among other things, to maintain the control of the United States over all the channels of radio transmission; and to provide for the use of such channels, but not the ownership thereof, by persons for limited periods of time, under licenses granted by Federal authority, and no such license shall be construed to create any right, beyond the terms, conditions, and periods of the license. No person shall use or operate any apparatus for the transmission of energy or communications or signals by radio (a) from one place in any State, Territory, or possession of the United States or in the District of Columbia to another place in the same State, Territory, possession, or District; or (b) from any State, Territory, or possession of the United States, or from the District of Columbia to any other State, Territory, or possession of the United States; or (c) from any place in any State, Territory, or possession of the United States, or in the District of Columbia, to any place in any foreign country or to any vessel; or (d) within any State when the effects of such use extend beyond the borders of said State, or when interference is caused by such use or operation with the transmission of such energy, communications, or signals from within said State to any place beyond its borders, or from any place beyond its borders to any place within said State, or with the transmission or reception of such energy, communications, or signals from and/or to places beyond the borders of said State; or (e) upon any vessel or aircraft of the United States (except as provided in section 303(t)); or (f) upon any other mobile stations within the jurisdiction of the United States, except under and in accordance with this Act and with a license in that behalf granted under the provisions of this Act.】

Radio facilities permission【SEC. 307. [47 U.S.C. 307] ALLOCATION OF FACILITIES; TERM OF LICENSES. (a) The Commission, if public convenience, interest, or necessity will be served thereby, subject to the limitations of this Act, shall grant to any applicant therefor a station license provided for by this Act. (b) In considering applications for licenses, and modifications and renewals thereof, when and insofar as there is demand for the same, the Commission shall make such distribution of licenses, frequencies, hours of operation, and of power among the several States and communities as to provide a fair, efficient, and equitable distribution of radio service to each of the same.】

Completely opening marketing【SEC. 257. [47 U.S.C. 257] MARKET ENTRY BARRIERS PROCEEDING. (a) ELIMINATION OF BARRIERS.--Within 15 months after the date of enactment of the Telecommunications Act of 1996, the Commission shall complete a proceeding for the purpose of identifying and eliminating, by regulations pursuant to its authority under this Act (other than this section), market entry barriers for entrepreneurs and other small businesses in the provision and ownership of telecommunications services and information services, or in the provision of parts or services to providers of telecommunications services and information services.】

Deprive any state from legislating to prohibit telecom market entering【SEC. 253. [47 U.S.C. 253] REMOVAL OF BARRIERS TO ENTRY. (a) IN GENERAL.--No State or local statute or regulation, or other State or local legal requirement, may prohibit or have the effect of prohibiting the ability of any entity to provide any interstate or intrastate telecommunications service.】

[相应的，入门许可被撤销，变成了入门后应当遵守的法定义务，比如，保证普遍服务、保护公共安全和福利、通信服务的持续质量保证、保护消费者权利，这些不是入门条件，而是入门后的义务。为保证没有网络资源的运营商，通过租赁网络资源或转售电信服务的方式，与具有网络资源的运营商公平竞争，美国1996年电信法规定了一系列保护措施。]首先，将竞争本地交换运营商（Competitive Local Exchange Carriers，CLEC）分为两类：其一，基于设备的运营商，其自己有设备或者用从现任本地交换运营商（Incumbent Local Exchange Carrier，ILEC，也译作传统本地交换运营商）处购买的非捆绑网络元素提供服务，由于买入价受到国家限制，所以在和自有设备商的竞争中没有明显劣势。其二，转售商从ILEC处购买服务，以自己的商标卖给用户，其与销售代理商的区别是，其以自己的名义和商标提供电信服务，自己承担责任。

批注：Correspondingly, the entrance admission is cancelled and became legal obligation after entrance, such as security for university service, protecting public security and welfare, continuous quality assurance for telecom service, protecting consumers' right, all of above are not admission condition but obligation after entrance. To ensure operators not possessing network resource could compete with operators possessing network resource, through leasing the resource from the latter, or resaling telecom service bought from the latter, the Act of Telecommunications (1996) stipulated a series of protecting measures.

由于 CLEC 必须从 ILEC 处租赁网络或转售服务才可以开展与 ILEC 同样的电信业务，美国为保护 CLEC 的顺利入门，对其入门要求非常简单，类似于我国注册普通的公司，其只需满足一般性许可要求即可，这些一般性要求只需遵守各州公共设施管理局(PUC)的规定，联邦通信委员会（FCC）并不附加更苛刻的条件（无论州内还是长途）。PUC 的要求包括：

（1）选择是基于设备的运营商还是转售商；

（2）指定服务内容；

（3）指定服务区域；

（4）财务能力要求（比如加利福尼亚要求资本金最低 10 万美元）；

（5）基于设备的运营商还要说明建设计划和环境影响评估；

（6）上报价目表[2]。

另外，促进竞争的必要手段就是反垄断。[电信市场的反垄断有其特殊性，它是在承认并接受基础电信业务的自然垄断特性前提下的反垄断。监管机构可以采纳以下策略应对本地运营商的反竞争策略：

（1）隔离——禁止进入特定业务，如禁止 Bell 电话公司进入电信终端设备制造或提供内部交换服务；

（2）结构分离——只能通过独立子公司提供竞争业务，并且接入费和接入条件和其他竞争对手一样；

（3）非结构性保护——通过财务审计、互联要求防止歧视接入和掠夺性定价；

（4）禁止或限制交叉补贴，通过其他方式提供普遍服务[3]。]

---

[2] Charles H, Kennedy. An Introduction to U.S. Telecommunications Law[M]. 2nd ed. Massachusetts: Artech House, Inc, 2001: 86-89.

[3] Charles H, Kennedy. An Introduction to U.S. Telecommunications Law[M]. 2nd ed. Massachusetts: Artech House, Inc, 2001.

批注：The antimonopoly of telecom market has its specific feature, which is under the condition of acknowledging and accepting natural monopoly as a characteristic of telecom business. Regulators have the following strategies to cope with the local operators' anti-competition methods:

(1) Quarantine, which is prohibit the local operator from entering some specific business areas, such as prohibiting Bell company from entering telecom terminal equipment production market or offering inner exchange business service.

(2) Structural separation, which is competition business could only be offered by independent subsidiary that must pay the same access fee and burden the same access condition as other competitors.

(3) Non-structural protection (the protection method does not intent to change the incumbent's company structure), which is to prevent from discriminatory access and predatory pricing through financial audit and interconnection requirement.

(4) Prohibit or restrict from cross-subsidization, as a result, the cost of universal service, burdened by incumbent operator in the name of cross-subsidization originally, is covered by alternative ways.

2. 管制的边界

[作为经济法的一个部门法,电信法需要不断思考的问题就是,什么样的经济行为需要政府规制?也就是划出管制和自由竞争的边界。这个问题似乎很容易回答,只有市场解决不了的才需要规制。]比如,有关价格规制,只有在市场失灵的领域,或者涉及竞争定价不能实现公众基本权利的领域,才需要国家干预——由国家定价或确定价格的浮动范围。[充分竞争的领域不需要规制,只需要国家维护公平竞争秩序,其他的就可以交给市场。]

> **批注**: As a branch of economic law, telecom law should think it over and over: what economic behavior should be regulated by government? That is to say, how to demarcate the boundary of regulation and free competition. That seems a piece of cake, and the key is on regulation only facing the market inability.

> **批注**: Completely competition fields do not need regulation, other than the government maintaining the fair completion order, and the rest could be left to the market.

具体到电信领域,简单来说,需要管制的是电信基础网络产业,而非在此之上建立的增值业务。因为只有前者是自然垄断的(网络资源本身),天然地不适合竞争。而在此之上建立的增值业务(网络上开展的服务),不需要管制,它们依赖竞争就可以获得市场效果。就像铁路需要管制,而铁路服务不需要管制;或者机场需要管制,航空服务不需要管制,基础电信需要管制,而增值业务可以交给市场。

[现实中电信管制边界的划分要复杂得多,尤其是电信新技术的日新月异,总能成为管制边界变化的原因。电信技术的发展使得规制经济学不得不重新认识电信的自然垄断性,因而,要重新划定管制的边界。电信技术的发展表现出从语音到数据、有线到无线的趋势,尤其随着三网融合,分业管制变成了完全开放竞争。][这些都使得原先需要管制的事项被推到了市场,管制的范围在缩小。从具体管制政策上看,技术使得原先受到管制的特定领域不再需要管制,比如,有关无线通信的价格,随着无线电通信技术的提高,尤其是智能频率分配的出现,虽然频谱的有限性对入门数

> **批注**: It's much complicated in reality to demarcate the regulation boundary, especially, the development of telecom technology is always the reason of boundary changing. The above development forces regulatory economy to reconsider the feature of telecom business. Therefore, it's necessary to redraw the regulation boundary. The telecom technology development tendency is from voice to date, from line to wireless. Especially with the convergence of tri-network, the separated regulation became complete competition.

> **批注**: All of the above factors push the businesses regulated originally into the market, and the regulation scope is smaller and smaller. In the perspective of specific regulatory policies, technology liberates some specific fields from restriction. For example, concerning the price of radio communication,

量构成理论上的限制,但技术已经使得频率的有限性对新进入者并不构成实质障碍,无线市场可以成为一个充分竞争的领域,不需要再规制无线通信的价格。]
[因此,美国不认为无线市场属于自然垄断行业,其完全开放了该市场,入门不需经过许可,只要入门后遵守专门的规则即可[4],并且,美国还放开了无线价格,"除非有证据显示无线运营商具有'主导'市场的地位,联邦和各州的规制者不得对无线资费进行规制"[5]。而在有线通信领域,技术尚未消除网络资源的自然垄断性,竞争不可能充分,有线价格仍受到规制。]

3. 电信法和竞争法的分工

研究电信法中管制的划界,还要搞清楚电信法和竞争法的关系。因为"政府该管的"不仅在电信法中规定了,在普通竞争法中也规定了,如何确定二者的效力显得很重要。这个问题类似于知识产权法与反不正当竞争法的关系,"中国的知识产权单行法确实已相当完备了,但这与反不正当竞争法的附加保护,并不矛盾。……知识产权单行法的保护要件(或前提),使一大部分本应受到某种保护的客体被'漏'掉了。……反不正当竞争法的附加保护,就显得十分必要了[6]。"

with the improvement of radio communication technology, especially appearing of intelligence frequency allocation technology, although the limitation of spectrum confines the market entering number theoretically, the present technology have cleared the substantial barrier, caused by spectrum scarcity, against new comer. Wireless communication market could became a fully competition market, whose price no longer need regulated.

批注:Therefore USA does not regard wireless communication market as a natural monopoly market, and opened it completely, that means the entrance permission has been eliminated, and the only thing operators should do is to obey the rules after entering that market. Furthermore, USA has loosened up the wireless communication prices. Unless evidence demonstrating the wireless operator obtaining the market dominating position, the regulator of federal and states should not control the wireless communication price. However, in the wire communication market, technology has not yet eliminated the natural monopoly of network, and the competition is not sufficient, consequently the wire communication price is controlled.

---

[4] Charles H, Kennedy. An Introduction to U.S. Telecommunications Law[M]. 2nd ed. Massachusetts: Artech House, Inc, 2001: 130.

[5] [美]罗伯特·W·克兰德尔. 竞争与混沌——1996年电信法出台以来的美国电信业[M]. 匡斌,译. 北京:北京邮电大学出版社, 2006:12.

[6] 郑成思. 知识产权论[M]. 3版. 北京:法律出版社, 2003: 263-264.

[电信法大量内容属于竞争法，其目的就是在自然垄断行业内模拟竞争的效果。因此，电信法与竞争法的关系就是特殊法和一般法的关系，电信法属于专业竞争法，除非电信法中有特殊规定，比如接入中的妨碍竞争性行为可以适用电信法处理，在此之外的其他妨碍竞争问题，就需要用竞争法解决。]电信法规范典型电信竞争行为、禁止典型反竞争行为，至于非典型性的反竞争行为，不具有电信法律关系的共性，或者行为手段时常变换，或者是将其他领域的反竞争手段用于电信行业，应使用更加一般性的竞争规范——竞争法。[在这些非典型性电信反竞争行为中，竞争法的价值目标足以实现电信法追求的价值目标，即保证消费者选择权、技术创新并将高科技带来的生产效率提高的福祉传递给消费者，保证行业的可持续发展。]

[以价格管制为例，电信法中反映典型电信法律关系的价格问题就是交叉补贴和接入价格。前者可能会被滥用，以垄断领域的高价格收入补贴竞争领域的掠夺性定价，并使这种掠夺性定价可持续[7]，后者是基础电信业务经营者为了维持垄断地位以明显高于成本的价格向增值业务运营商提供网络接入，限制后者与自己在增值业务领域的竞争。]
[禁止这样做，可以采用分业经营的方式，禁止基础运营商经营增值电信业务，或者政府对接入价格进行管制，使得租

批注：Many contents of telecom law belong to competition law, whose aim is to simulate competition effect in a natural monopoly business. The relation between telecom law and competition law is the relation of particular law and general law. Telecom law belongs to particular competition law. Therefore, unless telecom law has specific provisions, such as impediment competition behavior in access process, competition law should be applied governing other anti-competition behaviors instead of telecom law.

批注：Concerning these atypical anti-competition telecom behaviors, the value target of competition law is sufficient to achieve what telecom law pursuits, that is protecting the right of consumer's choice, maintaining technology innovation and passing consumer the welfare of productivity improvement caused by high science and technology, securing sustainable development of that business.

批注：Take price regulation for example, the typical legal problem concerning price in telecom law, is cross-subsidization and access price. The former could be abused by using the high profit collected from monopolized business to subsidize predatory prize in competition business, and making this cross-subsidization sustainable. The latter refers to that, basic telecom operator, intending to main its monopoly position, offers access network service to value-added telecom operators in obviously higher price than its cost, in order to restrict the latter's competition ability in value-added telecom field.

---

[7] 在普遍服务基金建立之前，交叉补贴是国家允许的为弱势群体提供普遍服务的一种方法。在VoIP流行之前，电信运营商以长途补贴本地、商业用户补贴家庭，目前由于VoIP和无线通信争抢了大量固话长途客户，长途业务收入萎缩，无法补贴本地固话，通行的办法是征收无线和VoIP税，取代征收长途业务税，用以补贴住宅本地固话。

用他人网络资源提供增值服务的运营商不至于支付过高的接入成本而损害竞争实力。这两种价格问题反映了电信法的典型法律关系,应当以电信法规制。][而其他的价格问题,与电信法律关系无关,是任何一个经济领域都可能出现的,比如拒绝交易(无正当理由不向竞争对手以批发价格提供产品或服务,甚至不以市场价格提供产品或服务)、价格歧视(同条件不同价)、掠夺性定价(低于成本定价,旨在消灭竞争对手,最终抬价)、强制搭售、滥用支配地位低价销售(利用某领域的支配地位谋求竞争领域的低价销售,如固网运营商提供低于成本价的互联网接入服务,旨在消灭纯粹网络接入商)[8]。上述行为不需要专门在电信法中规范,由一般的竞争法规范足矣。]

再将视角从价格扩大到其他电信领域,考察电信法和一般竞争法的管制边界。二者的区别不仅在于是否是典型性电信行为——产生、变更或者消灭电信法律关系的行为,二者在干预力度和启动干预的标准上也存在不同。比如,[拒绝互联,虽然也属于妨碍竞争的滥用支配地位行为,可以由竞争法管制,但该行为涉及典型性电信法律关系——互联法律关系,应由电信法管制,而非一般竞争法。而对于电信企业间的反竞争协议[9]的管制,则属于一般竞争法范畴。]

批注: To prohibit this behavior, the regulator could adopt separate operation mode to restrict basic operator from entering value-added business; or control the access price to protect value-added operator leasing network resource from others from paying too high access fee to jeopardize its competition ability. Both of the price problems reflect the typical legal relation of the Telecom Act, should be regulated by Telecom Act.

批注: Other problems besides the above, having nothing to do with telecom relation, could appear in any other economic field. For example, (1) refusing transaction, which means not offering product or service to competitor at wholesale price, even at market price, without justified reason. (2) price discrimination, which means different price on the same condition. (3) predatory price, which means the price lower than cost aiming at eliminating competitor, and raising price ultimately. (4) forced tie-in sale; (5) low price sale by abusing of dominant position, which means to set low price in competition field by using his dominating position in other field, such as incumbents operator offering internet access fee below cost, intending to eliminate internet access operator. All of the above behaviors need not regulated in telecom law, because the competition law is enough to work.

批注: To refuse interconnection belongs to the behavior of abusing dominant position intending to anti-competition, and could be regulated by competition law. However, this behavior relates to typical telecom legal relation, interconnection legal relation, so it should be governed by telecom law rather than ordinary competition law. On the other hand, anti-competition agreement between telecom enterprises belongs to ordinary competition law.

---

[8] 固网运营商由于已经有现成网络,其提供互联网接入服务的成本只是边际成本,不需支付额外成本。而其他没有固网的互联网接入运营商却要为租用固网线路支付成本或者自建网络的高昂成本。

[9] 反竞争协议是指以阻止、限制或干扰竞争为目的,或者产生其结果的企业间协议,以及建立企业联盟或一致行动的协议。

支配地位的极端形式就是垄断。在规制垄断方面，电信业的管制范围更宽，启动条件更低，对于监管者来说，使用电信法规制垄断比使用竞争法更得心应手。按照电信法，只要存在市场支配地位[10]，垄断规制程序就可以启动。而对于其他行业，竞争法规制的是行为而不是地位，只有行为构成滥用市场支配地位时，规制才可以启动。"根据通信规制体制，如果发现有市场支配地位存在，就要实施附加规制条款。其他行业则与此不同，发现企业处于市场支配地位本身并不会招致竞争法所规定的后果。只有当企业的行为被认为构成了市场支配地位滥用时，相关条款才会实施[11]。"比如英国《竞争法》第18（4）部分规定，一家或多家企业的任何行为，只要构成了市场支配地位的滥用，可能影响英国国内的贸易，就会被禁止[12]。

4. 规制赋予运营商的法定义务

[除去电信运营商与用户基于电信服务合同的义务，电信运营商还有依据电信法和竞争法等法律规范的法定义务。运营商依据电信法的法定义务可以分为：资质和技术要求、对其他运营商的义务、对消费者的义务、对国家的义务。每一项义务在电信法中都应当进行详细定义。]

（1）[资质和技术要求。比如：标准化服务、使用标准化/兼容性设备、设备入网的许可、最低服务能力和持续服务等等。

（2）对其他运营商的义务。比如：接入和互联互通、唯一路径的信道和设备共享、号码可携带[13]、向黄页编制者

批注：Besides the contract obligation based on contract with consumers, telecom operators have legal obligations based on law, such as telecom law and competition law. Telecom operators' legal obligation based on telecom law can be classified into the following: qualification and technology requirement, duty to other operators, duty to consumers, duty to nation. Any of the above duty should be stipulated in detail in telecom law.

批注：(1) qualification and technology requirement, such as standardized service, using standardized and compatible equipment, device access permission, minimum service ability and continual service etc.

(2) duty to other operators, such as access and interconnection, route and device sharing at non-alternative route, number portability,

---

[10] 确定是否具有支配地位，重点应考虑市场份额；而确定市场份额的前提是界定目标市场——确定产品和地域，从而确定在该地域该产品的可替代程度，即在该地域，地域内的企业和地域外的企业是否有机会平等地参与本地竞争。

[11] ［英］Ian Lloyd, 等．通信法[M]．曾剑秋，译．北京：北京邮电大学出版社，2006: 216.

[12] ［英］Ian Lloyd, 等．通信法[M]．曾剑秋，译．北京：北京邮电大学出版社，2006: 218.

[13] 号码可携带号码可携带是一切竞争的前提，没有客户的自由转移，其他竞争措施就没有意义。美国电信法153条定义了号码可携带，251条（b）(2)规定了用户号码携带自由选择运营商的权利。SEC. 3. [47 U.S.C. 153] DEFINITIONS. (30) Number portability.——The term "number portability" means the ability of users of telecommunications services to retain, at the same location, existing telecommunications numbers without impairment of quality, reliability, or convenience when switching from one telecommunications carrier to another. SEC. 251. [47 U.S.C. 251] INTERCONNECTION. (2) Number portability.——The duty to provide, to the extent technically feasible, number portability in accordance with requirements prescribed by the Commission. 英国电信法第51节（1）（a）第18条规定，"运营商应当满足用户在法律范围内在合理原因下提出号码可携带的要求。"

提供用户信息（不愿公开的客户除外）或者自己编制黄页。

（3）对消费者的义务。比如，紧急服务、号码目录服务、通话记录查询、话费清单查询、电信服务合同必备条款不得或缺（专业优势导致谈判能力不对等）、服务基本信息公示义务（用于客户比较其他运营商）、服务质量符合国家标准、话费清单保留最低时限、保证用户有权获得至少一个综合性的电话号码簿[14]。

（4）对国家的义务。比如，紧急状态下电信设施被征用、提供普遍服务和缴纳普遍服务基金、提供公共电话亭、提供残疾人服务、遵守频率和码号的管制。]

disclosing information to yellow pages compiler(except for the secret information requested by its owner) or compiling yellow pages personally.

(3) duty to consumers, such as emergency service, phone number directory service, call records inquiry, call list query, not lack of mandatory terms of contract(professional advantage causing asymmetric ability in negotiation), publicity of essential information about service(used for consumer comparing with various operators), service quality meets the national standards, the minimum period to reserve call list, to ensure consumers have the right to obtain at least one comprehensive phone directory.

(4) duty to the nation. Such as telecom equipment to be expropriated by government (right of eminent domain) in emergency states, the provision of universal service and to pay universal service fund, public phone booth, the provision of service for handicapped (disable) persons, compliance with the control for radio frequency and phone number.

第二节　不对称管制

Section 2　Asymmetric Regulation

[不对称管制，是指电信监管机构根据特定的区分标准对不同电信运营商，采取不同管制方式。其目的是扶持新兴电信运营企业，防止主导运营商滥用市场支配地位妨碍竞争，从而获得有效竞争的市场效果。上述区分标准通常选择市场占有率、年收入额、特定业务的收入额、网络资源占有率等参数。区分结果通常是将电信运营商区分为主导运营

批注：Asymmetric regulation, refers to regulator adopting different regulation policies to different telecom operators according specific distinction criteria, the aim of which is to support the emerging telecom enterprise to prevent the incumbent operators by abusing market dominant position, in order to obtain the market effect of effective competition. The above distinction criteria is usually according to such parameters as market share, annual revenue, specific business income, network

---

[14]　[英]劳埃德，等.通信法[M].曾剑秋，译.北京：北京邮电大学出版社，2006：134.

商和非主导运营商，或者本地网运营商和非本地网运营商两种；有时仅针对某特定运营商设定义务。]

[凡是管制机构旨在通过区别对待的方法规制市场主体，都可归结为不对称管制。因而，所有电信规制中的区别对待都属于电信不对称管制，其表现形式多种多样，比如：信息上报义务或者其他监管程度的区别对待（如主导运营商上报资费频率高于普通运营商）、码号可携带义务的区别对待、承担普遍服务义务的区别对待（如强制特定运营商铺设经济不理性地区的基础电信设施）、资费授权定价的区别对待（如允许特定运营商资费低于政府定价一定比例）、特许经营范围的区别对待（如我国只允许特定运营商经营小灵通业务）等。]

1. 不对称管制的法理学依据

不对称管制的法理学基础源于罗尔斯的正义论。实质公平是在承认主体差异前提下的结果公平。["如果平等的目标是让那些目标群体获得平等的结果而不只是形式上的平等，那么法律应该允许某些形式的区别对待[15]。"]基础电信业同铁路、自来水、燃气等行业一样，属于沉淀资本巨大、不宜重复投资、不适于充分竞争的自然垄断行业。电信管制的目的在于，通过合理的管制措施，在无竞争或寡头竞争的前提下，最大限度地模拟充分竞争的效果，比如降低资费、激励科技投入、行业进步的消费者

resource share, etc. The distinguish result is the classifying the telecom operator into dominant operators and non-dominant operators, or Incumbent Local Exchange Carrier(ILEC) and Competitive Local Exchange Carrier(CLEC). In some occasions, the duty is only imposed to specific operators.

批注：All of the regulation methods aiming to regulate market entity by the means of differential treatments can be classified into asymmetric regulation. Therefore, all of different treatments in telecom regulation belong to telecom asymmetric regulation, which have various demonstrations such as different treatment in information reporting institution and other supervision degree (for example, the price reporting duty for ILEC is more often than that of CLEC), different treatment in number portability obligation, different treatment in universal service obligation(for example some specific ILEC is forced to build the telecom infrastructure at economic irrational region(nonprofit region)), different treatment in authorizing pricing power (such as permitting some CLEC to price lower a certain percentage than government fixed price), different treatment in approving business scope(for example, in the early time of China, only specific operator was approved of business of Personal Handphone System(PHS, Little Smart)).

批注：The legal theoretical basis for asymmetric regulation

批注：If the aim of equality is to let target group obtain equality in essence rather than equality in form, the law should allow some forms of different treatments.

---

[15] 李薇薇. 禁止就业歧视：国际标准和国内实践 [M]. 北京：法律出版社，2006: 10.

分享等。[不对称管制制度就是以形式上的不公平（管制法为不同的市场主体设定的权利义务不对等），矫正已经存在的实质不公平（具备市场支配地位者滥用市场优势阻碍竞争），最终达到真正意义上的实质公平（充分竞争或模拟充分竞争效果）。]

虽然各国普遍建立了反垄断法律制度，但普通反垄断法主要是针对自由竞争的市场中存在的垄断行为；对于自然垄断行业，反垄断法并未重点关注。因此，其并不能够完全解决自然垄断行业的不正当竞争问题。而"不对称管制制度"正是电信法对普通反垄断法律制度的补充和完善。不对称管制规则规制电信垄断，比一般竞争法更严格：[不对称管制规则适用的条件是存在市场支配地位，而不需要妨碍竞争的行为出现。只要市场支配地位的状态存在，就进行规制；而我国的反垄断法是行为规制法，非地位规制法，没有妨碍竞争的行为，即使主导运营商处于垄断地位也不进行规制。在我国，只有具备市场支配地位且妨碍竞争的行为出现两个条件同时具备，才开始规制。具体到电信领域，如果主导运营商没有实施反垄断法禁止的行为，该法并不对其附加额外义务。故单纯适用反垄断法，无法达到要求主导运营商在未实施妨碍竞争性行为前提下，承担不对等义务的效果。这只有依赖于不对称管制措施。]

批注：Asymmetric regulation system is to use inequality in form, regulating rules imposing different right and obligation to different market entities, to correct the existing inequality in essence, which is the operators with market dominant position abusing of their market advantage for Significant Impediment to Effective Competition, at last to obtain a real sense of equality in essence, which is completely competition or fully simulating the effect of competition.

批注：The asymmetric regulation rules apply on condition that the existence of market dominant position, without the anti-competitive behavior. Only if market dominant position existing, the asymmetric regulation works. However, Chinese anti-monopoly law is behavior regulation law, other than status regulation law. Therefore, if lack of impediment competition behavior, even though ILEC takes monopoly position, the regulation is not initiated. In China, only if both of the conditions are met at the same time, which are taking the market dominant position and impediment competition behavior appearing, the regulation could be initiated. As for telecom field, if ILEC does not commit the behaviors prohibited by anti-monopoly law, then the law does not impose further duty to ILEC. Therefore, only depending on anti-monopoly law, we cannot require ILEC, without impediment competition behavior, to take asymmetric obligating, which should only rely on asymmetric regulation measure.

2. 不对称管制规范的结构

不对称管制表现在立法上，就是为不同的市场主体设定的权利义务不对等，其规范结构有两种。其一，通过设定区分市场主体的标准，进而设定不同的权利义务。

如我国《公用电信网间互联管理规定》第五条定义了区分标准,即"主导的电信业务经营者,是指控制必要的基础电信设施,并且所经营的固定本地电话业务占本地网范围内同类业务市场50%以上的市场份额,能够对其他电信业务经营者进入电信业务市场构成实质性影响的经营者。"第七条对区分出的主体设定了不对称互联义务,即"主导的电信业务经营者应当根据本规定制定包括网间互联的程序、时限、互联点的数量、用于网间互联的交换机局址、非捆绑网络元素提供或出租的目录及费用等内容的互联规程。"

其二,直接对特定主体设定"不平等"义务。[如美国1996年电信法第三章[16]专门规制地区贝尔公司,为其附加了多项不对称义务。该法第271~275条[17]为地区贝尔经营长途业务和电子出版、家庭电子安保、通信设备制造等业务附加了较苛刻的条件[18],而对其他公司无此要求,尤其是对于贝尔公司及其子公司经营长途业务,设定了极为苛刻的条件[19],]

批注:For example, Act Telecommunication (1996) of USA Part 3--SPECIAL PROVISIONS CONCERNING BELL OPERATING COMPANIES is used only for Bell Company, imposing many asymmetric obligations. Article 271-275 set strict conditions for a bell operating company, or any affiliate of that Bell operating company, on entry into interlata services, separate affiliate, safeguards, manufacturing by bell operating companies, electronic publishing, alarm monitoring services, to which other telecom operators is not required to satisfy. Especially, for a bell operating company, or any affiliate of that Bell operating compa-

---

[16] [47 U.S.C.] PART III--SPECIAL PROVISIONS CONCERNING BELL OPERATING COMPANIES
[17] [47 U.S.C. 271-275]法条名称分别为: BELL OPERATING COMPANY ENTRY INTO INTERLATA SERVICES、SEPARATE AFFILIATE; SAFEGUARDS、MANUFACTURING BY BELL OPERATING COMPANIES、ELECTRONIC PUBLISHING BY BELL OPERATING COMPANIES、ALARM MONITORING SERVICES.
[18] 同注17,即根据美国电信法271~275条,地区贝尔经营长途业务和电子出版、家庭电子安保、通信设备制造等业务必须满足苛刻的条件,如开放本地网、拆分独立公司经营且独立公司不得使用贝尔的名称和商标、禁止用基本电话业务提供电子出版服务、电信法生效日起五年内不得经营家庭电子安保业务、不得利用基本电话业务进行交叉补贴、向其他提供电子出版的公司提供互联互通等。
[19] 根据美国电信法SEC. 271(c)(2)(B),除非贝尔运营公司满足"竞争性一揽子规定competitive checklist",否则其及其子公司不可提供起始于本地并结束于外地的长途业务,即贝尔及其子公司可以提供起点在其他区域的但终点在本区域的长途业务,但提供起始于本地并结束于外地的长途业务,则需要满足下列"竞争性一揽子规定competitive checklist":
1. 与本地竞争者互联;
2. 网络元素接入;
3. 杆、路由、信道和路权接入;
4. 本地环路接续;
5. 非捆绑本地传输;
6. 非捆绑本地交换;
7. 接入911、地址本服务、话务员服务;
8. 电话号码库接入;
9. 数据库和信号接入;
10. 码号可携带和平等拨号;
11. 相互补偿协议;
12. 转售。

ny, carrying on **In-region interlata** (starting from its own state and terminating at other state, excluding of starting at other state and terminating at its own state, see SEC 271 (b)(4)) business, Telecommunication Act imposing extremely strict condition(see SEC271(C)(2)(B)).

SEC 271 (b)(4) Nothing in this section prohibits a Bell operating company or any of its affiliates from providing termination for interlata services, subject to subsection (j).

SEC271(C) REQUIREMENTS FOR PROVIDING CERTAIN IN-REGION INTERLATA SERVICES.--

(2)(B) COMPETITIVE CHECKLIST.--Access or interconnection provided or generally offered by a Bell operating company to other telecommunications carriers meets the requirements of this subparagraph if such access and interconnection includes each of the following:

(i) Interconnection in accordance with the requirements of sections 251(c)(2) and 252(d)(1).

(ii) Nondiscriminatory access to network elements in accordance with the requirements of sections 251(c)(3) and 252(d)(1).

(iii) Nondiscriminatory access to the poles, ducts, conduits, and rights-of-way owned or controlled by the Bell operating company at just and reasonable rates in accordance with the requirements of section 224.

(iv) Local loop transmission from the central office to the customer's premises, unbundled from local switching or other services.

(v) Local transport from the trunk side of a wireline local exchange carrier switch unbundled from switching or other services.

(vi) Local switching unbundled from transport, local loop transmission, or other services.

(vii) Nondiscriminatory access to——

(I) 911 and E911 services;

(II) Directory assistance services to allow the other carrier's customers to obtain telephone numbers; and

(III) Operator call completion services.

(viii) White pages directory listings for customers of the other carrier's telephone exchange service.

(ix) Until the date by which telecommunications numbering administration guidelines, plan, or rules are established, nondiscriminatory access to telephone numbers for assignment to the other carrier's telephone exchange service customers. After that date, compliance with such guidelines, plan, or rules.

(x) Nondiscriminatory access to databases and associated signaling necessary for call routing and completion.

(xi) Until the date by which the Commission issues regulations pursuant to section 251 to require number portability, interim telecommunications number portability through remote call forwarding, direct inward dialing trunks, or other comparable arrangements, with as little impairment of functioning, quality, reliability, and convenience as possible. After that date, full compliance with such regulations.

(xii) Nondiscriminatory access to such services or information as are necessary to allow the requesting carrier to implement local dialing parity in accordance with the requirements of section 251(b)(3).

(xiii) Reciprocal compensation arrangements in accordance with the requirements of section 252(d)(2).

(xiv) Telecommunications services are available for resale in accordance with the requirements of sections 251(c)(4) and 252(d)(3).

[原因在于地区贝尔具有本地网资源，为防止其利用本地网资源妨碍竞争，设定了上述"不平等"义务。]又如该法第五章[20]专门对电话公司经营视频服务设立了不对称管制义务，有线电视运营商进入通信领域和通信运营商进入有线电视领域的许可条件不同，对前者的限制较少，对后者限制较多[21]，原因在于通信运营商的竞争实力远大于有线电视运营商，故当该法开启混业经营大门时，立法者不得不考虑"锄强扶弱"。

批注：The reason for strictly restrict bell company operating competition business is that, Bell company controls the local network resource. To prevent it use the local network resource from impediment competition, the law established its asymmetric obligation.

我们再来看一下就互联互通，美国电信法给予弱小竞争者 CLEC 的优惠待遇，他们不需要提供地区贝尔被强制要求提供的非捆绑网络元素[22]、允许其他运营商以折扣价趸售服务等不对等义务，只需要满足通常运营商都需要履行的一般义务即可：

(1) 互联互通 SEC. 251（a）；
(2) 不得禁止他人转售 SEC. 252(b)(1)；
(3) 码号可携带 SEC. 252(b)(2)；
(4) 平等拨号权 SEC. 252(b)(3)；
(5) 共享其杆、路由、信道和路权 SEC. 252(b)(4)；
(6) 建立传输和终结电信服务的互相补偿机制 SEC. 252(b)(5)。

3. 不对称管制的反向歧视特征

[既然在间接歧视情况下，形式上的平等规则产生了实质上的不平等，那么，为恢复实质平等，就需要设立形式上的不平等规则。为恢复宪法平等权而设定的补偿性正义，就是反向歧视，它在日常生活中经常见到，比如西

批注：Even that in the condition of indirection discrimination, formal equality rules create essential (substantial) inequality, in order to restore essential equality, the formal inequality rules is required to be established. The compensating (corrective) justice, established for restitution of the constitutional equality right, is reverse discrimination, which could be often found in daily life, for example, the college admission score of western remote

---

[20] [47 U.S.C.]PART V—VIDEO PROGRAMMING SERVICES PROVIDED BY TELEPHONE OMPANIES
[21] [47 U.S.C. 571] REGULATORY TREATMENT OF VIDEO PROGRAMMING SERVICES
[22] 网络元素包括：
　　(1) 环路，包括用于 DSL;
　　(2) 网络接口设备；
　　(3) 本地电路交换器；
　　(4) 专有或共享的传输；
　　(5) 信令或与呼叫有关数据库；
　　(6) 操作支持系统；
　　(7) 话务员和电话号码目录辅助服务。

部偏远地区考生的分数线低于教育发达地区，企业的招工标准中残疾人优于正常人，少数民族可以生二胎等。]

[反向歧视本身也是一种区别对待，其规则在形式上不中立，类似于直接歧视，但形式上的不中立旨在挽回既有的实体不公正，]区分目的与总体行业目的或社会目的吻合。比如个人所得税法根据个人收入对公民进行区分，根据区分结果附加不同的征收义务，表面上违反了宪法平等权，但这种区分体现了能者多劳、辅助弱者的社会正义。又如《反垄断法》根据经营者的市场份额等因素区分具有市场支配地位者[23]，并限制其民事权利能力[24]，形式上违反平等权，但是，这种区别对待可以实现保证公平竞争的实质正义。

> 批注：region is much lower than developed region, qualification for recruiting workers is less strict for disabled people than for able-bodied people, minority has the privilege of generating more than one children.
>
> 批注：The reverse discrimination is a kind of different treatment, whose rules are not neutrality in form, similar to direct discrimination. However, the formal non-neutrality aims to correcting the existing substantial injustice.

不对称管制规则是反向歧视在电信法中的表现。由于网络资源的自然垄断特征，要想利用本地网提供电信服务，就必须向本地网所有人提出接入请求，如果所有人本身也在提供同样的电信服务，其很容易滥用市场支配地位，妨碍竞争。比如，收取高额网间互联费、增加网间阻塞、降低通话质量、拒绝提供足够容量或网络元素、拒绝分拆捆绑业务等。面对既有竞争实力的明显不对等，形式上完全平等的管制政策将无法保护弱小运营商，产生事实上的不公正。所以，面对既有的竞争力差别，不对称管制措施显得十分必要，其利用形式上不平等的规则，给本地网运营商附加特定义务，或者限制其特定民事权利能力，防止其滥用网络优势、排挤竞争对手，从而扶持弱小运营商，获得有效竞争的市场效果。比如，禁止本地网运营商涉足该领域，或者在一定时间段内不得经营该业务，或者要求其剥离出独立子公司经营该业务。

4. 不对称管制的合宪性

[不对称管制规范的本质是法人行为能力的区别对待。其形式上体现了不平等，表面看违反了法律平等原则，但这是否意味着侵犯了法人平等权呢？]这个问题不解决，不对称管制规范的效力就无从谈起。然而，在解决这个问题之前，

> 批注：The essential content of asymmetric regulation rules is different treatment to disposing capacity (behavior competence) of legal persons, which is inequality in form, and violates legal equality principle on the surface. However, does these mean to violate the right of equality of legal person?

---

[23] 《反垄断法》第18、19条。
[24] 《反垄断法》第17条。

首先要确定法人是否有平等权。

（1）法人平等权

[平等权的概念最初只赋予了自然人。美国《独立宣言》将"人人生而平等"作为先验的真理，但只确立了公民的平等权。]同样，我国确立平等权的《宪法》第三十三条，即"中华人民共和国公民在法律面前一律平等"也只适用于公民，无法将法人的概念涵盖于具有法定内涵的公民[25]之内。"……虽然法人不享有与自然人同样广泛的一般人格权，但是法人的人格也受到法律保护[26]。"在我国，法人人格权的概念虽然没有直接法律依据，但被大部分法学学者认可，"法人作为民事权利主体所享有的人格不受侵犯的权利，是以与法人财产利益相对应的法人人格利益为基础，与法人人格密不可分的权利"，法人人格的标的即为"法人人格独立"以及"法人人格平等"，"法人人格与自然人人格具有共同的性质，这就是平等性[27]。"即使将法人人格视为纯粹财产权益，也丝毫不影响法律对于这种财产权益的平等保护，即法人具有平等权。

批注：Originally, the concept of "equality right" was only used for natural person. In the Declaration of Independence, the maxim "all men are created equal" as a self-evidence truth, established the equality right only for citizen.

我们可以在宪法和其他法律中找到法人平等权的渊源：《宪法》第五条规定，"任何组织或者个人都不得有超越宪法和法律的特权。"《民事诉讼法》第八条规定，对当事人在适用法律上一律平等，《行政诉讼法》第七条规定，当事人在行政诉讼中的法律地位平等。上述宪法和法律渊源确定了法人的平等权，即法人在法律面前一律平等。

（2）[不对称管制是否侵犯了法人的平等保护权]

[早在1997年，美国南方贝尔通讯公司诉联邦通信委员会案[28]就提出了这个问题。南方贝尔公司就美国1996年电信法中第271~275条的合宪性提出诉讼，认为立法者指名道姓地在法律中规定仅对该公司的不对称管制措施[29]，限

批注：Does asymmetric regulation violate equal protection right of legal person

批注：As early as 1997, this issue was raised up in the case of SBC Communications Inc. Vs. FCC (981 F. Supp. 996 1997). Southwestern bell initiated that litigation for the constitutionality of Article 271-275 of Telecommunications Act of USA, which is PART 3--SPECIAL PROVISIONS CONCERNING BELL OPERATING COMPANIES. In the

---

[25] 宪法第三十三条 "凡具有中华人民共和国国籍的人都是中华人民共和国公民。"
[26] [德] 迪特尔·梅迪库斯. 德国民法总论 [M]. 2版. 邵建东, 译. 北京：法律出版社，2001：822.
[27] 王利明，等. 人格权法 [M]. 北京：法律出版社，1997：39-41.
[28] 王郁琦. 资讯、电信与法律 [M]. 台湾：元照出版有限公司，2004：203-207.
[29] 这些条款都属于美国电信法第三部分（47 U.S.C. PART III——SPECIAL PROVISIONS CONCERNING BELL OPERATING COMPANIES）中的内容。

制了其经营特定业务的权利，侵害了联邦宪法平等权，违反了联邦宪法第 1 条第 9 款第 3 项规定的"禁止制定权利剥夺法"[30]，以及宪法第 14 修正案所确立的"法律平等保护权"[31]。] 从立法角度看，作为一般性规范的法律，可以为一类人设定义务，但不应当专门为一个人（或法人）设定义务，否则就违反了"禁止制定权利剥夺法"，侵犯了法律对公民的"平等保护权"。一审法院判决原告胜诉，认定电信法第 271~275 条违宪。联邦通信委员会上诉，上诉法官认为该条款合宪，撤销了原判决，原告再上诉，联邦最高法院拒绝受理，上诉判决为终审判决。上诉判决理由是：有关"禁止制定权利剥夺法"，法官认为电信法第 271~275 条是非惩罚性条款，虽然限制了企业的行为能力，但该限制无处罚的意图，目的是促进公平竞争，符合公共利益，因而不属于"权利剥夺法"范畴。[针对"法律平等保护权"，法官认为宪法第 14 修正案所确立的"法律平等保护权"是针对公民的，非法人，法律可以针对特定法人进行专门管制。只要目的符合正当利益即不侵犯平等保护权。]

通过该案所确立的原则可以看出，即使针对一个法人立法，限制其民事权利能力，只要该限制不具惩罚性意图，并出于正当目的，就不侵犯法人平等权。

lawsuit, SBC complained that, legislators established the asymmetric regulation measure specifically used for one company, mentioning by its name in the Act, violated "bill of attainder" set by Constitution article 1- 9-3, and "the equal protection right" set by the fourteenth Amendment section 1, the result of which is its right of running specific business was restrained, and its constitutional equality rights was infringed.

Constitution article 1- 9-3 "No bill of attainder or ex post facto Law shall be passed."

The fourteenth Amendment section 1, "All persons born or naturalized in the United States, and subject to the jurisdiction thereof, are citizens of the United States and of the State wherein they reside. No State shall make or enforce any law which shall abridge the privileges or immunities of citizens of the United States; nor shall any State deprive any person of life, liberty, or property, without due process of law; nor deny to any person within its jurisdiction the equal protection of the laws."

批注：As for "legal equal protection rights", the judger held that, those rights are established by the fourteenth amendment of constitution, and only applying to citizen, other than legal person, which means laws are able to specially regulate particular legal person. Only if those aims conform to legitimacy interest, they do not violate equal protection rights.

---

[30] 美国宪法第 1 条第 9 款第 3 项禁止制定权利剥夺法（bill of attainder）和追溯既往的法律（ex post facto law），原文为 "No bill of attainder or ex post facto Law shall be passed."
[31] 美国宪法第 14 修正案（XIV - Citizen rights not to be abridged）

[美国宪法第 14 修正案所确立的"法律平等保护权"原则，源于"人人生而平等"的人身至上性，因而其适用范畴限于自然人。]对于法人，有些学者并不承认法人人格权，认为"法人的'人格权'无精神利益，实质上是一种财产权[32]。"[既然法人人格权的核心为财产权，而非人身权，就失去了至上性[33]。因而，出于公共利益或其他正当目的的需要，限制法人的财产权，或进行法人行为能力的区别对待（限制特定法人的民事权利能力），应属正当。]所以，对法人的不对称管制并不侵犯法人平等权。

5. 不对称管制措施的立法权

有些电信业内人士认为目前电信业通过市场主体的重组已经进入充分竞争时代，不对称管制已经没有存在的价值[34]。笔者认为，是否建立不对称管制制度属于经济学考虑，应视电信市场竞争的充分程度而定[35]，正如[欧共体在 2002 年《关于电子通信网及业务的共同管制框架（框架指令）》中要求成员国的：如果市场存在有效竞争，就应去除不对称管制；如果市场竞争不充分，就应建立或加强不

批注：The principle of "legal equal protection rights" established by the Fourteenth amendment of constitution of USA, stemmed from the body physical supremacy rooted in the maxim of "all people are created equal". Therefore the application scope of the principle of "legal equal protection right" is limited to natural person.

批注：Now that the kernel of legal persons' right is property right, other than physical right, it lost supremacy. Therefore, in need of public interest or other legitimate aim (reasonable aim), to restrict property right of legal persons, or differentiate treatment to disposing capacity of legal person (confine the civil rights capacity of specific legal persons) is justifiable.

批注：European Community Directive 2002/21/EC

"on a common regulatory framework for electronic communications networks and services" (Framework Directive)

Article 16 Market analysis procedure

3. Where a national regulatory authority concludes that the market is effectively competitive, it shall not impose or maintain any of the specific regulatory obligations referred to in paragraph 2 of this Article.

4. Where a national regulatory authority determines that a relevant market is not effectively competitive, it shall identify undertakings with significant market power on that

---

[32] 尹田.论法人人格权[J].法学研究，2004（4）：56.
[33] ［德］迪特尔·梅迪库斯.德国民法总论[M].2 版.邵建东，译.北京：法律出版社，2001：821.
[34] 白永忠.电信业热点法律问题透析[M].北京：法律出版社，2003：276.新华网.不对称管制的前提已不存在——中国电信总经理周德强答记者问[EB/OL].（2002-05-27）
http://news.xinhuanet.com/it/2002-05-27/content_410158.htm
[35] 从我国目前的竞争状况看，笔者认为有必要保留并加强该制度。目前还远未进入电信业的充分竞争时代，重要电信资源的分配仍由政府指定，电信行业的计划经济色彩相当浓厚，电信法迟迟未能出台，中国加入 WTO 后虽然开放了电信市场，但外资运营商并无实质竞争力等等，即使真的"进入充分竞争的时代"，新入门者仍需要该制度辅助逐渐获得竞争力。

对称管制[36]。] 本文讨论的是，如果要设立不对称管制规范，哪个部门有立法权？

[旨在恢复实质正义的不对称管制制度，要用形式上的不平等获得实质上的平等。作为一种反向歧视措施，不对称管制规则的制定机关应为有权制定反向歧视规则的机关。] "立法主体的立法权限范围，主要取决于它置身于何种国情之下[37]。" 国家或政府立法权的划分完全依赖于国内法，"不少国家的政府立法权的调整范围实际上比立法机关行使的立法权调整的范围还要广泛。……有的国家甚至规定政府在一定时期内可以通过行使立法权来调整属于宪法性法律调整的事项[38]。" [在美国，行政命令、法律都可以成为反向歧视规则的渊源[39]。所以，美国议会和联邦通信委员会都有权颁布不对称管制措施；] 而欧共体成员国有关互联互通的不对称管制措施如果超过了欧盟指令中规定的种类，必须由国内通信监管机构报欧共体委员会批准方可执行[40]。

那么，我国有权制定不对称管制规则的机关是谁呢？讨论这个问题有两条路径：其一，探讨制定不对称管制规则属于抽象行政行为还是立法行为；其二，从立法法

批注：Aiming to restoring essence justice, the asymmetric regulation system acquires essence equality by formal inequality. As a kind of reverse discrimination measure, the legislation organ of asymmetric regulation rules should be the organ who has the power to enact reverse discrimination.

批注：In USA, both administrative order and law could become source of reverse discrimination. Therefore, both congress and FCC have right to enact asymmetric regulation measure.

---

[36] 欧盟《电信管制框架指令》Directive 2002/21/EC (Framework Directive) Article 16, Section 3 "Where a national regulatory authority concludes that the market is effectively competitive, it shall not impose or maintain any of the specific regulatory obligations referred to in paragraph 2 of this Article. ……" Section 4 "Where a national regulatory authority determines that a relevant market is not effectively competitive, it shall identify undertakings with significant market power on that market in accordance with Article 14 and the national regulatory authority shall on such undertakings impose appropriate specific regulatory obligations referred to in paragraph 2 of this Article or maintain or amend such obligations where they already exist."

[37] 周旺生. 立法学教程. 北京：北京大学出版社，2006：223.
[38] 周旺生. 立法学教程. 北京：北京大学出版社，2006：233.
[39] 李薇薇. 禁止就业歧视：国际标准和国内实践 [M]. 北京：法律出版社，2006：63-64.
[40] 欧盟《接入与互联指令》Directive 2002/19/EC (Access Directive) Article 8, Sector 3, "In exceptional circumstances, when a national regulatory authority intends to impose on operators with significant market power other obligations for access or interconnection than those set out in Articles 9 to 13 in this Directive it shall submit this request to the Commission. The Commission, acting in accordance with Article 14(2), shall take a decision authorising or preventing the national regulatory authority from taking such measures."

划定的政府立法和国家立法的界限出发，探讨其立法权。

(1) 第一条路径

制定不对称管制规则到底属于抽象行政行为，还是立法行为？这个问题较难回答，因为订立不对称管制规则表现出行政和立法的两面性：其起源于政府对特定行业的管理，是政府为保护竞争环境进行的行政管理行为；而政府为实施该管理行为限制了特定法人的民事权利能力，设定了形式上"不平等"的民事权利能力。因而，不对称管制规则的设定不同于普通抽象行政行为。

普通的抽象行政行为可以赋予公民或法人权利，或者课以义务，但应当是平等的，不能设定形式上"不平等"的权利义务。而不对称管制立法，旨在设定形式上"不平等的"民事权利能力，故其不属于政府立法权范围。"政府立法权一般是专门调整行政关系的立法权[41]。""行政法律关系的内容都与国家行政权力直接有关[42]。"而设定"不平等的"民事权利能力不属于行政法五类内容之一[43]，应属于国家立法范畴。

根据《民事诉讼法》第八条规定，"对当事人在适用法律上一律平等"，以及《行政诉讼法》第七条规定，"当事人在行政诉讼中的法律地位平等"，任何法人在法律面前，一律平等。如果设定形式上"不平等"的权利义务，必须通过法律本身规定（在国外，对其合宪性可以提起违宪审查），而不是执行法律的行政法规。所以，有权制定不对称管制措施的立法机构是全国人大及其常委会。

(2) 第二条路经

我国立法法为政府立法和国家立法划出了明确的界限，立法法第五十六条限定了国务院的立法权限，即"为执行法律的规定需要制定行政法规的事项"（第一项政府立法权）和宪法第八十九条规定的"国务院行政管理职权的事项"（第二项政府立法权）。在讨论订立不对称管制规范的立法权时，假定前提是该规范尚未出台，这显然不属于已经有法律规定、仅需通过抽象行政行为具体执行的第一项政府立法权。

有关第二项政府立法权，表面上看，在对电信业进行管理过程中，制定不对称管制措施属于国务院实施宪法第八十九条赋予的职权，即"领导和管理经济工作和城乡建设"。另外，从立法法第八条规定的全国人大及其常委会专属立法权——制定"民事基本制度"，可以推定：非民事基本制度可以由国务院立法。因为在"民事基本制度"之外，还存在大量的设定民事权利义务的规范，立法法并未剥夺国务

---

[41] 周旺生. 立法学教程 [M]. 北京：北京大学出版社，2006：232.
[42] 胡建淼. 行政法学 [M]. 2版. 北京：法律出版社，2003：28.
[43] 胡建淼. 行政法学 [M]. 2版. 北京：法律出版社，2003：17.

院在此事项上的立法权。而不对称管制措施并不属于"民事基本制度",这样看来,国务院似乎有制定不对称管制的立法权。

然而,实施该政府立法权的结果是设定了"不平等的"权利或义务,"不平等地"限制特定主体的民事权利能力,违反了《宪法》第五条"任何组织或者个人都不得有超越宪法和法律的特权",侵犯了法人平等权。如果国务院在制定行政管理法规时"平等地"赋予了或剥夺了企业或法人的民事权利,该行政法规不涉及反向歧视,则为有效;否则,无效。因为设定"特权"的,只能是法律。因而,设定"不平等"的权利——反向歧视,应当属于我国《立法法》第八条规定的"必须由全国人民代表大会及其常务委员会制定法律的其他事项",而非国务院的行政法规,更不可能是工信部的部门规章。

综上,[不对称管制规则的立法权在于国家,而非政府。不过,鉴于我国全国人大及其常委会立法过程的烦琐,为提高立法效率,可以在即将出台的电信法中,通过授权立法的形式,授权电信监管机构在适当的时候,根据需要颁布不对称管制措施,以解决其无立法权又要保证监管及时的尴尬。]

批注:The legislative power of asymmetric regulation is at the nation other than government. However, as for the legislative procedure of The National People's Congress (NPC) and its standing committee being complicated, to improve legislative efficiency, we could set entrust provision in the upcoming telecom law, which authorizes telecom regulator to enact asymmetric regulation decree as needed, at appropriate time, to resolve its embezzling of guaranteeing the regulation efficiency but without legislative power.

生词和词组

第三章

1. 最大程度地模拟竞争效果 simulate the competition consequence to the maximum extent

2. 不充分竞争 incomplete competition

3. 自然垄断 natural monopoly

4. 持续质量保证 Continuous Quality Assurance
5. 终端设备 terminal devices
6. 独立子公司 independent subsidiary
7. 掠夺性定价 predatory pricing
8. 财务审计 financial audit
9. 交叉补贴 cross-subsidization subsidize
10. 分业管制 separated regulation
11. 智能频率分配 Intelligence frequency allocation
12. 妨碍竞争 impediment competition, anti-competition
13. 价值目标 value target
14. 生产效率提高 productivity improvement
15. 可持续发展 sustainable development
16. 无正当理由 without justified reason
17. 强制搭售 forced tie-in sale, forced tying
18. 低于成本价 below-cost price
19. 标准化服务 standardized service
20. 兼容设备 compatible equipment
21. 设备入网许可 Device access permission
22. 最低服务能力 minimum service ability
23. 持续服务 continual service
24. 唯一路径 non-alternative route
25. 号码可携带 number portability
26. 披露信息 disclose information
27. 黄页汇编人 yellow pages compiler
28. 紧急服务 emergency service
29. 号码目录服务 phone number directory service
30. 通话记录查询 call records query, call history inquire
31. 话费清单查询 bill list query

32. 合同必备条款 prerequisite clauses of contract, mandatory terms of contract

33. 电话号码本 phone directory

34. 国家征用权 right of eminent domain

35. 征用 expropriate

36. 缴纳普遍服务基金 render (pay) universal service fund

37. 有损失 suffer from losses, endure losses

38. 公共电话亭 public phone booth (box)

39. 提供服务 render service, provide service, supply service

40. 残疾人 handicapped (disable) persons

41. 遵守 comply with, abide by, obey, subject to

42. 新兴企业 emerging enterprise

43. 严重妨碍有效竞争：Significant Impediment to Effective Competition (SIEC)

44. 滥用市场支配地位 abuse market dominant position

45. 年收入额 Annual revenues

46. 市场占有率 market share

47. 资源占有率 resource share

48. 主导运营商 dominant operator, incumbent operator, Incumbent Local Exchange Carrier（ILEC，本地交换运营商）

49. 非主导运营商 non-dominant operator, Competitive Local Exchange Carrier（CLEC，与本地交换运营商竞争的运营商）

50. 设定义务 Impose duty, establish obligation

51. 区别对待 asymmetric treatment

52. 市场主体 market entity

53. 信息上报制度 information reporting institution

54. 监管程度 supervision degree

55. 电信基础设施 telecom infrastructure

56. 经济不理性地区 economic irrational region, nonprofit region

57. 授权定价权 authorize pricing power

58. 政府定价 government fixed price

59. 核准的经营范围 approve business scope

60. 小灵通 Personal Hand-phone System(PHS), Little Smart

61. 法理学依据 legal theoretical basis for

62. 形式上的平等 equality in form

63. 实质上的平等 equality in essence, equality in substance

64. 实质正义 essence justice, essential justice, substantive justice, material justice

65. 形式正义 formal justice

66. 程序正义 procedural justice

67. 目标群体 target group

68. 市场支配地位 market dominant position

69. 滥用市场优势 abuse of market advantage

70. 严重阻碍市场竞争 Significant Impediment to Effective Competition

71. 真正意义上的 a real sense of

72. 充分模拟竞争的效果 fully simulating the effect of competition

73. 中立 neutrality

74. 身体健全的 able-bodied

75. 高考录取分数线 college admission score

76. 招工标准 qualification for recruiting workers

77. 补偿正义（矫正正义）compensatory justice, restitutive justice, corrective justice

78. 间接歧视 indirect discrimination

79. 先验的真理 A priori truth, self-evidence truth

80. 表面上看 judging by appearance, on the surface, looking from outside

81. 权利剥夺法（剥夺公权法案）bill of attainder

82. 追溯既往的法律 ex post facto law

83. 正当利益 legitimate interests

84. 美国宪法第14修正案 The Fourteenth Amendment of constitution of U.S.A.

85. 人人生而平等 all men are created equal

86. 法律的平等保护权 law equal protection rights, the legal right of equal protection

87. 行为能力 disposing capacity, capacity, behavioral competence

88. 民事权利能力 the civil rights capacities

89. 自然人 natural person

90. 正当目的 justifiable aim, reasonable aim

91. 至上性 supremacy

92. 财产权 property right

93. 人身权 physical right

94. 人格权 right of personality, Personal right

95. 法人 legal person

96. 欧共体 European Community

97. 机关 organ, body, organization

98. 行政命令 administrative order

99. 反向歧视 reverse discrimination

100. 法律渊源 legal source, source of law

第 四 章
Chapter 4

电信市场准入
Telecom Market Access

按照传统观点，由于电信基础资源（电信网络、无线电频率、卫星轨道、电话码号）的稀缺，电信市场准入应当实行审批制度，属于《行政许可法》第十二条第（二）类行政许可事项[1]。我国《电信条例》和《电信业务经营许可管理办法》为电信企业入门资格设定了特许制度，以控制总量。然而，《电信条例》实施以来，其第十二条"颁发《基础电信业务经营许可证》，应当按照国家有关规定采用招标方式"规定的竞争性许可机制从未实施过，频率、码号、路权等稀缺电信资源通常采用国家指定的计划经济分配方式。另外，为履行入世开放承诺，我国2001年出台了《外商投资电信企业管理规定》，但到现在外资很少能够进入基础电信领域。面对欧盟电信框架指令和美国1996年电信法中撤销电信运营商入门许可、完全开放电信市场的国际趋势，在我国尚未出台的电信法中如何设定入门资格的行政许可，是在开放市场与加强监管之间寻求利益平衡的关键。

批注： How to institute administrative permission about entry qualification, is the key of acquiring interest balance between market opening and strengthening supervision.

---

[1] 《行政许可法》第十二条第（二）项"有限自然资源开发利用、公共资源配置以及直接关系公共利益的特定行业的市场准入等，需要赋予特定权利的事项"。

第一节　我国电信企业市场准入的行政许可类型

Section 1　The Classifications of Telecom Market Access in China

1. 基础电信业的自然垄断性和特许准入制

"自然垄断主要指依赖独特的资源优势，在规模经济和范围经济显著的条件下使得由一家企业或极少数企业经营比多家企业经营这类产品或服务的效率更高的现象[2]。" [根据规制经济学理论，对于自然垄断行业，竞争是不经济的，或者说是浪费社会资源的。由于缺乏竞争，仅凭"看不见的手"调节市场，无法达到社会总体利益最大化[3]。自然垄断性行业需要政府管制，尤其需要控制入门资格。]

批注：According to the theory of regulatory economics, as for natural monopoly business, competition is uneconomic, in other words, waste of social resources. Because of lack of competition, only through "invisible hand" adjusting market, social overall benefit cannot be maximized. The natural monopoly business needs governmental regulation, especially need controlling entry admission qualification.

电信业之所以被认为是自然垄断行业，原因在于电信网络不宜重复建设，深埋地下的管线不仅建设成本巨大，而且天然不适于竞争。网络自身的自然垄断性往往被推延至基于网络的服务，于是全体"某部门"被认为是自然垄断的。"问题是无论怎么引入竞争，可能最终仍然会有某些部门存在自然垄断，比如，永远不会存在同时建立两个彼此平行的输电网或铁路运输网的必要，这主要与其经济技术特征密切相关[4]。"在电信发展的初期，各国通常以保障国家安全、公民通信秘密权和民族利益为由，直接指定一家运营商垄断经营电信业。电信企业私有化后，除限制外资持股比例外[5]，对企业入门资格的限制性规定仍然存在。

[进入21世纪后，发达国家相继取消了除涉及稀缺电信资源的入门限制，完全开放了电信市场。而我国无论是对基础电信业务，还是增值电信业务[6]，均实行严格的准入审批制，这严重妨碍

批注：After entering 21th century, developed countries, one after another, cancelled entry admission restriction, and fully opened market, except for what are related to scarcity telecom resource. However, China implements strict examine and approval for

---

[2]　杨培芳.网络协同经济学——第三只手的凸现[M].北京：经济科学出版社，2000：138.

[3]　[美]卡尔·夏皮罗，等.信息规则：网络经济的策略指导[M].张帆，译.北京：中国人民大学出版社，2000：20.

[4]　张昕竹，等.网络产业：规制与竞争理论[M].北京：社会科学文献出版社，2000：3.

[5]　比如我国《外商投资电信企业管理规定》第六条"经营基础电信业务（无线寻呼业务除外）的外商投资电信企业的外方投资者在企业中的出资比例，最终不得超过49%。经营增值电信业务（包括基础电信业务中的无线寻呼业务）的外商投资电信企业的外方投资者在企业中的出资比例，最终不得超过50%。"

[6]　在以下论述中分别使用网络运营商和电信服务商的称谓，分别指电信网络的运营商和靠租用他人的电信网络提供电信服务者。这比我国《电信条例》第八条对基础电信业务和增值电信业务提供者的区分更科学。

了电信市场的自由竞争。]要探讨我国的电信准入行政许可的改革，首先要搞清我国的电信市场准入属于行政许可法上的哪一种行政许可。

2. 我国电信市场准入的行政许可类型及其弊端

[我国《行政许可法》第十二条规定了五种类型的行政许可，分别为：

（一）直接涉及国家安全、公共安全、经济宏观调控、生态环境保护以及直接关系人身健康、生命财产安全等特定活动，需要按照法定条件予以批准的事项（普通许可，也叫批准，无自由裁量权）；

（二）有限自然资源开发利用、公共资源配置以及直接关系公共利益的特定行业的市场准入等，需要赋予特定权利的事项（特许，也叫审批，资源分配型许可，这类许可有数量限制，根据《行政许可法》第五十三条，"实施本法第十二条第二项所列事项的行政许可的，行政机关应当通过招标、拍卖等公平竞争的方式作出决定。但是，法律、行政法规另有规定的，依照其规定。"）；]

[（三）特殊职业准入的资格资质认可，比如律师、医生、注册会计师，属于自由裁量权许可，应通过考试、考核等方式决定；

（四）对特定物的核准，比如电梯、汽车、电信终端入网许可，根据《行政许可法》第五十五条，行政机关应当按照技术标准、技术规范依法进行检验、检测、检疫；

market access of both basic business and value-added business. As a result, this system severely impedes free competition of telecom market.

批注：Administrative License Law of The People's Republic of China Article 12 stipulates 5 types of administrative license being established for any of the following matters:

(1) The special activities that directly bear on the state security, public security, macro-economic control, ecological environment protection, and those directly relate to the human health, safety of life and property, which shall be approved according to the legal requirements (ordinary permission, i.e. ratify, non-discretion)

(2) The development and utilization of the limited natural resources, allocation of public resources and the market entry of the special trades that directly concern public interests, which shall be entitled with special rights (charter, or special permission, or examine and approve, because of concerning to resource allocation approval, this kind of license has quantitative restriction, according to Administrative License Law, Article 53 When implementing the licensing matters listed in Article 12 (2) of the Law, the administrative organ shall make a decision by adopting fair competitive methods, such as bid invitation and auction, etc., but if it is otherwise provided for in the laws, administrative regulations, the latter shall prevail.);

批注：(3) special professional vocation admission, such as lawyer, doctor, registered accountant, belongs to discretion, approving by qualification test or check;

(4) Qualification for specific product to be used, such as elevator, car, telecom termination admission access to network. According to Administrative License Law, Article 55 When

（五）法人设立登记，如公司设立，是无自由裁量权的对主体的许可，主要是形式审查[7]。]

[与电信相关的许可涉及普通许可和特许。]普通许可是指行政机关准予符合法定条件的公民或法人从事特定活动的行为，其条件法定，符合条件的行政机关必须批准，不符合则不批准。例如，颁发持枪证、危险化学品的生产销售许可等。特许是指行政机关代表国家依法向相对人转让某种权利的行为，用于有限自然资源的利用、公共资源的限量以及直接关系公共利益的特定行业的市场准入等，其主要功能是分配稀缺资源。例如：采矿许可、取水许可、海域使用许可。根据《行政许可法》第五十三条，行政机关应当通过招标、拍卖等公平竞争的方式对特许做出决定。

[普通许可和特许的主要区别在于前者是免除相对人的不作为义务，后者是赋予相对人特权。前者无数量上的限制，属于羁束行政行为，行政机关没有自由裁量权；后者有数量限制，属于自由裁量行政行为，行政机关具有较大的裁量权。入门许可

implementing the licensing matters listed in Article 12 (4) of the Law, namely, conducting inspection, testing or quarantine according to the technical standards or criteria, the administrative organ shall make decisions according to the pertinent results.

(5) Legal person registration, such as company registration, this is non-discretion approval to subject, through formality examination.

批注：The administrative license concerning to telecom relates to ordinary permission (ratify) and special permission (charter, examine and approve)

---

[7] 《行政许可法》第十二条将行政许可分为五类：（1）普通许可（无自由裁量权的对行为的许可）。直接涉及国家安全、公共安全、经济宏观调控、生态环境保护以及直接关系人身健康、生命财产安全等特定活动，需要按法定条件予以批准的事项。例如，食品卫生许可、持枪证、危险化学品的生产销售许可等。这类许可依法律规定的条件规定，并无数量上的限制。根据《行政许可法》第三十四条，申请人提交的申请材料齐全、符合法定形式，行政机关能够当场作出决定的，应当当场作出书面的行政许可决定；需要对申请材料的实质内容进行核实的，行政机关应当指派两名以上工作人员进行核查。（2）特许（资源分配型许可）。有限自然资源的利用、公共资源的限量以及直接关系公共利益的特定行业的市场准入等，需要赋予特定权利的事项。例如：采矿许可、取水许可、海域使用许可、无线电频率许可（垄断行业）等。这类许可有数量限制，根据《行政许可法》第五十三条，行政机关应当通过招标、拍卖等公平竞争的方式作出决定。（3）认可（自由裁量权许可）。提供公众服务并且直接关系公共利益的职业、行业，需要确定具备特殊信誉、特殊条件或者特殊技能等资格、资质的事项。例如：医师、律师、会计师资格、建设企业的资质等。这类许可应通过考试、考核等方式决定。根据《行政许可法》第五十四条，赋予法人或者其他组织特定的资格、资质的，行政机关根据申请人的专业人员构成、技术条件、经营业绩和管理水平等的考核结果作出行政许可决定。（4）核准（对物的许可）。直接关系公共安全、人身健康、生命财产安全的重要设备、设施、产品、物品需要按照技术标准、技术规范，通过检验、检测、检疫等方式进行审定的事项：如电信终端设备的入网许可、电梯运行的核准、动物及动物产品的检疫等。根据《行政许可法》第五十五条，行政机关应当按照技术标准、技术规范依法进行检验、检测、检疫，行政机关根据检验、检测、检疫的结果作出行政许可决定。（5）登记（无自由裁量权的对主体的许可）。企业或者其他组织的设立等，需要确定主体资格的事项，这类许可主要是形式审查。根据《行政许可法》第五十六条，申请人提交的申请材料齐全、符合法定形式的，行政机关应当当场予以登记。需要对申请材料的实质内容进行核实的，行政机关应当指派两名以上工作人员进行核查。

赋予了企业特定的行为权利，决定着市场主体的数量，从而决定了竞争的充分性。] 如果可以将稀缺资源使用权与入门资格许可剥离，则选择普通入门许可还是特许入门，决定于行业法制环境、政府管制能力和市场对竞争充分性的要求。[一般行业的入门许可都经历了从特许（审批制）到普通许可（批准制）的演变。在行业诞生初期，管制机构体制薄弱、管制能力有限、行业立法不完备，入门限制就显得相对重要，这时的入门条件苛刻，行政许可采用特许制；一旦行业发展成熟，有了完备的行业立法和健全的管制机构，有效的管制手段可以渗透在入门后日常经营活动中，这时入门管制就显得不再重要，重要的是以清晰的权利义务规范为依据进行制度化管理，入门的特许通常会变为普通许可，以增大竞争程度。] 正如德国的公司制度对于新设公司许可经历了从特许制到登记制（普通许可）的演变，直到1870年德国修订《普通德意志商法典》之前，对股份公司都采取特许制，即"法人的权利能力由国家，而且是根据尽其本分的裁量授予[8]。"

[我国《电信条例》第七、九、十、十二、十三条规定了对于基础电信业务和增值电信业务实行严格的审批制；] 申请经营基础电信业务的，申请人必须达到《电信条例》第十条和《电信业务经

批注：The main difference between ordinary permission (ratify) and special permission (charter) is that, the former exempt the administrative counterpart from omission obligation (in-action obligation, not as obligation), and the latter grant the administrative counterpart privilege. The former has no quantitative restriction, belonging to restriction administrative action, and the administrative organs have no discretion. The latter has quantitative restriction, belonging to discretion administrative action, and the administrative organs have greater discretion power. Entry admission authorizes enterprises with specific behavior right, deciding the quantity of market players, thus determining the sufficiency of competition.

批注：To ordinary business entry admission, it evolves from charter (examination and approval) to ordinary permission (ratify). At the early stage of the birth of the business, the regulation institution is vulnerable (frail), the management ability is deficient, trade legislation incomplete, therefore, the entry restriction seems more critical. At that time, the admission is rigorous, and the permission adopts the form of chart (examine and approve). Once the trade becomes mature, having completely trade legislation and sound regelation organ, the effective regulative method could permeate into daily managing activities after entering into the market, entry admission seems no longer critical, and the critical is to systematically manage, according to rules with definite right and obligation. At this time, entry charter usually changes into ordinary permission to enhance the degree of competition.

批注：China's Telecommunications Regulations article 7、9、10、12、13 stipulate that, admission for both basic and value-added telecom business applies with strict examine and approve system (charter).

---

[8]　［德］迪特尔·梅迪库斯. 德国民法总论[M]. 邵建东，译. 北京：法律出版社，2001：815-816.

营许可管理办法》第五条规定的条件[9]。申请经营增值电信业务的，申请人必须达到《电信条例》第十三条和《电信业务经营许可管理办法》第六条规定的条件[10]。外资企业经营电信业务，除需满足上述条件外，还要满足《外商投资电信企业管理规定》第四～十条规定的额外条件[11]。在审批过程中，行政机关对提交材料的形式要件和申请人的实质要件都要审查，以此做出是否批准的决定。[行政机关具有很大的自由裁量权，有权进行数量限制，企业无法预见获得许可的可能性。对于基础电信业务，《电信条例》第十二条规定，"国务院信息产业主管部门审查经营基础电信业务的申请时，应当考虑国家安全、电信网络安

批注：The administration organ has great discretionary power, could restrict the quantity of market players, thus the market players could not prohibit the possibility of obtaining admission. As for basic telecom business, Telecommunications Regulations article 12 stipulates that, "When examining an application for the operation of Basic Telecommunications Services, the State Council's department in charge of the information industry shall consider such factors as State security, telecommunications network security, continuous usability of telecommunications resources, environmental protection and the state of competition in the telecom market, etc.

The issuance of Basic Telecommunications Service Operating Permits shall require the invitation of tenders in accordance with the relevant State regulations." Therefore, this kind of permission belongs to typical charter,

---

[9] 这些条件是：（一）经营者为依法设立的专门从事基础电信业务的公司，并且公司的国有股权或者股份不少于51%；（二）有业务发展研究报告和组网技术方案；（三）有与从事经营活动相适应的资金和专业人员；（四）有从事经营活动的场地、设施及相应的资源；（五）有为用户提供长期服务的信誉或者能力；（六）在省、自治区、直辖市范围内经营的，注册资本最低限额为1亿元人民币；在全国或者跨省、自治区、直辖市范围经营的，注册资本最低限额为10亿元人民币；（七）公司及其主要出资者和主要经营管理人员三年内无违反电信监督管理制度的违法记录；（八）国家规定的其他条件。

[10] 这些条件是：（一）经营者为依法设立的公司；（二）有与开展经营活动相适应的资金和专业人员；（三）有为用户提供长期服务的信誉或者能力；（四）在省、自治区、直辖市范围内经营的，注册资本最低限额为100万元人民币；在全国或者跨省、自治区、直辖市范围经营的，注册资本最低限额为1000万元人民币；（五）有必要的场地、设施及技术方案；（六）公司及其主要出资者和主要经营管理人员三年内无违反电信监督管理制度的违法记录；（七）国家规定的其他条件。

[11] 这些条件是外商投资电信企业的注册资本应当符合下列规定：（一）经营全国的或者跨省、自治区、直辖市范围的基础电信业务的，其注册资本最低限额为10亿元人民币；经营增值电信业务的，其注册资本最低限额为1000万元人民币；（二）经营省、自治区、直辖市范围内的基础电信业务的，其注册资本最低限额为1亿元人民币；经营增值电信业务的，其注册资本最低限额为100万元人民币。经营基础电信业务（无线寻呼业务除外）的外商投资电信企业的外方投资者在企业中的出资比例，最终不得超过49%。经营增值电信业务（包括基础电信业务中的无线寻呼业务）的外商投资电信企业的外方投资者在企业中的出资比例，最终不得超过50%。经营基础电信业务的外商投资电信企业的中方主要投资者应当符合下列条件：（一）是依法设立的公司；（二）有与从事经营活动相适应的资金和专业人员；（三）符合国务院工业和信息化主管部门规定的审慎的和特定行业的要求。外商投资电信企业的中方主要投资者，是指在全体中方投资者中出资数额最多且占中方全体投资者出资总额的30%以上的出资者。经营基础电信业务的外商投资电信企业的外方主要投资者应当符合下列条件：（一）具有企业法人资格；（二）在注册的国家或者地区取得基础电信业务经营许可证；（三）有与从事经营活动相适应的资金和专业人员；（四）有从事基础电信业务的良好业绩和运营经验。外商投资电信企业的外方主要投资者，是指在外方全体投资者中出资数额最多且占全体外方投资者出资总额的30%以上的出资者。经营增值电信业务的外商投资电信企业的外方主要投资者应当具有经营增值电信业务的良好业绩和运营经验。

全、电信资源可持续利用、环境保护和电信市场的竞争状况等因素。颁发《基础电信业务经营许可证》，应当按照国家有关规定采用招标方式。"这属于典型的特许行政许可，审批机关考虑的因素不客观、不透明。]对于增值电信业务，表面看属于普通许可（批准），但入门条件中的"有为用户提供长期服务的信誉或者能力"具有不客观、不透明因素，给行政机关留下了很大的解释空间；并且[《电信条例》和《电信业务经营许可管理办法》都规定了增值业务的实质审查程序，所以也属于特许。]

of which the approving authority considers factors is neither objective nor transparent.

批注：Both Telecommunications Regulations and Measures for the management of telecommunications business license stipulate the substantial review procedure for value-added telecom business. Therefore that review belongs to charter(examine and approve).

  特许对内资和外资企业入门都构成障碍，但对外资的影响要严重得多。有些专门针对外资入门限制的条文非常模糊，留给主管机关极大的自由裁量权。比如"符合国务院工业和信息化主管部门规定的审慎的和特定行业的要求""有从事基础电信业务的良好业绩和运营经验"。电信作为服务业的一种，被纳入到成员国承诺开放国内市场的范围，WTO要求各成员国开放国内市场的承诺不是要求各国放弃入门条件，而是入门条件的法定化和透明化，各国有权制定自己的入门规则，但不得靠不透明的政策作为管制入门的依据[12]。我国在《电信条例》中明确了开放电信市场[13]，该条例和《外资投资电信企业管理规定》对外资的持股上限进行了规定[14]。然而，外资电信企业入门的寥寥无几[15]。另外，《电信条例》第十二条虽然设计了采用招标方式获得许可证的机制，但"目前的基础运营商均由于历史延续取得了基础电信业务经营许可证，还没有一家公司是通过招标的方式取得[16]。"我国多年来电信主体间的兼并重组并未形成电信市场充分竞争的格局，其关键原因就在于市场准入门槛过严，大量有竞争实力的企业被限制在特许之外，市场缺乏竞争的数量。在这种背景下，在尚未出台的电信法中，重新设计适合我国国情的入门许可制度十分必要，以此将自然垄断的外延缩到最小，最大限度地开放市场。

---

[12] 1997年2月15日WTO达成的《服务贸易总协定》第四议定书（也称作《基础电信谈判协定》）要求各成员国可以全面提供市场准入或国民待遇，也可继续执行限制措施，但不可在承诺表之外采取其他措施限制外国电信业者进入本国提供服务。
[13] 我国《电信条例》第四条。
[14] 参见我国《电信条例》第十条第一项，以及《外资投资电信企业管理规定》第六条第一款、第二款。
[15] 阚凯力.入世一年："外资入侵论"可以休矣 [M] // 阚凯力.阚凯力观点：对电信业的思考与挑战.北京：北京邮电大学出版社，2005：164.
[16] 续俊旗，等.中欧电信法比较研究 [M].北京：法律出版社，2008：124.

第二节　传统电信特许理论及其面临的挑战

Section 2　The Concept and Challenges of Traditional Telecom Special Pormission

[传统管制理论认为，自然垄断并非绝对排斥市场竞争[17]，而是需要引入管控措施以规范竞争、保证竞争的有序和社会效益。电信网络资源的自然垄断性，以及无线电频率、电信网码号、信道路权[18]等资源的稀缺性构成传统电信管制理论的基础。]面对经济的管制需求，法律给出了行政特许的解决方案。然而，随着电信技术的发展，尤其是互联网的发展，话音和数据业务的边界逐渐模糊，对基础电信业务和增值电信业务的二分法越来越难以操作，原来根据电信产业目录确定行政许可的做法已经不再适应电信技术的发展。

> **批注**：Traditional regulation theory holds that, natural monopoly does not absolutely exclude competition, but needs to introduce management and control measures to regulate competition, protect competition order and social efficiency. The natural monopoly of telecom network resource, as well as the resource scarcity of radio frequency, code number, right of way, constitute the theoretical basis of traditional telecom regulation.

1. 传统特许理由之一：市场配置资源的失效与生产无效率

[主张特许者认为，在通常情况下，市场可以完成资源的最优配置。然而，对于具有自然垄断性的电信业，必须通过特许限制入门数量，]这是因为：（1）网络建设的"沉淀资本"巨大、不宜重复建设、收益周期漫长，由于市场的盲目性，如果政府不做入门限制，会造成社会总成本的消耗；（2）电信建设中不断开挖城市地下管路势必破坏市容市貌、交通环境；（3）虽然从长远看，市场可以控制总量[19]，但优胜劣汰需要过程。过程中，可能会侵害消费者利益（如无法提供持续电信服务）、公共利益（如无法承担普遍服务义务）和其他运营商利益（如无法保证互联互通、码号可携带义务的实现）。所以，不能完全依赖市场的长效机制控制总量，政府应在入门时通过特许严格审查，防止

> **批注**：The scholar who holds charter, suggest that, in the ordinary condition, market is competent to finish the optimal allocation of resources. However, as for telecom business with the feature of natural monopoly, the quantity of market players must be limited through examination and approval.

---

[17] 周其仁. 数网竞争：中国电信业的开放和改革 [M]. 北京：三联书店，2001：27.
[18] 主要指唯一地理通道，包括管道（孔）、杆路、线缆引入口及槽道等通信设施。《公用电信网间互联管理规定》第九、十条有相关规定，以及《关于推进电信基础设施共建共享的紧急通知》[工信部联通[2008]235号]第三条第二、三款说明了：铁塔、杆路、其他基站设施（包括基站的铁塔等支撑设施、天面、机房、室内分布系统、基站专用的传输线路、电源等其他配套设施）和传输线路（包括管道、杆路、光缆）。
[19] 如1996年时存在的互联网公司到2001年就关闭了三分之二。

日后大范围淘汰的发生;(4)网络安全、终端兼容、技术标准,是市场无法解决的,必须引入特许管制。

关于(1)网络自然垄断性不适于竞争的问题,目前技术的发展已经可以做到同一网络同时为多家服务商提供传输服务。随着波分复用、多路调制技术的发展,一路光纤上可以同时传输200万个双向话路。鉴于单一运营商日常大部分带宽都是冗余的[20],并且"距离死亡"使得长途和本地的区分不再重要[21],网络资源完全可以由多个服务商分享。一家服务商垄断使用一个网络不仅不利于服务竞争,还会造成社会资源总量的浪费。[网络和服务的拆分使得网络的自然垄断特征不会延及服务的有效竞争,除专门经营网络资源外,几乎所有电信服务都可以形成有效竞争的市场。因而,将整个电信业看作自然垄断的观念已经过时。从世界范围的电信立法来看,发达国家很早就采取了拆分管制、分业经营、为网络运营商设定不对称管制的办法,以将网络自然垄断性对服务竞争的影响缩小到最小。由于网络不可剥离的自然垄断性,网络自身需要垄断或寡头经营,其垄断者或寡头经营者经特许入门[22]](如后文所述:即使这种特许,在强制接入和接入费管制条件下,也变得没有必要)。[美国1996年电信法体现了这种对本地网运营商入门管制的理念转变,即将事先的准入许可,变为入门后的法定不对称义务,比如,强制无歧视接入、接入条件透明、接入价格管制、执行接入裁决等不对称义务。

举例来说,美国1996年电信法251(c)3规定,"任何在位本地交换网

> **批注**: The split of service and network could block natural monopoly characteristics of network from extending into the complete competition of telecom service, the result of which is almost all of telecom service could form a sufficient competition market, excepting for specialized network resource. Thus, the concept of regarding the telecom business as a whole natural monopoly business is out of date. From the perspective of the world's telecom legislation, the developed countries adopted the method of split regulation, separate operation, establishing asymmetric regulatory policy for network operator very early, in order to minimum the impact of network natural monopoly to competition of service. Because of the natural monopoly of network which can not strip, the network business needs monopoly or oligopoly, in which mode the monopolist or oligarch should obtain admission before entering market.

> **批注**: Act of Telecommunications (1996) of USA reflected this concept conversion of regulating local network operator admission, that is to change the admission before entering the market into asymmetric legal obligation after entrance, such as enforced no-

---

[20] 阚凯力.谈电信传输的"距离死亡"[M]//阚凯力.阚凯力观点:对电信业的思考与挑战.北京:北京邮电大学出版社,2005:57.
[21] [美]罗伯特·W·克兰德尔.竞争与混沌——1996年电信法出台以来的美国电信业[M].匡斌,译.北京:北京邮电大学出版社,2006:67-80.
[22] 如根据我国《行政许可法》第十二条第一款第二项设定的行政许可。

运营商有义务向任何提出请求接入的电信服务运营商在任何技术可行点上、以非捆绑为基础提供非歧视性网络元素接入，……"。

对于可以从网络上分离出的电信服务，作为一般营业范围，任何组织都可以自由经营，法律只为其设定义务（如互联互通、普遍服务、信息安全等），]而不设入门许可；或者仅设定如我国行政许可法第十二条第一款第一项的普通许可，而非特许。

为了强制网络运营商开放网络资源供电信服务商自由使用，国家需要确立网络运营商的接入义务和以成本为基础的网间结算办法。网络运营商从电信服务商处收取的接入费超过建网费和维护费部分，构成网络运营商的利润，这是市场手段调节网络运营商数量的价格杠杆。接入费定得过高，将把电信服务商阻挡在网络之外，无法形成电信服务的有效竞争；如果接入费定得过低，网络运营商就不愿意投资网络建设或开发新技术。

discrimination access, transparence of access condition, access price regulation, implement adjudication concerning access.

For example, Act of Telecommunications (1996) of USA, SEC. 251. [47 U.S.C. 251] INTERCONNECTION (c) ADDITIONAL OBLIGATIONS OF INCUMBENT LOCAL EXCHANGE CARRIERS. (3) UNBUNDLED ACCESS.---The duty to provide, to any requesting telecommunications carrier for the provision of a telecommunications service, nondiscriminatory access to network elements on an unbundled basis at any technically feasible point on rates, terms, and conditions that are just, reasonable, and nondiscriminatory in accordance with the terms and conditions of the agreement and the requirements of this section and section 252. An incumbent local exchange carrier shall provide such unbundled network elements in a manner that allows requesting carriers to combine such elements in order to provide such telecommunications service.

As for the telecom service which could be split away from network, it is regarded as ordinary business , which could be operated freely by any enterprise, and it should only take the burden of legal obligations, such as interconnection, universal service, information security, etc.

在确立了网络运营商的接入义务和以成本为基础的网间结算办法后，以特许方式通过行政手段限制网络运营商入门数量就没有必要了。美国1996电信法未对网络运营商入门进行数量限制，通过租赁、转售等方式使用他人网络提供电信服务的服务商远远超过自建网络提供服务的网络运营商。现在美国联邦通信委员会（FCC）担心的已经不是撤销入门特许后，网络运营商过多导致的网络资源的无序竞争、社会资源浪费，而是没有人愿意充当网络运营商，以及现有网络运营商没有热情投入新技术和资金进行网络建设的问题[23]。

---

[23] [美]罗伯特·W·克兰德尔. 竞争与混沌——1996年电信法出台以来的美国电信业[M]. 匡斌, 译. 北京：北京邮电大学出版社，2006：4.

关于（2）撤销入门许可后的市容市貌问题，完全可以通过提高城市道路开挖补偿标准等价格手段解决。关于（3）网络运营商破产无法履行社会责任等问题，可以通过设定严格的普通许可条件，而不是特许，比如注册资本金、从业人员、技术能力等指标，并在其运营过程中严密监控、预设破产后的客户转移程序等操作层面的措施解决，普通许可完全可以在自然垄断约束条件下模拟市场竞争的效果。关于（4）[网络安全、终端兼容和电信标准问题，可以将其设定为法定义务，强制入门后的企业履行，违反则惩罚，这些不应当成为入门条件，而是入门后义务，]欧盟和美国1996年电信法已经将其从入门条件中剥离到了入门后的企业义务中，后文专述。

批注：As for network security, terminal compatibility, and telecommunication standards, they could be set to legal obligations, enforcing the enterprise to obey, and punishing who violates. These obligations should not be set as admission condition, but duty after entering the market.

2. 传统特许理由之二：入门限制有助于实现普遍服务

电信运营商通常愿意向高端客户提供服务，而抛弃低端市场。因为向地理环境恶劣、人烟稀少、低收入群体等经济非理性地区提供服务的投入巨大，回报率却很小。普遍服务被视为带有道义性的社会责任，无法通过"看不见的手"实现。[国家一方面强制垄断运营商提供普遍服务，以实现公共利益；另一方面，默认或者允许垄断运营商进行交叉补贴，以其在垄断上的超额利润补贴普遍服务成本[24]。传统特许理论认为，保证垄断运营商从垄断业务中获得垄断利润，成了国家强制其履行普遍服务的前提。所以，国家会限制入门总量，保证垄断运营商赚取垄断利润，以便其通过交叉补贴弥补普遍服务成本。]美国20世纪70年代之前，一直采取这种措施。联邦通信委员会（FCC）在要求AT&T提供本地普遍服务的同时，允许其垄断长途业务，并用其超额利润交叉补贴本地业务的低价格亏损（普遍服务之一种）。

批注：The government enforces monopoly operators to supply universal service to realize public interest, on the other hand, acquiesces or allows monopoly operators to cross subsidize, which is using superprofit collected from monopolized business to subsidize the cost of universal service. Traditional concession theory holds that, it is precondition of enforcing monopoly operators to perform the universal service obligation that government safeguards the monopoly operators to collect monopoly profit. Therefore, the government should set the ceiling of admission, so as to safeguard monopoly operators to make monopoly profit used for covering the cost of universal service through cross subsidizing.

[交叉补贴最大的问题是造成不正当竞争，垄断经营者不仅用垄断业务高收费补贴普遍服务支出，还用其补贴竞争性业务的低价格亏损，以获得竞争优势。而其竞

---

[24] [加] Hank Intven，等. 电信规制手册[M]. 管云翔，译. 北京：北京邮电大学出版社，2001：272.

争对手，由于并不提供垄断服务，无从获得垄断利润，无法跟进竞争性业务的低价格，最终被赶出竞争业务市场[25]。所以，采用交叉补贴的方式提供普遍服务无异于饮鸩止渴。最有效的补偿普遍服务成本的办法是建立普遍服务基金[26]，将普遍服务义务赋予所有电信从业者，或者在不对称管制措施下将此义务赋予达到一定收入规模的运营商；然后，采用招标的方式寻求普遍服务提供者，并用该基金向其补偿。根据美国1996年电信法，所有经营跨州电信业务的公司都要提供普遍服务或缴纳普遍服务基金，该基金用于补偿普遍服务提供者的普遍服务支出[27]。

批注：The most problem caused by cross subsidization is unfair competition, monopoly operator, whose price is set lower than its cost to achieve competitive advantage, uses the superprofit collected from monopoly business to subsidize not only the loss of universal service, but also the loss of competition business. On the other hand, because of no superprofit collected from monopoly service, its competitor cannot afford to follow too low of the price to be compelled out of the market of competition business. Therefore, to supply with universal service by cross subsidization is temporary relief which would result in disaster. The most effective way to compensate the loss of universal service is to establish universal service fund, and impose the obligation of universal service to every telecom operator, or in the condition of asymmetric regulation, those whose income over a certain baseline. Then, the regulator designates the universal service provider by tendering, and uses the fund to compensate it. According to Act of Telecommunications (1996) of USA [47 U.S.C. 254] (d) ," Every telecommunications carrier that provides interstate telecommunications services shall contribute, on an equitable and nondiscriminatory basis, to the specific, predictable, and sufficient mechanisms established by the Commission to preserve and advance universal service."

Act of Telecommunications (1996) of USA[47 U.S.C. 254] (d) TELECOMMUNICATIONS CARRIER CONTRIBUTION.--Every telecommunications carrier that provides interstate telecommunications services shall contribute, on an equitable and nondiscriminatory basis, to the specific, predictable, and sufficient mechanisms established by the Commission to preserve and advance universal service. The Commission may exempt a carrier or class of carriers from this requirement if the carrier's telecommunications activities are limited to such an extent that the level of such carrier's contribution to the preservation and advancement of universal service would be de minimis. Any other provider of interstate telecommunications may be required to contribute to the preservation and advancement of universal service if the public interest so requires.

(e) UNIVERSAL SERVICE SUPPORT.--After the date on which Commission regulations implementing this section take effect, only an eligible telecommunications carrier designated under section 214(e) shall be eligible to receive specific Federal universal service support. A carrier that receives such support shall use that support only for the provision, maintenance, and upgrading of facilities and services for which the support is intended. Any such support should be explicit and sufficient to achieve the purposes of this section.

---

[25] 欧阳武. 美国的电信管制及其发展 [M]. 北京：中国友谊出版公司，2000：126.
[26] ［加］Hank Intven，等. 电信规制手册 [M]. 管云翔，译. 北京：北京邮电大学出版社，2001：278.
[27] ［47 U.S.C. 254］(d)、(e).

3. 传统特许理由之三：基础电信服务必须使用稀缺电信资源

[自然垄断理论认为，频率、码号、路权等电信资源的稀缺性对从业者数量构成限制，比如，考虑到频率资源稀缺，只能允许少数使用频率资源提供服务的运营商入门，否则就会造成无线电干扰。]如果在多个市场主体间平均分配电信稀缺资源，从技术角度看，会影响通信质量和信息安全；从经济学角度看，无法获得规模经济，由于市场不会考虑竞争主体之间的总体协调性，会出现所谓的市场势力和生产无效率[28]。故[分配电信稀缺资源应当考虑公共利益最大化，将有限资源分配给能够发挥资源最大效益的垄断或寡头经营者，并对其价格进行政府控制。因此，资源稀缺决定了入门特许和专有权制度，以控制从业者数量，德国老《电信法》第八条规定，管理者可以以频率有限作为拒绝颁发许可证的理由[29]。]

[其实，限制稀缺资源使用权与限制企业从事基础电信业务的行为权利是两个不同层面的问题。稀缺资源使用权是一种权益，企业获得该权益进而有"能力"从事电信服务，与该企业获得行政许可从而有"权利"从事电信服务，是两个性质不同的问题。]在法律上，有时行为主体有能力但无权利，比如《出版管理

批注：Natural monopoly theory hold that, the scarcity of telecom resource, such as frequency, code number, right of way etc., limits the market player's quantity. For example, considering the scarcity of frequency resource, the market can only afford little operator to provide service by using frequency resource, or the radio interference would occur.

批注：The allocating of telecom resource should consider the maximization of public interest, therefore, limited resource should be allocated to monopolizer or oligarch who could create maximum efficiency by using it, and the price should be controlled by government. Thus, the scarcity of resource determines admission and exclusive right system to control the number of practitioners. The old telecom law of Germany article 8 stipulated that, regulator has the right of refusal of permission for frequency scarcity.

批注：In fact, to restrict the right of using scarcity resource and to restrict the enterprise's behavior right of running basic telecom business are different issues on separate level. The right of using scarcity resource is a kind of rights, to which enterprises are authorized, then they have the capacity to operate telecom service. This right has different feature to administrative permission to "be granted to" operate telecom service.

---

[28] 张维迎. 信息、管制与中国电信业的改革[M] // 张昕竹. 中国规制与竞争：理论和政策. 北京：社会科学文献出版社，2000：238.

[29] 老德国电信法1996年生效，2004年被新电信法取代。老德国电信法第8条"……许可证申请在下述情况下应予以否决：1. 管理机构没有任何可用频率提供给准备使用无线链路的申请者，……"。

条例》第九条禁止个人从事出版活动，但《商标法实施条例》第二章规定的商标申请人资格并未排除个人申请，故个人可以获得图书出版的商标权，但不得使用这种商标从事出版活动，这是由于获得商标权并不以具有从事使用商标活动的行政许可为前提。[有时行为主体无能力但有权利，比如在房地产公司的入门许可中，没有拿到土地的房地产公司也被允许注册成立，其是否有土地"能够"开展房地产业务，与其是否被核准登记从而"有权"开展房地产业务不同，故不能借口土地稀缺而限制房地产公司总量。]

[同样，电信稀缺资源使用权也是私权利，与提供特定电信服务的行政许可是两回事。我们应当区分"电信稀缺资源使用权的特许"和"从事特定电信业务的登记许可"，并且为二者分别设计许可制度。这也是发达国家电信法在处理这个问题上的一种潮流：对于前者，应采用竞争性特许以限制使用人总量，如同国家出让土地等其他稀缺资源使用权一样，即通过招标、拍卖等竞争性方式特许电信稀缺资源使用权；对于后者，不设行政许可，而将经营任何电信业务作为一般经营范围，企业自注册之日即有从事该行为的权利，如果企业没有获得电信稀缺资源使用权，虽然其有权经营该电信业务，但从技术上看，其缺乏行为能力而无法实现其行为权利。]欧盟授权指令（2002/20/EU）第六条及附录A（一般授权条件）、B（无线电频率授权条件）、C（码号授权条件）规定了一

批注: Sometimes, the actor has no capacity but has right. For example, the real estate companies are allowed to be registered as incorporate without land. Whether they have land to "be capacity of" operating real estate business is different to whether they are approved to be registered as incorporate and then "authorized" to do the business. Therefore, the regulator could not use the excuse of land scarcity to restrict the quantity of real estate companies.

批注: Similarly, the right of using telecom resource is a kind of private right, entirely different from administrative permission for providing with specific telecom service. We should differentiate between "authorized of the exclusive right of utilization of telecom scarcity resource" and "permission to registering of operating specific telecom business", furthermore, devise respective permission systems for them. To deal with this question, it is a trend for developed countries. For the former ("authorized of the exclusive right of utilization of telecom scarcity resource"), government should adopt competitive tender to limit the quantity of users, just like granting the use right of land or any other scarcity resource, that is to say, through the competitive assignment methods, such as tender or auction, the government grants the exclusive right of using telecom scarcity resource. On the other hand, for the latter ("permission to registering of operating specific telecom business"), the government should not establish administrative permission, but regard providing with telecom service as ordinary business scope, which any enterprise has since existence registration. If the enterprise has not acquired the right of utilizing telecom scarcity resource yet, from technique perspective, although having the right to operate telecom business, it could not realize that right for lacking of behavior capacity.

般授权条件和电信资源使用权条件，而且第 4 款规定，授予稀缺电信资源使用权不得使用一般授权的条件，即他们的授权是分别进行的。

作为过渡，可以将涉及电信稀缺资源的主体入门许可由特许转为普通许可，不做总量控制，总量控制只限定在电信稀缺资源分配程序中，将申请人获得电信稀缺资源使用权作为入门许可的条件，即申请人首先获得了电信稀缺资源使用权才有权申请从事特定电信业务的普通许可。待行业规范完备、监管体制健全后，再撤销入门的普通许可。

第三节　欧盟和美国的电信准入立法实例

Section 3　The Specific Legislation Cases in EU and USA

放松市场准入、取消电信入门许可是适应电信技术发展、促进竞争的结果。欧盟和美国都将促进竞争作为电信法的立法目的之一[30]，[在欧盟和美国的入门许可制度中，最大程度地剥离了稀缺资源使用权分配和市场主体的入门登记许可，只对电信稀缺资源的分配进行总量控制，对主体入门不设行政许可。]

批注：As for admission system of EU and USA, the allocation of utilization right of scarcity resource and admission registration of market entity are stripped to maximized extension, they only control the total number of telecom scarcity resource, and have eliminated the administrative permission of market entities' entrance.

1. 欧盟

欧盟各国早期电信业都采用政府专营，不存在行政许可问题。20 世纪 80 年代开始了电信私有化改造，行业准入采用特许制。直到 1997 年，欧盟 97/13/EC 指令"建立了一套将电信领域的一般性授权和单独许可证区别对待的制度，……目的是促进许可证制度的自由化，如果可能，认为提供电信业务根本不需要许可，……[31]"。进入 21 世纪后，[欧盟通过授权指令 2002/20/EC 废除了电信行

批注：By authorizing directive 2002/20/EC, EU abolished the administrative permission to telecom business admission, and adopted concession system to scarcity resource and reporting system to operate telecom business, which means that, in case of obtaining scarcity resource such as frequency, code number, the enterprise should be grant of concession from the government; on the other hand, in case of operating telecom business, whatever is basic telecom business or value-added telecom business, the enterprise should only report to the government agent in charge of telecom affairs, not be required to obtain the license issued by the government.

---

[30] 美国 1996 电信法第 257 条，英国 2003 电信法第 4 条第 3 款，欧盟 2002 管制框架第 8 条第 2 款。
[31] 续俊旗，等. 中欧电信法比较研究 [M]. 北京：法律出版社，2008：128，131。

业准入的行政许可，而采用稀缺资源特许制和经营电信业务通知制，即企业要想获得频率、码号等稀缺资源，需要国家特许，而企业经营电信业务，无论基础电信业务还是增值电信业务，只需要通知电信行政主管部门即可，不需获得政府部门颁发的许可证。]

[根据欧盟授权指令[32]，获得电信稀缺资源使用权需经有数量限制的特许，并满足附件B（无线电频率）或C（码号）的条件，这些条件包括资源指定用途、缴纳使用费、号码可携带、提供查号服务和电话簿等义务。指令将该特许称为"单独许可"（grant rights）[33]。如果不涉及电信稀缺资源使用权，企业不需经过行政许可，经营之前只需通知电信管制机构即可。指令将这种自由经营权称为"一般授权（General authorization）"[34]。][欧盟2002/20/EC对电信市场的入门和许可条件都做了详尽的规定。]

批注：According to EU directive, obtaining the permission of utilization of telecom scarcity resource should be grant of concession with quantity limitation, and meet appendix B (as for radio frequency) or C (as for code number), which includes the designated usage of resource, paying occupation fee, number portable, providing with searching number service and providing with phonebook, etc. In the directive, concession is referred to as "grant rights". If the matter does not relate to the utilization right of telecom scarcity resource, enterprises do not be required to get permission, they are required only to report to telecom regulator. In the directive, the free right of operation is referred as "general authorization".

批注：Directive 2002/20/EC of the European Parliament and of the Council "on the authorization of electronic communications networks and services (Authorization Directive)"

Article 2-2-(a)"general authorization" means a legal framework established by the Member State ensuring rights for the provision of electronic communications networks or services and laying down sector specific obligations that may apply to all or to specific types of electronic communications networks and services, in accordance with this Directive;

Article 3-2. The provision of electronic communications networks or the provision of electronic communications services may, without prejudice to the specific obligations referred to in Article 6(2) or rights of use referred to in Article 5, only be subject to a general authorization. The undertaking concerned may be required to submit a notification but may not be required to obtain an explicit decision or any other administrative act by the national regulatory authority before exercising the

---

[32] 欧盟2002/20/EC 第2、3-2、6-1，6-2,6-3和附件A、B、C。
[33] 欧盟2002/20/EU 第五条第二款。
[34] 欧盟2002/20/EU 第三条第二款： "Article 3-2. The provision of electronic communications networks or the provision of electronic communications services may, without prejudice to the specific obligations referred to in Article 6(2)（接入和普遍服务义务，作者注）or rights of use referred to in Article 5（无线电频率和码号义务，作者注），only be subject to a general authorization. The undertaking concerned may be required to submit a notification but may not be required to obtain an explicit decision or any other administrative act by the national regulatory authority before exercising the rights stemming from the authorization. Upon notification, when required, an undertaking may begin activity, where necessary subject to the provisions on rights of use in Articles 5, 6 and 7."

rights stemming from the authorisation. Upon notification, when required, an undertaking may begin activity, where necessary subject to the provisions on rights of use in Articles 5, 6 and 7.

Article 5

Rights of use for radio frequencies and numbers

1. Member States shall, where possible, in particular where the risk of harmful interference is negligible, not make the use of radio frequencies subject to the grant of individual rights of use but shall include the conditions for usage of such radio frequencies in the general authorisation.

2. Where it is necessary to grant individual rights of use for radio frequencies and numbers, Member States shall grant such rights, upon request, to any undertaking providing or using networks or services under the general authorisation, subject to the provisions of Articles 6, 7 and 11(1)(c) of this Directive and any other rules ensuring the efficient use of those resources in accordance with Directive 2002/21/EC (Framework Directive).

Without prejudice to specific criteria and procedures adopted by Member States to grant rights of use of radio frequencies to providers of radio or television broadcast content services with a view to pursuing general interest objectives in conformity with Community law, such rights of use shall be granted through open, transparent and non-discriminatory procedures. When granting rights of use, Member States shall specify whether those rights can be transferred at the initiative of the right holder, and under which conditions, in the case of radio frequencies, in accordance with Article 9 of Directive 2002/21/EC (Framework Directive). Where Member States grant rights of use for a limited period of time, the duration shall be appropriate for the service concerned.

Article 6

Conditions attached to the general authorisation and to the rights of use for radio frequencies and for numbers, and specific obligations

1. The general authorisation for the provision of electronic communications networks or services and the rights of use for radio frequencies and rights of use for numbers may be subject only to the conditions listed respectively in parts A, B and C of the Annex. Such conditions shall be objectively justified in relation to the network or service concerned, non-discriminatory, proportionate and transparent.

2. Specific obligations which may be imposed on providers of electronic communications networks and services under Articles 5(1), 5(2), 6 and 8 of Directive 2002/19/EC (Access Directive) and Articles 16, 17, 18 and 19 of Directive 2002/22/EC (Universal Service Directive) or on those designated to provide universal service under the said Directive shall be legally separate from the rights and obligations under the general authorisation. In order to achieve transparency for undertakings, the criteria and procedures for imposing such specific obligations on individual undertakings shall be referred to in the general authorisation.

3. The general authorisation shall only contain conditions which are specific for that sector and are set out in Part A of the Annex and shall not duplicate conditions which are applicable to undertakings by virtue of other national legislation.

ANNEX

The conditions listed in this Annex provide the maximum list of conditions which may be attached to general authorisations (Part A), rights to use radio frequencies (Part B) and rights to use numbers (Part C) as referred to in Article 6(1) and Article 11(1)(a).

A. Conditions which may be attached to a general authorisation

1. Financial contributions to the funding of universal service in conformity with Directive 2002/22/EC (Universal Service Directive).

2. Administrative charges in accordance with Article 12 of this Directive.

3. Interoperability of services and interconnection of networks in conformity with Directive 2002/19/EC (Access Directive).

4. Accessibility of numbers from the national numbering plan to end-users including conditions in conformity with Directive 2002/22/EC (Universal Service Directive).

5. Environmental and town and country planning requirements, as well as requirements and conditions linked to the granting of access to or use of public or private land and conditions linked to co-location and facility sharing in conformity with Directive 2002/22/EC (Framework Directive) and including, where applicable, any financial or technical guarantees necessary to ensure the proper execution of infrastructure works.

6. "Must carry" obligations in conformity with Directive 2002/22/EC (Universal Service Directive).

7. Personal data and privacy protection specific to the electronic communications sector in conformity with Directive 97/66/EC of the European Parliament and of the Council of 15 December 1997 concerning the processing of personal data and the protection of privacy in the telecommunications sector(1).

8. Consumer protection rules specific to the electronic communications sector including conditions in conformity with Directive 2002/22/EC (Universal Service Directive).

9. Restrictions in relation to the transmission of illegal content, in accordance with Directive 2000/31/EC of the European Parliament and of the Council of 8 June 2000 on certain legal aspects of information society services, in particular electronic commerce, in the internal market(2) and restrictions in relation to the transmission of harmful content in accordance with Article 2a(2) of Council Directive 89/552/EEC of 3 October 1989 on the coordination of certain provisions laid down by law, regulation or administrative action in Member States concerning the pursuit of television broadcasting activities(3).

10. Information to be provided under a notification procedure in accordance with Article 3(3) of this Directive and for other purposes as included in Article 11 of this Directive.

11. Enabling of legal interception by competent national authorities in conformity with Directive 97/66/EC and Directive 95/46/EC of the European Parliament and of the Council of 24 October 1995 on the protection of individuals with regard to the processing of personal data and on the free movement of such data(4).

12. Terms of use during major disasters to ensure communications between emergency services and authorities and broadcasts to the general public.

13. Measures regarding the limitation of exposure of the general public to electromagnetic fields caused by electronic communications networks in accordance with Community law.

14. Access obligations other than those provided for in Article 6(2) of this Directive applying to undertakings providing electronic communications networks or services, in conformity with Directive 2002/19/EC (Access Directive).

15. Maintenance of the integrity of public communications networks in accordance with Directive 2002/19/EC (Access Directive) and Directive 2002/22/EC (Universal Service Directive) including by conditions to prevent electromagnetic interference between electronic communications networks and/or services in accordance with Council Directive 89/336/EEC of 3 May 1989 on the approximation of

the laws of the Member States relating to electromagnetic compatibility(5).

16. Security of public networks against unauthorized access according to Directive 97/66/EC.

17. Conditions for the use of radio frequencies, in conformity with Article 7(2) of Directive 1999/5/EC, where such use is not made subject to the granting of individual rights of use in accordance with Article 5(1) of this Directive.

18. Measures designed to ensure compliance with the standards and/or specifications referred to in Article 17 of Directive 2002/21/EC (Framework Directive).

B. Conditions which may be attached to rights of use for radio frequencies

1. Designation of service or type of network or technology for which the rights of use for the frequency has been granted, including, where applicable, the exclusive use of a frequency for the transmission of specific content or specific audiovisual services.

2. Effective and efficient use of frequencies in conformity with Directive 2002/21/EC (Framework Directive), including, where appropriate, coverage requirements.

3. Technical and operational conditions necessary for the avoidance of harmful interference and for the limitation of exposure of the general public to electromagnetic fields, where such conditions are different from those included in the general authorisation.

4. Maximum duration in conformity with Article 5 of this Directive, subject to any changes in the national frequency plan.

5. Transfer of rights at the initiative of the right holder and conditions for such transfer in conformity with Directive 2002/21/EC (Framework Directive).

6. Usage fees in accordance with Article 13 of this Directive.

7. Any commitments which the undertaking obtaining the usage right has made in the course of a competitive or comparative selection procedure.

8. Obligations under relevant international agreements relating to the use of frequencies.

C. Conditions which may be attached to rights of use for numbers

1. Designation of service for which the number shall be used, including any requirements linked to the provision of that service.

2. Effective and efficient use of numbers in conformity with Directive 2002/21/EC (Framework Directive).

3. Number portability requirements in conformity with Directive 2002/22/EC (Universal Service Directive).

4. Obligation to provide public directory subscriber information for the purposes of Articles 5 and 25 of Directive 2002/22/EC (Universal Service Directive).

5. Maximum duration in conformity with Article 5 of this Directive, subject to any changes in the national numbering plan.

6. Transfer of rights at the initiative of the right holder and conditions for such transfer in conformity with Directive 2002/21/EC (Framework Directive).

7. Usage fees in accordance with Article 13 of this Directive.

8. Any commitments which the undertaking obtaining the usage right has made in the course of a competitive or comparative selection procedure.

9. Obligations under relevant international agreements relating to the use of numbers.

(1) OJ L 24, 30.1.1998, p. 1.

(2) OJ L 178, 17.7.2000, p. 1.

(3) OJ L 298, 17.10.1989, p. 23. Directive as amended by Directive 97/36/EC of the European Parliament and of the Council (OJ L 202, 30.7.1997, p. 60).

(4) OJ L 281, 23.11.1995, p. 31.

(5) OJ L 139, 23.5.1989, p. 19. Directive as last amended by Directive 93/68/EEC (OJ L 220, 30.8.1993, p. 1).

根据指令，任何电信业务都属于企业自由经营范围，但经营者入门后必须履行附件A中的义务，比如普遍服务、互联互通等。可以发现，对电信稀缺资源的单独许可属于我国行政许可法第十二条第一款第二项规定的特许，行政机关可以进行总量控制。该指令所述的一般授权，不是行政许可，因为企业只需通知管制机关，并不需要获得管制机关的批准。有的学者将其称为"许可证制度的取消"或"从许可证制度到普遍授权"[35]。

2. 美国

[美国电信业经历了专利垄断、自由竞争、管制垄断和完全竞争四个时期[36]。] 在管制垄断时期，出台了世界上最早的准入管制。当时，美国本地涌现出了6000家独立电话公司，竞争使得电话价格下降了一半，但市场变得无序并且消费者使用各家的电信业务变得极为不便。美国1934年电信法将管制权交由联邦通信委员会（FCC）行使，管制权中的一项重要内容就是行业准入。任何企业要想进入电信市场必须提交申请，获得批准方可经营。这段时期一直持续到1984年AT&T解体，期间电话公司由多寡头经营[37]。[美国1996年电信法取消了准入许可，除涉及稀缺资源外，不限制数

批注：American's telecom business experienced four stages, i.e. patent monopoly, freely competition, regulative monopoly and full competition.

批注：Act of Telecommunications (1996) of USA abolished the entry permits, in addition to the scarcity resource, it does not limit the number, so to encourage fully completion. The law adopted the strategy at federal level similar to EU Framework Directive (2002/21/EC) and Authorization Directive (2002/20/EC). Sec 253 stipulates that, unless establishing operator's obligations for public interest or competition requirement, states should safeguard operators' free management right, especially to wireless carriers.

SEC. 253. [47 U.S.C. 253] REMOVAL OF BARRIERS TO ENTRY.

(a) IN GENERAL.--No State or local statute or regulation, or other State or local legal requirement, may prohibit or have the effect of prohibiting the ability of any entity to provide any interstate or intrastate telecommunications service.

---

[35] ［英］Ian Lloyd, 等. 通信法 [M]. 曾剑秋, 译. 北京：北京邮电大学出版社，2006：54.

[36] 欧阳武. 美国的电信管制及其发展 [M]. 北京：中国友谊出版公司，2000：19-38.

[37] 包括 AT & T、GTE、Central 和 United 等.

量,以促进全面竞争。该法律在联邦层面采取了和欧盟电信框架指令(2002/21/EC)、入门许可指令(2002/20/EC)相同的策略,其253条(a)~(e)规定,各州除出于公共利益或竞争需要设定运营商义务外,必须保障电信运营商的自由经营权,尤其是无线运营商的自由经营权。"任何州或地方法律、规章,或者其他法律不得禁止任何实体提供任何州内或跨州的电信服务,或者对其具有禁止性影响。"该法还规定,在其生效后15个月内以及每隔三年,联邦通信委员会应当清理构成电信市场入门障碍的任何法律和规定[38]。这说明,美国在联邦层面并未设定入门的行政许可,而将电信业务视为一般经营范围,任何企业都可以自主经营;而在各州层面,电信法授权联邦通信委员会监督其不得制定入门许可。[当然,入门后企业应当履行法定义务,不过,这些义务并不构成入门限制或条件。美国电信法详细规定了入门后义务,如接入义务[39]、互联义务[40]、使用符合电信标准的设备的义务和本地网运营商的转售(resale)、号码可携带(number portability)、平等拨号(dialing parity)、路权接入(access to rights-of-way)、分账(reciprocal compensation)的义务[41],所有跨州(长途)电信运营商具有缴纳普遍服务基金的义务[42]等。]

(b) STATE REGULATORY AUTHORITY.--Nothing in this section shall affect the ability of a State to impose on a competitively neutral basis and consistent with section 254, requirements are necessary to preserve and advance universal service, protect the public safety and welfare, ensure the continued quality of telecommunications services, and safeguard the rights of consumers.

(c) STATE AND LOCAL GOVERNMENT AUTHORITY.--Nothing in this section affects the authority of a State or local government to manage the public rights-of-way or to require fair and reasonable compensation from telecommunications providers, on a competitively neutral and nondiscriminatory basis, for use of public rights-of-way on a nondiscriminatory basis, if the compensation requirement is publicly disclosed by such government.

(d) PREEMPTION.--If, after notice and an opportunity for public comment, the Commission determines that a State or local government has permitted or imposed any statute, regulation, or legal requirement that violates subsection (a) or (b), the Commission shall preempt the enforcement of such statute, regulation, or legal requirement to the extent necessary to correct such violation or inconsistency.

(e) COMMERCIAL MOBILE SERVICE PROVIDERS.--Nothing in this section shall affect the application of section 332(c)(3) to commercial mobile service providers.

批注:Of course, after entering the market, enterprises should fulfill statutory obligations, however, these obligations do not constitute entry restrictions. Act of Telecommunications of USA stipulates those obligations after en-

---

[38] [47 U.S.C. 253].
[39] [47 U.S.C. 201](a).
[40] [47 U.S.C. 251](a).
[41] [47 U.S.C. 251](b)、(c).

通过研究美国和欧盟的电信市场准入制度，可以发现，美国和欧盟的电信法制健全、监管完善，入门制度除涉及电信稀缺资源外，不需要行政许可，电信服务落入企业的一般经营范围，只需承担入门后义务。而涉及稀缺资源的电信业务的入门许可，与稀缺资源的特许分配相分离，稀缺资源采用竞争性的特许分配方式，而使用稀缺资源的电信业务本身仍不设入门许可。这种弱化入门许可的结果是市场主体众多，竞争激烈。

trance in details, such as obligation of access (Sec.201 (a)), interconnection (Sec. 251(a)), using device comply with telecom standard, and incumbent local exchange operator's (ILEO) resale, number portability, dialing parity, access to right of way, reciprocal compensation (Sec.251 (b) 、(c)), as well as paying universal service fund imposed to all interstate operators. (Sec.254 (d)).

生词和词组

第四章

1. 设定行政许可　create administrative licensing requirements
2. 创设行政许可　establish of an administrative license
3. 规制经济学　regulatory economics
4. 不经济的　uneconomic
5. 看不见的手　invisible hand
6. 社会总体利益　the total benefit of the whole society
7. 社会总体利益　social overall benefit
8. 市场准入审批　examination and approval of market access
9. 市场准入　market access, market admission

---

[42] 〔47 U.S.C. 254〕(d).

10. 自由竞争 free competition

11. 妨碍 impede, hamper, obstruct, hinder, interfere with, in the way of, Block

12. 宏观经济控制 macro-economic control

13. 自由裁量权 discretion

14. 无自由裁量权 non-discretion

15. 特许 concession, charter, special permission

16. 审批 examine and approve

17. 数量限制 quantitative limitation, quantitative restriction

18. 形式审查 formality examination, check the formality

19. 豁免 exempt from, release from, Immunity, remit, waiver

20. 行政相对人 administrative counterpart, opposite person for administration

21. 不作为 negative act, non-action, omission, inaction

22. 不作为的义务 omission obligation, not as obligation, inaction obligation, obligation of negative act

23. 行政不作为 administrative omission

24. 羁束行政行为 Restriction administrative act

25. 自由裁量行政行为 discretionary administrative act

26. 行政机关 administrative organs, administrative agency

27. 市场主体 market players, market entity, market subject

28. 竞争的充分性 sufficiency of competition, adequacy of competition

29. 行业立法 trade legislation, industry legislation

30. 法制不完备 incomplete of legal institution

31. 竞争程度 the degree of competition

32. 招标 the invitation of tenders

33. 电信资源可持续利用 continuous usability of telecom resources

34. 审批机关 approving authority

35. 不客观 non-objective

36. 不透明 opaque, non-transparent

37. 实质审查程序 substantial review procedure

38. 排斥竞争 exclude competition

39. 管控措施 management and control measures

40. 码号 code number

41. 路权 right of way

42. 理论基础 theoretical basis

43. 资源最优配置 optimal allocation of resources

44. 拆分管制 split regulation

45. 将服务从网络业务中拆分出来 to carve service out of network business

46. 分业经营 Separate Operation, Segregated Operation

47. 寡头垄断 oligopoly

48. 垄断者或寡头 monopolist or oligarch

49. 终端兼容 terminal compatibility

50. 电信标准 telecommunication standards

51. 超额利润 superprofit

52. 特许理论 concession theory

53. 垄断利润 monopoly profits

54. 履行义务 perform an obligation

55. 未履行义务 failure to perform an obligation

56. 底线 baseline

57. 自然资源的专有使用权 the exclusive right of natural resources

58. 自然资源的特许权 be granted of (be authorized of) the exclusive right of natural resources

59. 两个不同层面的问题 two different issues at separate levels

60. 权益 rights

61. 行为主体 the body of behavior, action body

62. 竞标 competitive tender

63. 履行义务 carry out obligations; perform obligations; comply with one's duty

64. 履行的义务 duty of performance

第 五 章
Chapter 5

接入和互联互通
Access Network and Interconnection

基础电信网络资源严格的计划性和巨大的沉淀资本，使得 [基础电信业具有自然垄断性，其竞争应受到管制，] 而借助线路提供信息服务的增值电信业可以完全放开竞争。虽然按照服务自愿和所有权原则，电信业务经营者有权拒绝向非用户（同业竞争者）提供服务，线路所有者有权拒绝非用户（同业竞争者）租用线路的请求，但是，考虑到拒绝向同业竞争者开放业务或者禁止向同业竞争者出租线路会形成基础电信垄断，最终损害全体电信用户的利益。因此，[基础业务主要经营者或线路所有人的经营权或所有权应当从法律上加以限制，确立其开放共享义务和接入义务，在请求人提出请求并支付接入费[1]前提下，必须向请求人开放线路、允许接入或者实行互联。如果接入义务人拒绝履行义务，或故意拖延履行该义务的期限，或提出的接入费超过法律规定，申请人可以向管理者提出行政救济或向司法机关提出司法救济请求。] 电信管理机关查证属实后，应当确定在请求人支付合理费用的前提下强制要求

批注：Basic telecom business has a feature of natural monopoly, therefore its competition should be regulated.

批注：The right of management and ownership of basic telecom business operators and line owners should be limited, their obligation of sharing and access should be established. Under the premise of the claimant's request and payment for access fee, they are obliged to open lines, allow access in and carry out interconnection. If the obligator of access duty refuses to carry out the above duty, or intentionally delays to fulfil the duty, or charges for access fee more than state fixed price, applicant could apply for administrative remedy to administration organ or apply for judicial remedy to judicial organ.

---

[1] ［加］因特温，等．电信规制手册[M]．管云翔，译．北京：北京邮电大学出版社，2001：99．

线路所有人开放线路。[这种做法类似于专利实施的强制许可[2]，二者都是通过法律对权利人的权利进行限制，使得他人在特定条件下可以使用该权利的标的物，并且在他人申请使用权利标的物受阻时可以申请行政机关给予救济。] 德国《电信法》第33条规定了业务共享的义务[3]，第35条规定了接入的义务[4]，第37条规定了强制互联的行政救济[5]。

[在基础电信业的竞争中，最常用的妨碍竞争的手段就是设置障碍，限制转售和拒绝接入。因此，各国电信法都对转售和接入做出了强制性规定，并且提供行政和法律救济措施。]

批注：This method is similar to compulsory license for patent enforcement, because both of them limit the rights of oblige by law, so that others could use the object of the right in specific condition, and in case of frustration in requesting to use the object of the right, the applicants could apply for administrative relief.

批注：In the competition of basic telecom business, the most common means is to impede competition that means setting obstacles, limiting resale and refusal of access. Therefore, telecom law of various countries established mandatory provisions for resale and access, furthermore, providing with administrative and judicial relief.

1. 背景和意义

互联是基于以下原因产生的。电信服务是一个复杂的过程，包括发送、传递和接受电子信号的全过程。有些电信从业者只经营其中的一部分业务，其向用户提供的完整的机到机的服务必须借助其他电信从业者的帮助。比如无线业务只涉及信号的接收、空中传输、进入固定网络的过程，当手机用户拨打固定用户时，信号在固定线路中的传输必须借助固定电信经营者。因此，[互联是无法提供端到端通信服务

---

[2] 类似于这种情况的对专利实施的强制许可可见于我国《专利法》第四十八条"具备实施条件的单位以合理的条件请求发明或者实用新型专利权人许可实施其专利，而未能在合理长的时间内获得这种许可时，国务院专利行政部门根据该单位的申请，可以给予实施该发明专利或者实用新型专利的强制许可。"以及第五十条"一项取得专利权的发明或者实用新型比前已经取得专利权的发明或者实用新型具有显著经济意义的重大技术进步，其实施又有赖于前一发明或者实用新型的实施的，国务院专利行政部门根据后一专利权人的申请，可以给予实施前一发明或者实用新型的强制许可。"

[3] 德国《电信法》第33条"任何为公众提供电信业务并在这一市场上具有《反竞争限制法》§22所指的统治地位的业务提供者应在一视同仁的基础上，让这类市场的竞争者们能够接入内部使用和向市场提供的业务，……，权力滥用发生在一个在相关市场具有《反竞争限制法》§22所指的统治地位的业务提供者让他自己接入到内部使用和提供给市场的业务时，有着比他为者使用这些业务进行业务提供而提供的条件优越得多，……"

[4] 德国《电信法》第35条"为公众提供公共电信服务并依从反竞争限制法第22条享有市场统治地位的电信公司应允许其他用户接入自己的部分或全部电信网络，接入方式可通过供所有用户使用的一般网络接入方式进行连接，亦可通过特殊网络接入方式而连接，以上第1句所指的通信公司应特别促成它自身的电信网与其他公司的公共电信网的互联。"

[5] 德国《电信法》第37条"若某地公用电信公司间未达成有关互联协议，有关管理机构可在了解上述各方情况后，应某方提出的互联要求的第一天起6周内命令各方互联，在这段时间内，管理机构将延长时间最多达四周，四周内必须作出决定。"

的非全过程电信经营者参与竞争的基本保障,离开了互联,非全过程电信业务经营者就无法提供完整的电信服务。] 随着通信技术的发展,一条线路可以传递多路信号,这就为多家电信公司分享一根电话线路提供了技术上的可行性。很难设想每一家电话公司都要单独布线,如果能做到线路共享,不仅节约前期投入,可以使用户的电信费用降低,而且线路的分享也给用户带来了使用上的便利,比如更容易达到编码标准和传输标准上的统一。

批注:Interconnection is the basic protection for operators, who have no capacity for providing entire process service to realize end-to-end communication, to participate competition. Without interconnection, the above operators could not supply the whole process telecom service.

批注:Access system is devised for the need of competition.

[接入的产生则是出于竞争的需要。] 对于被接入者,允许接入意味着增加竞争对手的同时,也获得了接入者给其补偿的机会,接入对于被接入者的有利方面被法国新规制经济学家拉丰描绘于其《电信竞争》中:"进入者补偿了ILEC(在位的本地交换经营商)的机会成本,即服务的零售价格与当服务被进入者转售时ILEC所节省的成本之间的差额[6]。"然而,接入行为对被接入者的竞争优势构成的不利影响是明显且明确的,而其机会成本的补偿却是预测和潜在的,故大部分线路所有者并不愿意竞争者接入。[向自己的竞争对手开放网络资源无异于帮助自己的对手与自己争夺电信市场。所以,即使各国电信法都有向竞争对手提供接入服务的义务性规定,掌控基础电信资源的主导运营商一般都会采用一些隐蔽的方法故意阻碍接入,妨碍竞争,比如:]

[(1)收取高额网间接入费;
(2)增加网间阻塞,降低通话质量;
(3)拒绝提供足够网络容量或网络元素;
(4)关键地理位置拒绝共享;
(5)拒绝分拆捆绑业务。]

批注:Opening network resource to competitors is the same as helping them to contend for telecom market. Therefore, even though providing with access service to competitors is a mandatory provision in various countries, the dominant operator, who master basic telecom resource, usually adopt some hidden measures deliberately so as to block access and impediment to competition, such as:

批注:(1) Charge high access fee
(2) Create network jam to decrease call quality
(3) Refuse to provide enough network capacity or network element
(4) Refuse to share critical geographic position
(5) Refuse to spin-off bundled business

---

[6] [法]让·雅克·拉丰,让·泰勒尔.电信竞争[M].胡汉辉,等译.北京:人民邮电出版社 2001:21.

因此，[为促进基础电信从业者之间的竞争，就需要管理者为接入提供法律上的保证，包括设定网络所有者的接入义务、明确接入程序和时限，以及当接入请求被拒绝时的救济措施。]

[接入义务属于不对称义务，接入谈判中的各方权利义务并不对等，比如，被申请人应当开放所有与接入有关的技术信息（商业秘密受限）、制定格式合同（交易条件相同，对任何申请人不得歧视）、英国电信法对显著市场地位者还课以更加严格的互联批发义务，互联批发条款由管制机构制定。制定这些不对称义务的目的是用形式上的不对等恢复实质正义，削弱主导运营商的优势地位，维护新进入者在与主导运营商谈判中的平衡。]

[为避免被申请者以畸高的接入费阻挡申请人租用网络与其竞争[7]，接入费一般由国家定价，定价的原则是以成本为基础。接入费定价对于接入权的实现具有决定意义；如果接入费定价过高，申请者就会放弃接入而考虑自行铺设网络，当其无力承担自建网络的巨大沉淀资本时，将选择退出市场；如果接入费定价过低，被申请人就没有动力投资建网以及进行与网络有关的科技研发。]"假如新进入者在强制性要求下，能迅速以低廉的、受规制的费率租用在位运营商

批注: To promote competition among basic telecom business providers, regulator needs to provide with legal protection for access, including establishing access duty for network owner, elaborating access procedure and time limit, and preparing relief measure when access request was refused.

批注: The duty of access belongs to asymmetric duty. In the access negotiation, rights and obligations of different parties are not equal. For example, respondent should open (allow access to) all technology information concerning access (except for commercial secret), design standard contract (the same trade terms, no discrimination to any applicant). In Britain, telecom law imposed more strict wholesale duties for interconnection to SMP(significant market power), and the terms of interconnection wholesale are designed by regulator. The aim for designing these asymmetric obligations is to restore substantial justices with unequal in form, weaken dominant operators' advantage position, so as to balance the position between new comers and dominant operators in negotiate.

批注: For the sake of preventing the responds from resisting applicant to rent network to compete through extraordinary high access fee, access fee is set by government, and the principle of pricing is cost-based. The access fee price is critical to realize the right of access. If the fee is over high, the applicants would give up accessing and try to build network by themselves, and when they could not afford the great capital precipitation using for building network, they would be expelled out of the market. If the access fee is over low, the respondents would lost the impetus to invest in network building, as well as researching and developing project concerning network.

---

[7] 除了以高昂的接入费阻挡申请人进入外，被申请者拒绝接入的另一个理由就是：不存在可行的网络接入点，因为法律要求的接入义务是在"任何技术可行点"，被申请人可以借口网络设计时并未预见到将来有申请人要从某点接入。所以，电信法的一个趋势是，在任何一个运营商建网时就要给其附加留出未来接入点的最低要求。

的网络设施，这些本地在位运营商还会投资此类网络设施吗[8]？"[美国1996年电信法实施以来，该问题已经凸现，美国为了鼓励竞争，强迫主导运营商以受规制的批发价格向进入者提供网络及其设施，由于价格过低，主导运营商不再愿意进行大规模网络建设和技术升级，]"因为他们被迫以较低的全要素长期增量成本（TELRIC）与竞争者共享自己的投资成果"[9]。如何确定接入费，不是一个法律问题，是电信经济学者需要解决的。

[有关接入或互联的交易条件，各国电信法都规定了非歧视原则，即不得歧视任何接入申请人，这就是接入的"最惠国待遇"，被请求者给予任何一个互联请求者的优惠，必须给予其他请求者。][歧视，就是同样对价条件下的区别对待，]比如，某接入申请人比其他人先收到系统元素调整的通知，就属于歧视。而价格区分不应当视为歧视。[除普遍服务外，价格区分在任何经济行为中都是合法的，]有钱的坐头等舱、没钱的坐经济舱，再没钱的坐火车，或者走路。愿意支付高对价的申请者，可以获得接通优先权。歧视是在所有申请人愿意支付同样对价前提下，被申请人区别对待了申请人，比如，其选择交易对象，拒绝与特定申请人交易；或者给与申请人的

批注：After USA implementing Act of Telecommunications (1996), this problem has already arisen. In order to encourage competition, USA enforced dominant operators to provide with network and corresponding equipments to new comers at the regulated wholesale price, which is too low to impetus dominant operators to further invest in large-scale network building and technology upgrading.

批注：As for access and interconnection trading terms, telecom laws of various countries stipulate the principle of non-discrimination, which requires not to discriminate any applicant. This term is called MFN(most favored nation) treatment for access, that is to say, any privilege respondent favored to one applicant, should be favored to all of the others.

批注：Discrimination is different treatment in the same condition of consideration.

批注：Except for universal service, differentiating by price is legitimate in any economic behavior.

批注：Discrimination refers to as, applicants, in the condition of being willing to pay the same consideration, are differently treated by respondent.

---

[8]　[美]罗伯特·W·克兰德尔．竞争与混沌——1996年电信法出台以来的美国电信业[M]．匡斌译．北京：北京邮电大学出版社，2006：4.

[9]　[美]罗伯特·W·克兰德尔．竞争与混沌——1996年电信法出台以来的美国电信业[M]．匡斌译．北京：北京邮电大学出版社，2006：60.

服务有区别。一个典型的例证就是，在接入服务中，被申请人向没有购买自己推荐的产品（或服务）的申请人提供服务的质量低于购买了自己推荐的产品（或服务）的申请人。

2. 定义

[接入是指根据规定的条件，在排他性或非排他性的基础上向其他企业提供线路、网络、设施和/或业务。它包括：接入网络元素和相关设施与业务（或包括以无线或有线的方式将设备连接起来）；进入包括建筑物、管道和电视塔在内的设施；进入软件系统（包括辅助操作系统）；进入码号传译或提供相同功能的其他系统；进入移动电话网络（特别是在漫游时）；进入用于数字电视业务的权限系统[10]。主导电信业者开放网络资源是以收取接入费为条件的，而公平合理的接入费是接入者能够实现接入的前提。]在主导电信服务提供者的网间成本不透明条件下，由信息不对称造成的主导服务者的寻租利润必然限制了接入者的数量。在这种情况下，为保证市场竞争的存在，必须保护接入者利益，因而[政府有必要专门颁布法律管制接入价格，以保护接入的实现。]

批注：Access means, in the stipulated condition, on the exclusive or non-exclusive base, providing other enterprises with line, network, device and (or) service. It includes, access to network elements, relevant device and service (or includes connecting devices by wire or wireless); access to equipment at building, duct and TV station etc.; access to software system (includes auxiliary operating system); access to code interpretation system or any other system with the same function; access to mobile phone network(especially when roaming) access to permission system for digital TV business. The condition for dominant telecom providers opening network resource is charging access fee, and the fair and reasonable access fee is the precondition for accessing.

批注：To protect for realizing access, it's necessary for government to enact a law to regulate access fee.

批注：Interconnection, also called interoperability, or interconnection and interworking, is a specific access between public network, excluding end user accessing, which refers to physical and logical connection between public telecommunication networks belonging to the same or different enterprises, so as to make an enterprise's end user could communicate with another user of the same or different enterprises, or could obtain services provided by different enterprises.

[互联，也叫互联互通或网间互联，是在公共网络之间实施的一种特定的接入（但不包括最终用户的进入），是指同一或者不同企业所使用的公共电子通信网络的物理和逻辑连接，以使一个企业的用户能够与同一企业或其他企业的用户进行通信交流，或者能够获得由其他企业提供的业务[11]。]我国《电信条例》第十七条规定了电

---

[10] 因特温，等.电信规制手册[M].管云翔译.北京：北京邮电大学出版社，2001：74.
[11] 因特温，等.电信规制手册[M].管云翔译.北京：北京邮电大学出版社，2001：74.

信网络所有者进行互联的义务[12]，第十八条规定了互联的具体措施[13]。我国2001年5月10日生效的《公用电信网间互联管理规定》进一步细化了基础电信业务经营者的互联义务，并详细规定了互联点的设置及互联费用的分摊与结算、互联协议与工程建设、互联时限与互联监管、互联后的网络管理，以及互联争议的调处等问题。有关互联的行政救济措施以及互联费用协议不成的解决措施，各国法律也都做出了相关规定。我国《电信条例》第二十、二十一、二十二条也作了相应的规定[14]，我国2002年1月1日起生效的《电信网间互联争议处理办法》进一步明确了互联争议的调处机关、程序、时限，以及在调处中不能及时解决的情况下作出强制互联行政命令的程序和依据。

3. 区别和联系

[接入是互联的上位概念，包括所有接入他人网络提供服务，或接入他人网络接受服务的行为。互联仅指网络之间物理的或逻辑的连接，目的是让本网的用户可以与他网的用户通信或者享受他网的服务。接入，除去互联之外，主要是指单向地利用他人的网络向他网的用户提供服务，直接与他网客户建立合同关系，比如利用他人的有线电视网向有线电视用户提供上网服务就是接入。]

[接入的目的是实现竞争。在电信法意义上，接入权保证了没有电信网络资源的运营商与一个或多个基础电信运营商所控制的基础电信网络资源的物理和

批注：Access is the upperseat concept of interconnection, includes all behaviors of access to others' network to provide service, or accept service. Interconnection only refers to physical or logical connection between networks, aiming to make the users of the requesting network communicate with the users of the responding network, or accept the service provided by the responding network. Except for interconnection, access refers to providing the users of the responding network with services through the responding network unidirectionally, and establishing contract relationship with the users of the responding network directly, for example, providing the cable TV users with internet service through cable TV network belonged to other operator.

---

[12] 我国《电信条例》第十七条"电信网之间应当按照技术可行、经济合理、公平公正、相互配合的原则，实现互联互通。主导的电信业务经营者不得拒绝其他电信业务经营者和专用网运营单位提出的互联互通要求。"

[13] 我国《电信条例》第十八条"主导的电信业务经营者应当按照非歧视和透明化的原则，制定包括网间互联的程序、时限、非捆绑网络元素目录等内容的互联规程。互联规程应当报国务院信息产业主管部门审查同意。该互联规程对主导的电信业务经营者的互联互通活动具有约束力。"

[14] 我国《电信条例》第二十条"网间互联双方经协商未能达成网间互联协议的，……，任何一方均可以按照网间互联覆盖范围向国务院信息产业主管部门或者省、自治区、直辖市电信管理机构申请协调；……自网间互联一方或者双方申请协调之日起４５日内经协调仍不能达成协议的，由协调机关随机邀请电信技术专家和其他有关方面专家进行公开论证并提出网间互联方案。协调机关应当根据专家论证结论和提出的网间互联方案作出决定，强制实现互联互通。"第二十一条"网间互联双方必须在协议约定或者决定规定的时限内实现互联互通。未经国务院信息产业主管部门批准，任何一方不得擅自中断互联互通。……" 第二十二条"网间互联的费用结算与分摊应当执行国家有关规定，不得在规定标准之外加收费用。网间互联的技术标准、费用结算办法和具体管理规定，由国务院信息产业主管部门制定。"

逻辑连接，在没有电信网络资源前提下，也可以通过租网参与电信竞争。接入权是各国电信法规定的一种重要权利，赋予了非主导运营商在不具备电信网络资源的条件下提供电信服务的可行性。]接入不仅可以节约投入、扩大竞争，还有利于形成标准。

[双向接入与互联的概念比较接近，比如两个运营商，一个是互联网接入运营商，另一个是有线电视接入运营商，双向接入的结果是互联网运营商的客户可以使用互联网接受有线电视，有线电视运营商的客户可以使用有线电视网上网。这种双向接入构成了互联，本网运营商向他网客户提供服务的同时，本网客户享受到了他网运营商的服务。]

[互联的目的是方便电信用户，即通过互联确保电信用户能够：

（1）给任何一个普通的电话号码拨打电话或实现其他类型的电信传输；

（2）接收到他人打过来的任意电话或传输的电子通信信息，而该服务是由普通的电话号码识别设备来实现的[15]。]

[简单地说，对于非互联型接入，网络是人家的，客户是自己的，通过别人的网络为自己的客户提供服务，在客户与运营商之间建立了电信服务合同关系。比如，固话运营商通过接入他人的有线电视网向自己的客户提供电话服务。]

批注：The aim of access is to realize competition. On the significance of telecommunication law, the right of access securities that the operators without telecom resource could access to basic telecom network resource physically and logically controlled by one or more basic telecom operators, in order to take part in telecom competition through leasing network without telecom network resource. The right of access is an important right stipulated by various countries, which empowers non-dominant operators the feasibility to supply telecom service without telecom network resource.

批注：Di-direction access is similar to interconnection. For example, two operators, one is internet access operator, the other is cable TV access operator. Di-direction access can reach the effect that the clients of internet operator can access cable TV through internet, as well as the clients of cable TV operator can access internet through cable TV network. This kind of di-direction access constitutes interconnection, incumbent network operators supply clients of others operators with service, meanwhile, clients of incumbent network operators enjoy the service supplied by other operators.

批注：The aim of interconnection is to facilitate users, that is to say, through interconnection the users could: (1) phone to any ordinary telephone and realize other type of telecom transmission; (2) receipt of any call dialed by others and electronic message send by others, and the service is supplied by ordinary phone number identification equipment.

批注：In brief, as for non-interconnection access, the network is leased from others, but the clients are ours, who supply with service through others' network, and the telecom service contract is built between the operators and the clients. For example, fixed-line phone suppliers offer service to their clients through accessing into other's cable TV network.

---

[15] ［英］Ian Lloyd，等．通信法[M]．曾剑秋，译．北京：北京邮电大学出版社，2006：77．

[互联的典型例证就是在无线通信领域的手机漫游，如出国后运营商的网络无法覆盖，就需要接入其他运营商的网络，运营商之间可以通过签订漫游协议（互联协议）实现无线通信的漫游互联。］"1997年，欧洲委员会批准了一项约200家移动网络运营商之间的协议，制定了一份标准合约"，即漫游协议[16]。
[对于互联，会出现两种情形。其一，自己的客户使用别人的网。以本地移动运营商为例，其手机用户拨打固话时或者漫游时，就会使用别人的固网或无线网；其二，别人的客户使用自己的网。仍以本地移动运营商为例，固网运营商的客户拨打本地手机，或者外地无线运营商客户拨打本地手机，都将使得本地无线运营商向其他运营商客户提供服务。］

[在第二种情况下，接受电信服务的客户是其他电信运营商的客户，本地运营商依据与外地运营商的互联互通协议向非自己的客户提供了服务，而没有直接和客户建立法律关系，一旦客户要追究本地运营商责任，只有向自己的运营商提出请求，自己的运营商再依据互联合同，向本地运营商主张权利。其实，大部分情况下，漫游客户并不知道到底是哪一个服务商提供的互联服务，其仅与自己的运营商建立了电信服务合同关系，而整个通信路径可能有多个服务商参与。这样，在互联诉讼中就非常不方便，漫游用户可以将漫游地服务商作为第三

批注：The typical example of interconnection is mobile phone roaming. When in abroad, the operator's signal scope cannot cover the clients, they need to access into others' network. The operator could sign roaming contract (interconnection contract) with another operator to realize roaming interconnection for radio communication.

批注：There are two cases of interconnection: first, the clients of one operators use the network of other operators. Taking local mobile operator as example, when its clients using mobile phone dial a fixed-line phone or in roaming, they would use other operators' fixed-line network or wireless network. Second, the local operator's network is used by other operators' client. Take local mobile operator as example too, clients of fix-line phone operator dial local mobile phone, or clients of ecdemic (non-local) wireless operator dial local mobile phone. Both of the circumstances make the local wireless operator provide service to other operators.

批注：In the second circumstance, the client accepting telecom service is from other operators', to whom the local operator supplies service according to the interconnection agreement with ecdemic (non-local) operators, and with whom the local operator does not built legal relationship directly. Once the clients want to investigate the local operator for legal responsibility, they could only claim to their own operator, who afterwards claims to the local operator according to the interconnection agreement. In fact, in most circumstances, the roaming clients do not know which operator provides them with interconnection service on earth, and they build telecom service contract relationship only with their own operator, however, there are

---

[16] ［英］Ian Lloyd，等．通信法［M］．曾剑秋，译．北京：北京邮电大学出版社，2006：203．

人纳入到电信服务合同诉讼,而被告只能是其签约运营商。]

[互联有可能被恶意利用,借以形成互联双方的业务兼并,从而可能引发进一步的行业垄断。如果管理者放任任何互联动议的执行,则容易引发请求者和被请求者企图通过互联的方式进行更大规模的行业垄断;另一方面,如果管理者对互联互通的请求过于慎重,又会造成请求者因不能及时完成互联而退出市场,弱化了市场竞争。在平衡了这对矛盾后,对互联请求的准许作为一般规定,而将互联双方是否构成垄断的审查作为特例。]如德国《电信法》第38条规定了竞争限制协议的无效情形,"所有依据本法§35所许可的协议,若可能因无客观正当原因而侵害其他公司竞争机会时,该协议将无效。"

4. 法律关系

接入可以实现三赢:对于被申请人,冗余容量达不到规模经济,构成资源浪费;对于申请人,大规模的沉淀成本构成入门壁垒,无法进入市场;对于电信用户,服务提供者数量少,无法充分竞争。国家规制接入费条件下的接入,可以消除三方的上述不利。[通过电信法,赋予具有网络资源的电信运营商强制接入义务,是电信市场得以有效竞争的前提。比如,美国电信法就要求被申请者向申请者提供非捆绑的接入,价格受FCC规制,美国电信法251(c)3规定,"在位运营商有义务向任何提出接入请求的运营商在任何技术可行点上、在非捆绑

many operators serving in the whole telecommunication route. Thus, in interconnection litigation, it's inconvenient for the roaming clients, who could list the roaming operator as the third part in the litigation concerning the telecom service contract, and the defendant should definitely be the operator, who signed contract with them.

批注: Interconnection could be used maliciously, with which both of interconnection entities would integrate business merge, causing further business monopoly. If the regulator adopt the police of Laissez-faire, not interfering with any kind of implement of interconnection motivation, it's easy to cause further large scale merging through interconnection by applicant and respondent intending to acquire further business monopoly. On the other hand, if regulator's attitude to interconnection is too prudent, that will delay the applicant from achieving interconnection and be expelled of market, in which consequently, the competition is weakened. In the balancing the pair of contradictions, the regulator adjusted the police to that, it's general to permit to interconnection request, and it's special to inspect and decide whether both of entities intent to monopoly by interconnection.

批注: It's precondition of effective competition in telecom market to impose the mandatory duty of access to telecom network operators. For example, the Act of Telecommunication of USA, require the respondent to provide non-bundling access to applicant, and the access price is regulated by FCC. Sec 251(c) 3 provision says, UNBUNDLED ACCESS.--The duty to provide, to any requesting telecommunications carrier for the provision of a telecommunications service, nondiscriminatory access to network elements on an unbundled basis at any technically feasible point on rates, terms, and conditions that are just, reasonable, and nondiscriminatory

的基础上提供非歧视性的网络元素接入，其资费、条款和条件必须是公正的、合理的和非歧视性的。"]

[在互联互通之外的接入，主要指利用他网将自己的服务延伸到他网客户，可以有两种实现途径：由他网运营商转售，或者直接在本网运营商和他网客户之间建立法律关系。]举例来说，申请接入本地电话网提供互联网宽带业务，属于强制接入，美国FCC要求本地网运营商非捆绑地、以公正且合理的价格向互联网服务提供者开放本地电话网供网络宽带接入，并且如果互联网服务提供者有转售要求，也要以规定的折扣提供转售业务。

[有关如何确定强制接入范围的问题，美国电信法251（d）2给出了认定方法，"在决定何种网络元素应该是可获得的……委员会应最低限度地考虑：（a）是否接入此类网络元素本质上是必需的；（b）是否不能提供此类网络元素的接入，将损害电信运营商寻求接入以提供其试图提供的业务的能力……"。]
[根据上述认定，"进入者仍应能够从其竞争者即在位运营商那里以受规制的批发价格，实际上获得在位运营商的所有设施"[17]，包括交换设施、传输设施、码号资源、运营系统等。因此，在这样的强制接入下，申请者不需拥有网络就可以开展一切电信业务，比如，其不需

in accordance with the terms and conditions of the agreement and the requirements of this section and section 252. An incumbent local exchange carrier shall provide such unbundled network elements in a manner that allows requesting carriers to combine such elements in order to provide such telecommunications service.

批注：Except for interconnection, access refers to extending telecom operator A's service into another operator B's clients through the network of B. There are two ways to realize the above effect, resale A's service by B; or directly establish telecom service contract relationship between A and B's clients.

批注：As for how to define the enforced access scope, the Act of Telecommunications of USA Sec. 251(d) 2 gives a set of metheds for considering, which are:

ACCESS STANDARDS.--In determining what network elements should be made available for purposes of subsection (c)(3), the Commission shall consider, at a minimum, whether--

(A) access to such network elements as are proprietary in nature is necessary; and

(B) the failure to provide access to such network elements would impair the ability of the telecommunications carrier seeking access to provide the services that it seeks to offer.

批注：According to the above consideration, the new comer could actually acquire all equipments from its competitor, i.e. incumbent operator in wholesale price, which includes: exchange device; transmission device; code resource; operation system etc. Therefore,

---

[17] [美]罗伯特·W·克兰德尔. 竞争与混沌——1996年电信法出台以来的美国电信业[M]. 匡斌，译. 北京：北京邮电大学出版社，2006：9.

有固话网，就可以靠接入被申请人的固话网来提供宽带业务。] 在认定一个业务是否属于强制接入范围时，政策因素是相当重要的，在一定时期内，结论可能反复。比如，有线电视网使用调制解调器的宽带业务不属于强制接入范围，FCC"将电缆调制解调器业务归类于'信息'业务的最初裁决被联邦法院推翻"[18]，有线电视运营商不需要向ISP开放此线路，也就是说，这种业务不属于强制接入范围。造成这种双向不对称权利的原因是出于非对称管制的需要[19]，ISP 有义务向有线电视运营商开放网络，使其可以利用互联网提供有线电视服务；而有线电视运营商没有义务向 ISP 开放有线电视网，使其可以利用有线电视网提供互联网服务[20]。

批注：in the above enforced access circumstance, applicants could exploit any kind of telecom service no matter whether they have possess network or not. For example, the operator, without fixed-line network, could provide broadband service through access another operator's (the respondent) network.

5. 互联诉讼中的第三人

接入和互联是电信技术概念，从法律层面看，[互联只是利用他网实现本网客户呼叫他网客户，或者他网客户呼叫本网客户，本网运营商并未建立与他网客户的合同关系。互联并未在本网运营商和他网客户之间设立法律关系，也未

批注：The third person in interconnection lawsuit.

批注：Interconnection enables operator A's clients to contact with operator B's clients through B's network, or B's clients to contact with A's clients through A's network. Neither A nor B builds a contract relationship with clients of the other. Interconnection achieves two aims: (1) enable one operator's clients to

---

[18] ［美］罗伯特·W·克兰德尔. 竞争与混沌——1996年电信法出台以来的美国电信业[M]. 匡斌，译. 北京：北京邮电大学出版社，2006：104.

[19] 不对称管制，是指电信监管机构根据特定的区分标准对不同电信运营商，采取不同管制方式。其目的是扶持新兴电信运营企业，防止主导运营商滥用网络优势妨碍竞争，从而获得有效竞争的市场效果。不对称管制表现在立法上，就是为不同的市场主体设定的权利义务不对等，其规范结构有两种。其一，通过设定区分市场主体的标准，进而设定不同的权利义务。如我国《公用电信网间互联管理规定》第五条定义了区分标准，即"主导的电信业务经营者，是指控制必要的基础电信设施，并且所经营的固定本地电话业务占本地网范围内同类业务市场50％以上的市场份额，能够对其他电信业务经营者进入电信业务市场构成实质性影响的经营者。"第七条对区分出的主体设定了不对称互联义务，即"主导的电信业务经营者应当根据本规定制定包括网间互联的程序、时限、互联点的数量、用于网间互联的交换机局址、非捆绑网络元素提供或出租的目录及费用等内容的互联规则。"其二，直接对特定主体设定"不平等"义务。如美国1996年电信法第三章（PART III--SPECIAL PROVISIONS CONCERNING BELL OPERATING COMPANIES）专门规制地区贝尔公司，为其附加了多项不对称义务。该法第271～275条为地区贝尔经营长途业务和电子出版、家庭电子安保、通信设备制造等业务附加了较苛刻的条件，而对其他公司无此要求。原因在于地区贝尔具有本地网资源，为防止其利用本地网资源妨碍竞争，设定了上述"不平等"义务。

[20] 美国电信法第五章（PART V--VIDEO PROGRAMMING SERVICES PROVIDED BY TELEPHONE OMPANIES）专门对电话公司经营视频服务设立了不对称管制义务，有线电视运营商进入通信领域和通信运营商进入有线电视领域的许可条件不同，对前者的限制较少，对后者限制较多（见 [47 U.S.C. 571] REGULATORY TREATMENT OF VIDEO PROGRAMMING SERVICES），原因在于通信运营商的竞争实力远大于有线电视运营商，故当该法开启混业经营大门时，立法者不得不考虑"锄强扶弱"。

在本网客户和他网运营商之间设立法律关系。互联实现的两个目的——让本网客户与他网客户通信以及让本网客户享受他网服务，从用户层面看并没有改变原来的法律关系，各用户仍然只和自己的运营商发生法律关系，只是在运营商之间建立了新的法律关系。其中，让本网客户享受他网服务，属于本网运营商向本网客户的转售服务，一旦发生电信服务争议，本网客户只能找本网运营商解决，由本网运营商找他网运营商理论。]

而他网用户使用了本网服务商的服务，也没有与本网服务商建立法律关系，一旦出现侵权，其只能起诉他网运营商。[比如，中国移动的用户在美国打手机，接受了美国本网服务商AT＆T依据与中国移动的互联合同提供的本网电信服务，但该用户并没有与AT＆T建立法律关系，如果AT＆T经常无法接通或掉线，或者泄露了用户隐私，用户不得起诉AT＆T。在这种情况下，用户只能起诉电信服务合同的相对方中国移动，将AT＆T列为无独立请求权第三人参加诉讼，如果法院判决AT＆T承担民事责任，其有权提起上诉。因为中国移动与第三人AT＆T之间的互联关系与本诉具有牵连性，如果法院确认本诉讼被告中国移动承担法律责任，该法律责任最终可能由AT＆T承担[21]。]

communicate with other operator's clients; (2) enable one operator's clients to enjoy other operator's service. From the perspective of users, the contract relationship does not be changed by interconnection, clients only establish contract relationship with their original operator. Interconnection establishes new legal relationship between operators merely. The second aim of interconnection, enabling one operator A's clients to enjoy operator B's service, belongs to A resale of B's business, in which, once telecom dispute emerged, A's clients could only claim to A, then A claims to B afterwards.

批注：1、For example, a China Mobile's client uses mobile phone in USA, enjoying the service of American local operator AT & T according to interconnection contract between China Mobile and AT&T, however, the client has never built contract relationship with AT & T. If AT & T could not connect or off-line constantly, or have leaked the client's privacy, the client could not prosecute against AT&T, but his telecom service contract counterpart, China Mobile. In the litigation, the client could list AT & T as the third party without independent claims. If the court imposes civil liability on AT & T, it shall be entitled to file an appeal. Because the interconnection relationship between China Mobil and AT & T has implication with action, in which if the court imposes civil liability on China Mobile, the liability could be taken by AT & T.

---

[21] 根据我国《民事诉讼法》第五十六条第二款的规定，无独立请求权的第三人是指对当事人双方的诉讼标的没有独立请求权，但是案件处理结果同他有法律上的利害关系，申请参加诉讼或者由人民法院通知他参加诉讼的人。无独立请求权第三人参加诉讼的根据是本诉讼案件的审理结果与其有法律上的利害关系，即无独立请求权第三人与本诉讼的当事人存在另一个法律关系，而且本诉讼当事人争议的法律关系和该第三人与本诉讼当事人之间的法律关系具有一定的牵连性。

然而，我国合同法仅列出了三种无独立请求权的第三人情形：代位权诉讼、撤销权诉讼、合同转让[22]。因此，我国电信法应当专门就互联互通诉讼规定无独立请求权的第三人情形：[电信服务商通过互联互通合同，未经客户同意转移电信服务债务的，可以将电信服务的实际提供者列为无独立请求权的第三人。]

批注：If telecom service operators transfer obligations by signing interconnection contract, without clients' consent, the clients could list the actual service provider as the third party without independent claims.

生词和词组

第五章

1. 经营权 right of management
2. 所有权 ownership, proprietary rights; title; proprietorship
3. 国家定价 state fixed price
4. 行政救济 administrative remedy
5. 司法救济 judicial remedy
6. 行政机关 administrative body, administrative organsm, administration, Administrative agency, executive
7. 司法机关 judicial office; judicial authority; judicial organ
8. 实施专利的强制许可 compulsory license for patent enforcement
9. 权利人，债权人 obligee, creditor
10. 权利人的权利 the right of the obligee

---

[22]《中华人民共和国合同法》第74条和最高人民法院《关于适用〈中华人民共和国合同法〉若干问题的解释》（法释〔1999〕19号）第12条、第16条、第24条、第27条、第29条规定了合同案件中特别适用无独立请求权的第三人的情形。

11. 权利标的物 the object of the right
12. 妨碍竞争 impediment to competition
13. 强制性规定 mandatory provisions, obligatory provisions, compulsory provisions, peremptory provisions
14. 全过程电信服务 whole (entire, overall) process telecom service
15. 端到端服务 end-to-end service
16. 争夺市场 contend for markets, capture markets, seize markets
17. 掌握主动权 master (grasp) the initiative in hand,
18. 主动的 active, initiative
19. 阻碍接入和妨碍竞争 block access and impediment to competition
20. 网间阻塞 Network jam
21. 通话质量 call quality
22. 网络容量 network capacity
23. 网络元素 network element
24. 分拆 carve out, spin-off, list partly, partition
25. 分拆捆绑业务 spin-off bundled business
26. 促进竞争 promote competition
27. 被申请人 respondent, defending party to the application
28. 开放信息 open information, allow access to information
29. 制定格式合同 design standard contract
30. 交易条件 terms of exchange, trade terms, terms of the transaction
31. 明显市场优势 Significant Market Advantage
32. 具有市场支配地位者 Significant Market Power
33. 以成本为基础的定价 set cost-based price
34. 沉淀资本 the deposit of capital, sunk capital, capital precipitation
35. 技术升级 technology upgrading
36. 最惠国待遇 most-favored-nation clause, most-favored-nation-treatment
37. 价格区分 differentiating by price
38. 价格区分在任何经济行为中都是合法的 differentiating by price is legitimate

in any economic behavior

39. 辅助操作系统 auxiliary operating system

40. 码号传译系统 code interpretation system

41. 双向接入 di-direction access

42. 固定电话 fixed-line telephone

43. 手机漫游 mobile roaming

44. 固网 fixed network, fixed-line phone network

45. 无线网 wireless network, radio network

46. 外地运营商 ecdemic operator, non-local operator

47. 无线运营商 wireless carrier, wireless operator

48. 被追究法律责任 be investigated for legal responsibility

49. 主张权利 claim for right

50. 放任 adopt police of laissez-faire, not interfere with

51. 互联请求 interconnect request

52. 宽带业务 broadband services

53. 掉线 lost connection, Dropped, off-line

54. 电话无法接通 subscriber unable to connect; unreachable

55. 起诉某人 Bring an action against SB; prosecute against SB; take SB to court; sue SB

56. 合同相对方 counterpart of contract

57. 无独立请求权的第三人 the third party without independent claims

58. 法院判决承担民事责任的无独立请求权的第三人有权提起上诉 The third party without independent claims on which the court imposes civil liability shall be entitled to file an appeal.

59. 牵连性 implication, implicating nature, indivisibility

60. 本诉 action in chief

61. 反诉 counterclaim, countercharge

第六章 Chapter 6

普遍服务
Universal Service

[在通信作为基本人权的社会，为高成本地区、弱势群体提供电信服务，无法依赖利润的驱动，只有靠强制性义务，因而电信普遍服务被看作是企业的社会责任。普遍服务是全体运营商的义务，但其具体执行又只能落在少数企业头上，故如何补贴提供普遍服务的企业成为设计普遍服务制度的关键。纵观电信管制史，曾出现过多种普遍服务制度，有交叉补贴、接入费补贴、普遍服务基金等。]

批注：When telecommunication becoming a society's basic human right, it could not depend on the profit motivation to supply telecom service in high cost region or for vulnerable groups, but on mandatory duty, therefore, telecom universal service is regarded as enterprise's society responsibility. The universal service is a duty for all of telecom operators, however, the duty of executor is laid on a few operators. Therefore, how to subsidize the universal service provider is critical to devise system thereof. Surveying of the history of telecom regulation, there have been various universal service systems, such as the type of cross-subsidization, access fee subsidization, universal service fund, etc.

第一节　电信普遍服务
Section 1　Telecom Universal Service

[普遍服务指通过政策激励或者补贴促进并维持每一个家庭都能与公共电信

批注：Universal service refers that, through police stimulation or subsidization to encourage

网络连接。将所有或者大部分家庭同公共电信网络相连的目标，通常被称作"普遍服务义务"。普遍服务保证了公民参与社会交往和言论自由的基本权利，其具体内容包括：保证任何人在任何时间、任何地点都可以方便地享受到电信服务，以及电信服务标准的统一和无歧视、普通家庭经济能力可以承受的资费价格。]

[美国1996年电信法将普遍服务定义成一个随着电信和信息技术与服务演变的概念，包含以下要素：(1) 对教育、公共健康和公共安全至关重要；(2) 被绝大多数居民用户使用；(3) 由电信运营商在公众网上提供服务；(4) 符合公共利益、便利且是必需的[1]。][按照这一定义，其特征包含：可接入性（在任何地点都可以享受全面覆盖的电话服务）、平等性（价格、服务和质量无歧视）和可购性（服务价格普通消费者可消费得起）。普遍服务的主要对象是人口稀少地区；教育等公益机构；低收入等弱势群体；火警、匪警、急救等紧急救助电话。]

1. 有关普遍服务的必要性

从经济学视角看，["普遍服务义务是收入在个人之间或地区之间重新分配的重要工具。换句话说，就是商业和城市用户补贴住宅或农村用户，长途业务、增值业务和无线业务补贴固定的本地业务[2]。"] 由于扭曲了价格信号、造成了市场的无效率和整个社会福利的损失，

and maintain the access of every family to public telecom network. The aim of access of every or almost every family to public telecom network, is usually called "the duty of universal service", which guarantees the basic right of civilian to participate social intercourse and speech freedom. The content of universal service includes: guarantee everyone, at any time and any place, to enjoy telecom services conveniently, as well as the telecom service standard being unification and non-discrimination and the affordable price to ordinary family.

批注：The Act of telecommunications of USA (1996) defined "universal service" as a concept evolving with the telecom and information technology and service, consisting the following factors: (1) critical to education, public health and security; (2) used by majority residential users; (3) provided by telecom operator on the public network; (4) according with public interests and being convenient and indispensable (necessary).

批注：According to this definition, the features of universal service include that, (1) accessible, meaning that the user could enjoy telephone service covering all-around at any place; (2) equality, meaning that non-discrimination on price, service and quality; (3) affordable, meaning that service price is affordable by ordinary consumer. The main target of university service is sparsely populated region; public interest organization such as education organization; vulnerable groups such as low income persons; emergency service call such as fire, police, ambulance.

批注：The necessity of universal service

批注：Universal service duty is an important

---

[1] [47 U.S.C. 254]（c）1.
[2] 让·雅克·拉丰，让·泰勒尔. 电信竞争[M]. 胡汉辉，等译. 北京：人民邮电出版社，2001：14.

有些学者反对这种强制性的财富再分配政策[3]。还有的学者在考察了公平和效率后，认为应当实施该政策[4]。另外还有学者认为 [普遍服务的目的在于确保公民最基本的通信权利，是一种基本人权，其政治性要高于经济性[5]。]

探讨普遍服务存在的必要性，首先应当确定其是否属于应当由政府买单的公民的基本需求。公民有多项需求，按照马斯洛的需求层次理论[6]，[电信需求应当属于安全需求（紧急救援电话服务）和社交需求（短信聊天服务）。这些都不属于人的基本需求。我们需要研究的问题是，如果公民无法自力满足某种需求，国家是否应当免费提供救济，即应当将什么需求列入国家福利范围、进行国家救济的问题是一个很复杂的社会问题。][通常情况下，各国对于人的基本需求都提供国家救济，最低生活保障、廉租房、免费医疗都是国家买单来满足公民的基本需求的例证，但并不是所有基本需求无法自我满足的人，国家都应当提供救济，][比如性，虽然按照马斯洛的需求层次论，性属于人的基本需求，但除了战争时期特定国家为士兵提供这种救济（慰安妇）外，通常都不认为国

> income reassignment tool among persons or regions. In other words, commercial users and urban users subsidize residents users and rural customers, and long distant business, value-added business and radio business subsidize local business.

批注：The aim of universal service is to guarantee the basic communication right of civilians, being a kind of basic human right, whose political feature is superior to economic feature.

批注：The demand of communication belongs to security needs, such as emergency service, as well as social needs such as SMS (short message service) chat, which do not belong to human's basic needs. We should research that, if civilians can not satisfy some needs by themselves, should government offer relief free of charge, that is to say, what kind of needs should be included in the scope of national welfare and national relief. This is a complicated social question.

批注：Normally, to protect for human's basic needs, various countries offer national relief, minimum living guarantee, low-rent housing, free medical care, which are examples of national paying for satisfying the human's basic needs. However, not every basic needs that could not be satisfied by the person's own, should be offered by the national for free.

批注：Taking sex as an example, according to Maslow's theory of needs hierarchy, although

---

[3] 李丹. 中美电信普遍服务政策之比较研究 [D]. 武汉：中南财经政法大学，2006.
[4] 石文华. 电信普遍服务在中国必要性研究 [D]. 北京：北京邮电大学，2004.
[5] 唐守廉. 电信管制 [M]. 北京：北京邮电大学出版社，2001: 268.
[6] 马斯洛的需求层次论，亦称"基本需求层次理论"，是行为科学的理论之一，由美国心理学家亚伯拉罕·马斯洛于1943年在《人类激励理论》论文中所提出。马斯洛理论把需求分成生理需求、安全需求、社交需求、尊重需求、自我实现需求五类，依次由较低层次到较高层次排列。在这五类需求中，基本需求是首先要满足的，其包括呼吸、水、食物、睡眠、生理平衡、分泌、性，如果这些需要（除性以外）任何一项得不到满足，人类个人的生理机能就无法正常运转，人类的生命就会受到威胁。

家应当向有正常需求但无力满足者（如残疾人）提供这种福利[7]，甚至还要在特定的时间、地点、对特定主体，限制这种需求的实现[8]。][相反，对于并不是基本需求的其他需求，国家却可能向无力满足者提供救济，比如交通、教育、医疗、电信、邮政。]

[紧急救援电话服务满足了人的安全需求，普遍接入满足了人的社交需求，可见，电信需求并不是人的基本需求，远不如性需求更基础，但却应当得到救济。其原因就在于，电信是实现基本人权的必要手段。][在电信成为了信息社会的基本沟通手段后，言论自由权的实现已经无法脱离这个手段。技术提供了"说"的基本工具，延伸了"说"的权利形式。不"听"无以"说"，没有听的机会，就没有说的能力。所以，保障公民的基本交流需求，就是保障公民的言论自由权的实现。因此，电信普遍服务是一种基本人权。]

2. 普遍服务内涵和外延的变化

[普遍服务的概念随着电信技术发展在不断变化。在无线通信出现之前，普遍服务仅指通过有线电话的服务。在无线通信时代，在偏远地区架设固话的成本远远高于无线通信，普遍服务的概念

sex belongs to basic needs, except for in wartime, specific country offered this kind of relief (as comfort women) to soldiers, it is regarded that nation should not offer sex relief as a welfare to the person who has this kind of need but incapable such as handicap people. Furthermore, the government could restrict this kind of needs on specific time, at specific place, to specific subject.

批注：On the contrary, as for other needs not belonging to basic needs, nation could offer relief to inability, such as traffic, education, medical care, telecom, post.

批注：Emergency call service satisfies security needs, and universal service satisfies social communication needs. The telecom needs is not human's basic needs, far less basic than sex, but required national relief, for which the reason is telecom is an indispensable measure to realize basic human right.

批注：After telecom becoming a basic measure to communication in information society, and the right of speech freedom could not get rid of this measure. Technology offers us basic tool of saying, and extends the form of right to saying. We could not say without listening. If we lost the chance of listening, we are incapability of saying. Therefore to protect civilin's basic communication needs is to protect freedom of speech. The universal service is a basic human right.

批注：The change of connotation and denotation of universal service

---

[7] 国家救济的基本需求满足，满足的方式必须是纯粹经济化的，不能以牺牲他（她）人的人权为满足方式。医疗、教育、贫困人口的衣食住行都可以通过纯粹经济方式提供，但性救济不是单纯经济问题，会牺牲他（她）人的人权，为道德所不能接纳。因此，虽然性也属于基本人权（有关繁衍），但国家不提供救济。对有性需求的但无法自我满足的人士（如残疾人、战时的军人），国家不应建立救济体制。

[8] 搜狐IT. 美禁航天员太空性行为 [EB/OL]. (2010-07-04) http://it.sohu.com/20100630/n273184064.shtml.

相应做了调整,由"保证接入公众电话网"变为"保证接入公众网络[9]"。]

普遍服务的外延也随着电信技术的发展而改变。每一项新电信技术的出现,都会带来新的电信通信产品,或者彻底改革原有的通信模式。但[并不是每一项新的电信技术都会纳入普遍服务的外延。只有涉及公民基本通信权利的通信服务才被纳入普遍服务范围。比如,提供电文电话[10]在英国被认为是国家应当对聋哑人提供的救济,属于普遍服务范畴。][互联网出现后,宽带服务是否应当纳入普遍服务范畴就是一个值得讨论的问题。英国的普遍服务并不包括宽带接入业务,理由是:第一,公民使用其他媒体可以弥补没有宽带的不足,并不一定通过宽带才可以满足基本学习生活需要,比如发邮件可以到公共图书馆利用免费互联网进行。因此,宽带不是公民的基本通信权利,不应当被列入普遍服务范畴。]第二,经常上网的人群不是无力支付网络接入费的穷人,反而是较富裕用户。如果普遍服务基金用于宽带,意味着所有电信用户为这部分较富裕用户买单[11]。

批注: The concept of universal service is constantly changing with the telecom technology developing. Before the appearance of wireless communication, universal service only referred to service by line phone. In the era of wireless communication, the cost of setting up fix-line in remote region is much higher than wireless communication. So the concept of universal service changed correspondingly, from "to guarantee access to public phone network" to "to guarantee access to public network".

批注: Not every new telecom technology would be incorporated into universal service. Only the communication service which is related to citizen basic communication right would be absorbed into the scope of universal service, for example, to supply with text phone is regarded as national relief for deaf-mute people in Britain, which belongs to universal service.

批注: After internet appearing, it is a question worth discussing whether broadband service should be included in universal service or not. In Britain, the universal service does not include broadband service, for which the reason is: (1) citizen could use alternative media to replace broadband. It is not only broadband that could satisfy basic needs for study and life, for example, if sending email, the person could go to public library to use free internet. Therefor broadband is not belongs to citizen's basic communication right, should not be included in universal service.

---

[9]　[英]Ian Lloyd,等.通信法[M].曾剑秋,译.北京:北京邮电大学出版社,2006: 135-136.
[10]　通话一方将要说的话用文本打印出来,经特定装置转化为语音.
[11]　[英]Ian Lloyd,等.通信法[M].曾剑秋,译.北京:北京邮电大学出版社,2006: 117.

第二节 普遍服务制度中的信息披露义务

Section 2 The Information Disclosure Duty in The Universal Service Institution

[无论哪一种普遍服务制度，都必须解决两个问题：如何获得普遍服务费，以及如何向提供普遍服务的企业提供补偿。这两个问题的解决都需要建立运营商的信息披露义务。]

批注：No matter which kind of universal service institution, the two questions should be resolved firstly, how to get universal service fee, and how to subsidize the enterprise that supplied universal service. It is necessary to establish the operator's information disclose duty to resolve both of the above questions.

1. 建立普遍服务信息披露义务的必要性

[电信普遍服务制度包含很多重要内容，比如如何分配普遍服务义务、如何补偿普遍服务成本、如何选择普遍服务提供者。自从普遍服务提出以来，各国建立了各种普遍服务制度，包括交叉补贴、接入亏损补偿、普遍服务基金等。然而[12]，无论哪一种普遍服务方式，都离不开建立严格的电信运营商信息披露义务。]

批注：Telecom universal service institution includes a lot of important content, such as how to assign the universal service duty thereof, how to subsidize universal service cost, how to select the universal service provider. Since the concept of universal service being put forward, various countries have established various universal service institutions, such as cross-subsidization, access loss subsidization, universal service funds etc., however, no matter which kind of universal service, it could not be independent of strict duty of information disclosure for telecom operators.

[从宏观上说，任何普遍服务补偿制度都需要涉及两个重要环节：普遍服务提供者的实际损失和征收普遍服务费时各缴纳义务人的具体财务信息。有关第一个问题，普遍服务提供者的实际损失，从理论上说，监管机构与企业之间存在严重的信息不对称。]按照规制经济学理论，"政府规制的代理人——政府官员也受有限理性、信息不对称、偏好不合理等因素的束缚……"[13]，[监管机构无法从企业获得足够的信息实施有效监管。]"决策者的选择是否合乎'理性原则'不再是一

批注：Macroscopically speaking, any universal service subsidization institution relates to two critical steps, which are the actual loss of the universal service provider, and the detail financial information of tax payer when collecting universal service fee. As for the first question, namely the actual loss of universal service provider, theoretically, there is a severe of information asymmetry between regulatory agency and the provider.

批注：The regulatory agency could not

---

[12] Hank Intven，等. 电信规制手册[M]. 管云翔，译. 北京：北京邮电大学出版社，2001：252.
[13] 曲振涛，杨恺钧. 规制经济学[M]. 上海：复旦大学出版社，2006：23.

个不必回答的问题，……而是一个需要加以分析的问题了[14]。"在电信市场上，信息从业者之间、信息从业者和服务对象之间、政府管理者和信息从业者之间都存在信息不对称现象，"实际上，[规制的核心或者说规制的难点正是政府的信息不对称，即政府知道的有关垄断企业的信息远远少于企业所知道的相应信息[15]。"]退一步讲，即使监管机构从企业获得了足够的信息，"……利益集团通过贿赂来收买规制机构，使其向国会提供对他们有力的信息，从而发生规制俘获[16]。"

[有关第二个问题，征收普遍服务费时各缴纳义务人的具体财务信息，同样也存在政府信息不对称问题。]以目前被认为是最佳方案的普遍服务基金制为例，向所有电信企业（不对称管制下可能会有选择）征收普遍服务基金的数额是按照企业的营业额或者利润为基数计算的，向提供普遍服务的企业提供补偿的数额依赖于企业提供普遍服务的实际支出或亏损额。然而，企业所了解的自身情况永远比监管机构对它了解要多，即使建立了各种经济学模型，监管机构从理论上讲也不可能获得征税基数和补贴额的准确信息。

[这个问题在税收制度中得到了很好的解决，但普遍服务与税收征缴制度不同，普遍服务义务人仅限于电信运营商，义务人数量极少，制度设计不应当过于复杂、解决信息不对称成本不应过高。因而类似于增值税发票似的复杂的监管制度不是首选。简单易行的解决之道就是建立信息披露制度和审计制度。]各国电信法都规定了企业的信息披露义务，要求企业主动披露收益额和普遍服务支出。然而，企业的

批注：acquire enough information from the provider to implement effective supervision.

批注：The kernel of regulation, or in other words, the difficult of regulation, is the information asymmetry for government. Namely, all the information that the regulator could acquire about the monopoly operator is far less than what the operator knows about itself.

批注：As for the second question, the detail financial information of tax payer when collecting universal service fee, there is a information asymmetry for government, too.

批注：This question has been well resolved in the tax system, but universal service is different from tax collection, the obligor of universal service is limited to telecom operator, which is few. So the institution design should not be too complicated, and the cost for resolving information asymmetry should not be too high. Therefore, the intricate supervision institution similar to value added tax invoice is not first choice. The easy and feasible solution is to establish information disclosure and audit system.

---

[14] 黄淳，何伟.信息经济学[M].北京：经济科学出版社，1998：31.
[15] 张昕竹，等.网络产业：规制与竞争理论[M].北京：社会科学文献出版社，2000：4.
[16] 曲振涛，杨恺钧.规制经济学[M].上海：复旦大学出版社，2006：25.

信息披露义务能够解决问题吗？企业如果透露了不实信息如何承担责任？监管机构定期验证企业会计信息真假的成本极高，在这种情况下还有没有其他办法可以在信息不对称情况下公平合理地分配普遍服务义务？这些都应当是设计普遍服务制度时应当解决的问题。

2. 交叉补贴阶段的信息披露义务

[由于电信从业者是以追求商业利润为目的而存在的，管理者必须建立一定的机制给予普遍服务提供者利益补偿，否则就不能保证用户长久地、稳定地享受该项服务。为解决这一问题，管理者在最初的时候允许普遍服务提供者存在一定程度的交叉补贴，用以弥补因提供该服务而损失的利益。] [在众多的普遍服务制度中，交叉补贴是最早的也是应用最广泛的。我国至今仍实行的是该补贴方式。以美国曾经实施的交叉补贴为例，20世纪50年代，为保证当时普遍服务提供者美国电报电话公司（AT＆T）的经济利益，联邦通信委员会（FCC）允许了AT＆T交叉补贴，] [包括：(1)不同业务之间的交叉补贴（长话补市话、国际补国内）；(2)不同地区之间的交叉补贴（低成本地区补高成本地区）；(3)不同用户之间的交叉补贴（商业用户补居民用户、一般用户补贴低收入用户）。] [在20世纪70年代末，AT＆T长途业务收入的26%用于补贴本地业务[17]。

交叉补贴的第一个弊端在于政策上必

批注：As the telecom enterprises regarding pursuit of commercial profit as their existing aim, the regulator should establish some system to render the universal service provider with indemnity, or the customer could not enjoy that service long and steadily. To resolve this question, originally the regulator allowed the universal service provider to cross-subsidize to a certain degree, in order to compensate the indemnity caused by offering this service.

批注：Among various of universal service systems, cross-subsidization is the first and the most extensive used method. Until now, our country is using this kind of rendering method. Taking the cross-subsidization method used ever by USA in the 1950s in order to guarantee the economic interest of AT&T who offered universal service at that time, FCC allowed AT&T to cross-subsidize.

批注：That cross-subsidization includes: (1)subsidization among different business such as revenue of long-distance business subsidizing local phone indemnity, international revenue subsidizing domestic indemnity; (2)subsidization among different regions such as revenue of low cost region subsidizing indemnity of high cost region; (3) subsidization among different customers such as revenue from commercial customers subsidizing revenue of resident customers, ordinary customers subsidizing low-income customers.

批注：In the end of 1970s, the 26 percent of long-distance revenue was used to subsidize local business. The first drawback of cross-subsidization is to guarantee the universal service provider to acquire the monopoly position in the business of getting subsidizig revenue.

---

[17] 欧阳武. 美国的电信管制及其发展 [M]. 北京：中国友谊出版公司，2000: 319.

须保证普遍服务运营商在获得补贴收入领域的垄断地位。]当时的管理者FCC认为,只有长途业务补贴本地业务才能保证本地业务在低价格下的普遍服务,而[要维持长途对于本地的交叉补贴,就必须保证长途的高利润。对长途高利润的保障只有通过垄断,否则长途市场的充分竞争会使得价格趋于成本而不可获得用于补贴本地业务的高利润。这就是一直被诟病的政策性垄断。第二个弊端是,交叉补贴还会导致普遍服务运营商将通过政策性垄断获得的优势地位渗透到竞争领域。]比如在已经竞争充分的增值服务领域,普遍服务运营商可以以低于成本的价格提供服务,而用垄断服务的高利润补贴竞争性业务亏损。[这样势必挤垮了竞争对手,因为他们没有垄断业务,无法获得超额利润补贴竞争性业务低价格产生的亏损。这也是后来各国纷纷放弃交叉补贴的原因。]

[在通过交叉补贴实现普遍服务的过程中,管制者必须课以普遍服务运营商至少两项信息披露义务,以消除管制中的信息不对称[18]。其一是普遍服务成本,其二是各项业务的收支情况。前者用于计算补贴数额,从而核定提供补贴的服务价格(比如长途资费)。后者是为了防止将补贴用于竞争性业务亏损而做的分业管制。]比如英国《电信法》第77条第3款规定:管理机构可以要求电信从业者向其提供所经营业务的详细信息,包括现有及预计的业务收入、现有及预计的销售和成本量、

批注:In order to maintain long-distance business subsidizing local business, the high profit from long-distance business must be guaranteed. It is only through monopoly to guarantee the high profit of long-distance, otherwise the completely competition in long-distance business market would cause the price tending to cost, then to gain the high profit to subsidize local business is impossible. This is criticized as policy monopoly. The second drawback of cross-subsidization is to cause universal service provider penetrating its advantage by policy monopoly into competition business.

批注:The behavior of cross-subsidization would make the competitors suffer so heavy loss that they could be bankrupted, because they could not gain enough surplus profit from monopoly business to subsidize the loss in competition business. This is the reason for various countries giving up cross-subsidization.

批注:In the process of implementing universal service by cross-subsidization, it is required for regulator to impose two duties of information disclosure to universal service provider, in order to eliminate the information asymmetry in regulation. One of the duties is disclosing the information of universal service cost; the other is disclosing the information of incoming and expenses for every business of that provider. The former is used to calculate the amount of subsidization for setting the price of the business being subsidized, such as the price of long-distance call; the latter is a kind of segregating regulation method to prevent the provider from transferring subsidization into compensating the loss of competition business.

---

[18] 张昕竹,等.网络产业:规制与竞争理论[M].北京:社会科学文献出版社,2000:247-257.

可预见的用户和竞争者的反应,电信业者应写一份成本计算表,其形式应能够让管理机构得到实行价格管理所必需的成本数据。我国《电信条例》第二十六条[19]也有类似的规定。[欧盟普遍服务指令第21条规定,普遍服务补偿仅限于与普遍服务直接相关的成本,必须排除与普遍服务不是直接相关的支出。第25条规定,向所有运营商征收的普遍服务税必须仅用于补偿与普遍服务直接关联的净支出。]

批注:The Clause 21 of the Directive of Universal Service of EU stipulates that, the universal service subsidization could only be limited to the cost which is directly related to the universal service, mandatorily exclude the expenditure indirectly relating to universal service. The Clause 25 stipulates that the universal service tax collected from all operators is mandatorily limited to subsidizing the net expense directly relating to universal service.

3. 普遍服务基金制度中的信息披露义务

在交叉补贴方式的普遍服务妨碍竞争到了不得不改变的时候,管制者决定开放长途市场,保障该市场竞争。为解决普遍服务提供者的补贴问题,开始实行普遍服务基金制度。这种制度不再把长途业务作为垄断允许业务,而是开放该市场,保护同业竞争者利益,[普遍服务提供者损失的利益不再靠政策性或默认的垄断业务的收入提供交叉补贴,而是靠普遍服务基金补[20]。现代通行的普遍服务补偿基金制度中,对于普遍服务的义务主体、基金来源、基金分摊都要由法律做出合理公平的规定,并且适时调整,免除普遍服务基金被认为是政府帮助特定技术尽快发展的一种手段,类似于免税[21]。]

批注:The loss of universal service provider does not depend on the cross-subsidization offered by the income from monopoly business supported by the police or tacitly approved from regulator any more, but indemnity paid by universal service fund. In the modern system of universal service subsidization, the law should stipulate reasonably and fairly and adjust in time about subject of duty (obligation-bearing party), source of fund, fund contributions. The exemption of contributions for universal service funds, which is similar to tax exemption, is regarded as a means of government assisting specific technology to develop rapidly.

美国的普遍服务基金建立于1983年,[根据美国电信法规定,所有经营跨州电信业务的公司都要提供普遍服务或缴纳普遍服务基金,但是从事国际电信服务、有线电缆租赁、开放式视频系统、卫星广播

批注:According to Act of Telecommunication of USA, all enterprises providing with

---

[19] 我国《电信条例》第二十六条 "……电信业务经营者应当根据国务院信息产业主管部门和省、自治区、直辖市电信管理机构的要求,提供准确、完备的业务成本数据及其他有关资料。"

[20] [加]因特温,等.电信规制手册[M].管云翔,译.北京:北京邮电大学出版社,2001:278.

[21] 比如,美国并未将宽带业务列入征收普遍服务基金的范围,因此,VoIP在美国发展很快,其不仅不需要缴纳普遍服务基金,也不要向本地运营商缴纳接入费,所以成本远低于传统长途运营商。

和信息服务的公司可以豁免该义务。] 德国《电信法》第17~19条规定了普遍义务的定义、主体、提供的方式和补偿，在电信市场中获得某类服务或产品总销售至少4%的利润或居统治地位的从业者为普遍服务的义务主体，管理机构可以责成任何居统治地位的电信业者提供该项义务，但是履行普遍服务义务不得造成被指定者相对于其他电信业者增大损失。如果被强制方要求补偿，管理者也可以通过招标的方式确定普遍服务的提供者。享受普遍服务补偿的主体是提供该义务并能够证明其提供该义务的长期附加费用超过了公司由此获得的收益，补偿的数额为提供普遍服务的长期附加费用加上投入资金的利息再减去该服务的收入。德国普遍服务基金来源于纳税，纳税主体是未提供该服务的普遍服务义务人，即在电信市场中获得某类服务或产品总销售至少4%的利润或居统治地位的从业者中未提供普遍服务者，纳税额按照纳税人收入与所有纳税义务人总收入的比例确定，所有纳税人的纳税总额等于付给实际提供普遍服务者的损失补偿费。为保证准确核准普遍服务义务人和义务人分摊的普遍服务税的税额，第22条[22]规定了所有从业者的收入披露义务。

interstate telecom service have a duty to providing with universal service or paying contributions to the funds thereof, but the enterprises providing with the following telecom services could exempt from the above duty: international telecom service, cable lease, opening video system, satellite broadcasting, information service.

[普遍服务基金制度中的关键环节是信息披露制度，企业必须按照法律规定主动披露收益额和普遍服务支出。普遍服务基金制度的成败在相当程度上依赖于监管机构对普遍服务基金纳税人和普遍服务提供者的财务信息的了解，因为税额与其财务收入、利润等财务信息有关，而补贴额与普遍服务成本有关。因此，准确掌握纳税主体的财务信息是征收普遍服务基金的关键，而确切了解普遍服务成本既是核定补贴额的必要步骤，又是确定来年征收基金数额的根据。]

监管机构对企业信息的获得，主要依靠企业信息的披露制度实现，这一点

批注：The critical step of the universal service system is information disclosure system, which requires enterprises to actively disclose income and expenditure for universal service complying with law provision. Whether the universal service system success or fail relays significantly on regulation agent knowing of the financial information of the contributors of universal service funds and universal service providers, because tax amount relates to financial information such as financial revenue and profit, and subsidization amount relates to universal service cost. Therefore, it is a key for collecting universal service funds to grasp the accurate financial information of contributors, in the meanwhile, knowing the exact universal service cost is not only the indispensable step of evaluating subsidization amount, but also the basis to determine the amount of the fund in the next year.

---

[22] 德国《电信条例》第22条规定"……在相关市场上提供许可证规定的可用电信业务的许可证持有者，应按照要求每年向管理机构汇报相关市场的收入，否则管理机构可以进行估算。"

类似于税收申报制度。监管机构的抽查是不定时的，不是获取企业信息的主要途径，而日常性的信息披露义务是监管机构了解企业财务信息的主要途径，比如每周披露、每日披露，甚至实时信息披露。这种披露义务应当是电信法规定的，是全体电信运营商的义务。信息披露义务构成整个监管体制的一个重要组成部分，监管的前提是获得足够的企业信息，这样监管才有针对性。而企业财务信息是企业经营信息的重要部分，所以信息披露义务是整个电信监管的基础。

国家获取商业信息的权力源于国家对商业机构进行有效管理的需要。为保证及时了解企业信息，国家通过立法建立了企业对国家的信息披露制度，但企业的商业秘密也应得到尊重。[电信法规定的运营商的财务信息披露制度，不能侵犯企业合法的商业秘密。也就是说，监管机构一方面有权利要求企业提供这些信息，但必须保证这些信息仅用于电信监管目的，并承担保密责任。]这一点类似于证券法[23]、会计法[24]和统计法[25]，只不过披露的意图不同：证券法是出于保护广大投资人的公共利益，会计法是出于宏观经济监管和税收监管的需要，统计法是国家为了了解国民经济和社会发展情况，即时制定或调整国家政策的需要。

批注：The provision of telecom law about financial information disclosure system for telecom operators, should not infringe their legitimate commercial secrets. That is to say, the regulation agency has the right to require the enterprises to report such information, but it should guarantee such information to be used only for telecom regulation, and undertake confidential liabilities.

为防止企业披露不实信息，一方面应当加重虚假信息披露责任，包括行政处罚和刑事制裁；另一方面，应建立替代性机制，[在监管机构不了解企业真实信息的前提下，也可以实现普遍服务基金的有效征收

批注：In the condition of the regulation agency not knowing the enterprises true information, it is possible to implement effective collection and assignment of

---

[23] 法律对上市公司和证券交易机构规定了严格的信息披露制度，例如，我国《证券法》专门规定了上市公司的持续信息公开义务，要求公司在发行股票或者债券时，公告招股说明书、公司债券募集办法，发行新股或者公司债券的，还应当公告财务会计报告（《证券法》第五十八条）。另外还要求上述信息必须真实、准确、完整，不得有虚假记载、误导性陈述或者重大遗漏，（《证券法》第五十九条），并规定了公司将经营信息和公司状态信息进行中报（《证券法》第六十条）、年报（《证券法》第六十一条）、及时报（我国《证券法》第六十二条）的义务和法律责任（《证券法》第一百七十七条）。证券法中对于信息的强制披露条款出于保护体现了公众利益的公众投资者利益，公司不得以商业秘密的信息安全为理由拒绝提供上述信息。

[24] 会计法中对企业信息披露的要求是出于国家为了维护市场经济秩序、监督企业的经营状况和纳税情况，以利于对企业的经济和财务状况进行有效监管，该义务包括保证财务信息的真实性和完整性义务（《会计法》第五条、第十三条），以及向相关国家行政管理部门提交财务信息载体的义务（《会计法》第三十三条、第三十五条）。

[25] 统计法是国家为了了解国民经济和社会发展情况、即时制定或调整国家政策，而规定的公民或社会团体在国家进行统计时的信息披露义务（《统计法》第三条）。

和发放。监管机构要想在信息不对称情况下公平合理地分配普遍服务义务，必须使用激励性和博弈性方案。征收中采用激励性方案，发放中采用博弈性方案——招标或拍卖。]

批注：universal service fund. If the regulation agency wants to fairly and reasonably assign the duty of universal service in the condition of information asymmetry, it must use stimulating and competing plan, stimulation plan used in the phrase of collection, and competing plan, referred to as tender and auction, used in assignment.

有关征收中的激励性方案，根据经济学原理，理性人的行为规制可以通过经济性制度设计获得，只要奖励（守法收益）和惩罚（违法成本）适当，是可以将理性人的行为导向立法者期望的方向的。征收中的激励性方案可以这样设计，如果监管机构对企业信息的抽查结果与主动披露结果一致，给予奖励；如果不一致，给予惩罚。奖励的数额（守法收益）应当大于惩罚的数额与被逮到的几率（违法成本），其中，被逮到的几率与监管机构抽查的频率、抽查全面性、调查深度等因素有关。

发放中的博弈型方案，就是被世界各国广泛采用的有限资源的分配方案。只要竞标主体超过两个且不串谋，招标或拍卖的交易方式，通过制造投标人或竞拍人之间的博弈，保证招标人或拍卖人在不知道、也不试图知道对方自身状况前提下，最大化地获得交易受益。[具体到普遍服务的招标，可以通过在两个以上的普遍服务竞标者之间制造博弈性压价，监管机构就可以在不了解普遍服务成本的前提下，以最少的普遍服务补偿金获得最好的普遍服务。]

批注：As for the tender for universal service, by the means of competing bid among two or more bidders who are universal service candidates, the regulator could acquire the best service at the lowest subsidization, under the premise of not knowing universal service cost.

生词和词组

第六章

1. 弱势群体 vulnerable groups, disadvantaged groups
2. 社会责任 society responsibility

3. 纵观电信管制史 survey of telecom regulation history, make a comprehensive survey of telecom regulation history, through telecom regulation history

4. 社会交往 social interaction; social communication; social intercourse

5. 标准统一 unification of standard

6. 绝大多数居民用户 overwhelming majority residential users

7. 全面覆盖的 Universal coverage, covering all-around

8. 人口稀少地区 sparsely populated area, underpopulation area, thinly peopled area; low population area

9. 公益机构 public interest organizations, social welfare organization

10. 弱势群体 vulnerable groups; disadvantaged groups

11. 短信聊天 SMS (short message service) chat

12. 免费 gratuitous, free of charge

13. 国家福利 national welfare

14. 国家救济 national relief

15. 最低生活保障 subsistence allowances, basic cost of living allowances, Minimal living standard, the minimum living guarantee

16. 廉租房 low-rent housing

17. 需求层次论 hierarchy of needs theory

18. 内涵和外延 connotation and denotation

19. 信息披露 information disclosure

20. 从宏观上说 From a macro point of view

21. 信息不对称 information asymmetry

22. 义务人 obligor

23. 增值税发票 value added tax invoice

24. 给予补偿 pay an indemnity, give compensation, render compensation, give repayment

25. 弊端 drawback, disadvantage

26. 默认 acquiesce in, tacitly approve, give tacit consent to

27. 超额利润 surplus profit, excess profit, superprofit

28. 收支 revenue and expenditure, income and expenses, receipts and disbursements,

incomings and outgoings, balance of payment

29. 分业管制 segregating regulation, business separation regulation
30. 转移补贴 transfer subsidization
31. 净支出 net expense
32. 依靠 depend on, rely on, count on, be dependent on
33. 公平合理的 reasonable and fair
34. 义务主体 subject of duty, subject of obligation, obligation-bearing party
35. 基金分摊 fund contributions
36. 财务收入 financial revenue, financial income
37. 合法的 legitimate
38. 承担保密责任 undertake confidential liabilities
39. 博弈 competition, game, game playing, gambling
40. 招标 tender, invitation for bids, call for bids, invitation of tender, bid inviting
41. 拍卖 auction
42. 在此前提下 under this premise, on the premise of
43. 投标人之间的竞争性出价 competing bid among bidders

第 七 章
Chapter 7

无线电频率管制
Radio-frequency Control

[无线电波是指频率在 3 000 GHz 以下的电磁波],其波峰之间的距离为波长,单位时间内通过某一点的波峰数为频率。频谱是指按照电磁波频率排列起来所形成的谱系,即从低到高排列的全部频率的集合。[无线电频率、电话码号和静地卫星轨道等用于实现电信功能且有限的资源,被视为电信资源[1],广义上的电信资源还包括域名、通信管道和可使用的公共区域和设施[2]。由于电信资源的稀缺,如何公平合理地分配该资源自然被列入了管制范围[3]。]

我国《电信条例》第二十七条将无线电频率认定为电信资源,[《物权法》第五十条和《无线电管理条例》第四条规定"无线电频谱资源属国家所有",

批注: Radio wave refers to electromagnetic wave whose frequency below 3 000 GHz.

批注: The limited resource to realize telecom function, such as radio frequency, phone number, static satellite orbit, is considered as telecom resource. The definition of telecom resource in general also includes domain name, communication pipeline and the public region and facilities which are used for communication. In sake of the scarcity of telecom resource, how to allocate telecom resource fairly and reasonably belongs to telecom regulation.

批注: "Real Right Law" Clause 50 and "Radio Management Regulations" Clause 4 stipulate that, radio-frequency spectrum is owned by the nation, legal circle thinks that radio-frequency spectrum is natural resource owned by the nation.

---

[1] 由于有用且稀缺,频率、码号和静地卫星轨道一直被视为世界性稀缺资源。国际电信联盟(ITU)的主要工作就是负责分配和协调该资源。
[2] 周光斌,蔡翔. 电信政策与管制 [M]. 北京:北京邮电大学出版社,2001: 251-252.
[3] Thomas G. Krattenmaker. *Telecommunications Law and Policy* [M]. Durham: Carolina Academic Press, 1994: P38-39.

法学界也认为无线电频谱属于国家所有的自然资源[4]。]

第一节 无线电频谱的特征及管制

Section 1　The Characteristics and Regulations of Radio-frequency Spectrum

"虽然无线电频谱可以根据空间、时间、频率和编码方式进行复用，即不同无线电业务和设备可以复用和共用频率，但就某一频段或频率而言，在一定区域、一定时间和一定技术条件下的利用是有限度的[5]。"这就是频谱的稀缺性。"稀缺和有用"使得频谱看起来像是一种资源，但其本质上却是无线电波的一个物理特征（频率）的集合。无线电波是物质，频率只是无线电波的物理参数，就像振幅、相位一样，不是物质。作为频率集合（谱系）的频谱当然也不是物质。无线电频谱本质上不是物质形态的自然物，不会因为使用而消耗，不具备自然属性[6]，这是其与自然资源的本质区别。美国经济学文献分配表为自然资源经济学作的分类中也不包含频谱资源[7]。频谱具有准自然资源特征——特定含义下的"有用"和"稀缺"。与自然资源的有用和稀缺不同，频谱的有用和稀缺具有特定含义。自然资源有用性是指自然资源本身具有使用价值，包括直接使用价值（直接用于生产和消费）、间接使用价值（生态功能）、选择价值（未来不可预知的价值）[8]。频谱有用是指其所表征的物理特征（频率）促成了无线电波的有用性，即无线电波必须具有特定频率才是有用的。自然资源的稀缺性是指有限的自然资源对人类无限需求表现出的使用竞争性[9]。频谱的稀缺性指在特定时空和技术条件下，仅能允许一个无线电波具有特定频率，否则会相互干扰。因此，在接受具有特定内涵的"有用"和"稀缺"概念前提下，可以称频谱为"资源"。正是在这种语境下，可以称之为"频谱资源"。

[由于稀缺和容易产生干扰，无线电管制势在必行。我国《电信条例》第二十七条规定了电信资源的分配可以采

批注：Due to the scarcity and prone to be disturbed, it is imperative to control radio. Chinese "Telecommunication Regulations" stipulates that the allocation of telecom

---

[4] 黄松有，最高人民法院物权法研究小组．《中华人民共和国物权法》条文理解与适用 [M]．北京：人民法院出版社，2007：180．
[5] 工业和信息化波无线电管理局．无线电频谱知识百问百答 [M]．北京：人民邮电出版社，2008：3．
[6] 钟水映，简新华．人口、资源与环境经济学 [M]．北京：科学出版社，2007：173-174．
[7] 章铮．环境与自然资源经济学 [M]．北京：高等教育出版社，2008：5．
[8] 周珂．环境与资源保护法 [M]．北京：中国人民大学出版社，2007：397-398．
[9] 周珂．环境与资源保护法 [M]．北京：中国人民大学出版社，2007：398．

取指配或拍卖的方式。][《无线电管理条例》专门用于：(1) 规范在我国境内设置、使用无线电设施；(2) 研制、生产、进口无线电发射设备；(3) 使用辐射无线电波的非无线电设备行为。其明确了：(1) 无线电频谱资源属国家所有，国家对无线电频谱实行统一规划、有偿使用的原则；(2) 国家无线电管理机构对无线电频率实行统一划分和分配；(3) 国务院有关部门对分配给本系统使用的频段和频率进行指配；(4) 任何单位和个人未经批准，不得转让频率，禁止出租或者变相出租频率。][《无线电管制规定》规定，为维护国家安全、保障国家重大任务、处置重大突发事件等需要，国家可以实施无线电管制。无线电管制，是指在特定时间和特定区域内，依法采取：(1) 限制或者禁止无线电台（站）、无线电发射设备和辐射无线电波的非无线电设备的使用；(2) 对特定的无线电频率实施电磁干扰等技术阻断措施；(3) 对无线电波的发射、辐射和传播实施的强制性管理。]

[美国电信法第三部分（Title III Provisions Relating To Radio）都是有关无线电的管理规定（SEC.301~SEC.399），其中第301条[10]列明，"本法的目的之

resource could adopt the way of designating or auction.

批注：Chinese "Radio Management Regulation" is used specially to regulate the following behaviors within Chinese territory: (1) to install, use radio equipment; (2) to research, manufacture, import radio emission equipment; (3) to use non-radio equipment radiating radio waves. This Regulation makes clear that, (1) the radio-frequency spectrum resource is owned by the nation, whose principle about radio-frequency spectrum is unified planning, compensated use; (2) the national radio management agency has the power to devide and allocate radio-frequency spectrum; (3) the corresponding agent of state council designates the frequency band and frequency assigned into its jurisdiction. (4) no entity and person has the right to transfer, rent, in disguised form of rent frequency without being ratified.

批注："Radio Management Provision" stipulates that, to maintain national security, protect national significant task, deal with important emergency affairs, the government has the power to carry out radio control. Radio control refers to as hereunder, at specific time, on specific region, subjected to law: (1) restricting or prohibiting the use of radio station, radio emission equipment, and non-radio equipment with radio radiation; (2) carrying out technical blocking measure such as electromagnetic interference to specific radio frequency; (3) implementing the enforced management to radio emission, radiation and transmission.

---

[10] SEC. 301. [47 U.S.C. 301] LICENSE FOR RADIO COMMUNICATION OR TRANSMISSION OF ENERGY: It is the purpose of this Act, among other things, to maintain the control of the United States over all the channels of radio transmission; and to provide for the use of such channels, but not the ownership thereof, by persons for limited periods of time, under licenses granted by Federal authority, and no such license shall be construed to create any right, beyond the terms, conditions, and periods of the license. No person shall use or operate any apparatus for the transmission of energy or communications or signals by radio, …except under and in accordance with this Act and with a license in that behalf granted under the provisions of this Act.

一就是要保证美国对无线电传输的所有频道的控制,并根据联邦管制机构颁发的许可证向个人提供一定时期的上述频道的使用权,而非所有权,上述许可证不得被解释为产生了超越其所附条款、条件和期限的权利。除非根据本法获得了许可证并遵循本法,任何人不得使用或操作任何设备用于无线电能量、通信或信号的传输。"]

[就无线电频率的管理层次,要经过频率划分(allocation)、频率分配(allotment)、频率指配(assignment)等三个阶段。由于无线电频率的跨地域性,对其管制不仅是国内法意义上的,还是国际法意义上的。国际电信联盟就是负责分配和管理全球无线电频谱与卫星轨道资源、制定全球电信标准的一个联合国的专门机构,简称"国际电联"(ITU),其成立于1932年,《国际电信联盟组织法》第一条规定了国际电联的任务:(1)无线电频谱的频段划分;(2)频率的分配、指配;(3)静地卫星轨道位置登记;(4)消除国家间无线电台的干扰;(5)世界电信标准化;(6)技术援助和国际合作。]

批注:The 3rd Title of "Act of Telecommunications of USA" is Provisions Relating To Radio, in which SEC. 301. [47 U.S.C. 301] is LICENSE FOR RADIO COMMUNICATION OR TRANSMISSION OF ENERGY.SEC. 301. [47 U.S.C. 301]: It is the purpose of this Act, among other things, to maintain the control of the United States over all the channels of radio transmission; and to provide for the use of such channels, but not the ownership thereof, by persons for limited periods of time, under licenses granted by Federal authority, and no such license shall be construed to create any right, beyond the terms, conditions, and periods of the license. No person shall use or operate any apparatus for the transmission of energy or communications or signals by radio, ……except under and in accordance with this Act and with a license in that behalf granted under the provisions of this Act.

批注:Concerning the hierarchy of radio frequency management, there are 3 steps: frequency allocation, frequency allotment, frequency assignment. On account of the transregional feature of radio frequency, to which regulating is not only the sense of domestic law, but also the sense of international law. International Telecommunication Union(ITU), established in 1932, is one of specialized organizations of the United Nations in charge of assignment and management global radio-frequency spectrum and satellite orbit resource, setting global telecom standard. The first Clause of "Organization Law of ITU" definitely specifies the task of ITU: (1) allocation of radio frequency band; (2) allocation and assignment of frequency; (3) registration of static satellite orbit; (4) eliminate the interference of radio station among countries; (5) global telecom standardization; (6) technology assistance and international cooperation.

第二节　技术发展对频谱法律性质的影响

Section 2　The Development of Technology Effects The Legal Characteristic of Radio-frequency Spectrum

[虽然表面上看，无线电频谱资源也具有排他性，在一定时空下，一个频谱不能被两个人同时使用，否则相互干扰。然而，频率使用权的排他效力完全建立在技术瓶颈和法律限制基础上[11]，而非对物的直接控制，这不同于物权的排他效力。频谱独占源于技术瓶颈，同频率的无线电波会相互干扰。如果技术发展可以做到同频率不干扰，频率的排他性也就不存在了[12]。]这类似于知识产权，知识产权的排他许可依赖于知识产权所有人的意志，而非知识本身的不可同时复用。而物的排他性源于有形物在一个时间只能由一个人控制，不可同时复用。[本质上看，无线电频率并没有排他效力，只是受制于技术水平，只有排他，才可防止干扰。目前的频谱许可制度虽为独占许可，但与物权出于有形物唯一控制权的排他性有本质区别。]

[随着动态频谱分配（DSA）技术的发展，美国已经建立了 3 650 MHz 的频

批注：Although radio-frequency spectrum seemingly has the characteristic of exclusiveness, that is to say, under a certain space-time, a specific radio frequency spectrum could not be used by two persons at the same time, otherwise mutual interference will occur. However, being different from exclusiveness of real right, the exclusiveness of frequency using right is completely stemmed from technology bottleneck and legal prohibition, other than direct control of property. The sole occupation of frequency spectrum derives from technology bottleneck, interference between the same frequencies will occur. If the developed technology can avoid interference between the same frequencies, the exclusiveness of frequency would not exist.

批注：Essentially, radio frequency does not possess the exclusive effect, however, subject to undeveloped technology, exclusiveness is the only way to prevent interference. Although, radio frequency spectrum system adopts exclusive license at present, this system has substantial distinction from the exclusiveness of real right derived from real property's sole right of control and occupation.

---

[11] 根据《无线电管理条例》第二十五条，国家保证无线电频谱资源使用权人的独占使用权，其有权排除他人使用其被许可的无线电频谱资源。

[12] Jerry Brito. The Spectrum Commons in Theory and Practice[J]. Stan. Tech. L. Rev. 1. 2007. "Spread spectrum is one of these technologies. ... This has the effect of allowing many users to use the same frequencies at the same time, thus increasing the communications capacity of spectrum....Other technologies that allow multiple use of the same spectrum include time-division multiple access (TDMA) and spectrum use etiquettes such as "listen before talk" (LBT)." "Because these technologies allow multiple users to efficiently share the same spectrum, some scholars ... propose a 'commons' or an 'open spectrum' regime in which anyone could use any bit of the spectrum and avoid interference using the new technologies."

谱共享平台[13]。在技术层面实现了频谱共享之后，现有的围绕频谱独占权建立起来的频谱规范将面临转型，国外电信法专家已经开始争论转型的方向，是由目前的"命令-控制"型转向私有权利型，还是共享型[14]？]美国联邦通信委员会（FCC）2002年专门成立了频谱政策任务组（SPTF）用于分析现有频谱管制模式的利弊和探索建立新的管制模式[15]。

批注：With the development of dynamic spectrum allocation (DSA) technology, USA has built a platform for 3 650 MHz spectrum sharing. After achieved spectrum sharing in the technology level, the existing spectrum regulations built around the exclusive right of spectrum is facing transformation, whose orientation is controversy of foreign telecom experts. Should it be changed from type of "demand-control" at present into type private right, or type sharing?

将频谱看作自然资源后，对其设计的制度就是用益物权制度。然而，频谱用益物权无法适应无线电技术的发展。有的学者混淆无线电波和无线电频谱的概念，将前者的物质性强加于后者，进而将后者归入自然资源范畴[16]；有人提出按照自然资

---

[13] Jerry Brito. The Spectrum Commons in Theory and Practice [J]. Stan. Tech. L. Rev. 1. 2007."Recently the FCC designated a 50 MHz block of spectrum in the 3650 MHz band as a commons.""The FCC created a commons by making the 3650 MHz band open to anyone who acquires a nonexclusive license, but subject to certain usage rules." "It resulted in a March 2005 FCC order designating the 3650 MHz band for nonexclusive licensed use--a very unique commons. Although users of the band will have to acquire a license to use the band, the license does not give them the exclusive right to use the spectrum; that is, licensees will have to share the spectrum with every other licensee. An unlimited number of licenses will be issued on a national basis. Licensees will be required to "make every effort" not to interfere with each other. Additionally, there is no first-in-time right, meaning that an initial licensee does not have superior rights to a subsequent licensee."

[14] Daniel Sineway. WHAT'S WRONG WITH WIRELESS?: AN ARGUMENT FOR A LIABILITY APPROACH TO ELECTROMAGNETIC SPECTRUM REGULATION[J]. 41 Ga. L. Rev. 671. "The SPTF's findings identified three main theories of possible spectrum regulation in the future: the command-and-control model, the exclusive rights (private property) model, and the spectrum commons model.""The command-and-control model represents the present-day system of regulation… First, the government allocates a certain frequency band to a given service, …Next, the government prescribes certain use restrictions on the given band, such as how much geographic area the given license will cover, the size of the actual frequency band, and allowable power limits. Third, the actual licenses to use certain spectrum bands are assigned via lotteries, auctions, comparative hearings, or other methods. Finally, the FCC polices these broadcasters and ensures that they are not violating the terms of their licenses. … Exclusive Rights (Private Property) Model…states the theory that use of spectrum should be treated as private property. The reasoning behind this assertion is essentially an economic one-if resources are to be used most efficiently and economically, they must have the characteristics of property rights: universality, exclusivity, and transferability. …this approach places no restrictions on the licensees as long as technical minimum standards are met. Spectrum Commons Model is rooted in technology, not economics. Proponents of this view argue that spectrum scarcity, the basic ground on which both the Act of 1927 and the exclusive rights approach are based, is no longer an issue thanks to newer technologies. In fact, not only is spectrum scarcity not a concern, but vast wireless networks will be unable to flourish if the current system continues…."

[15] Daniel Sineway. WHAT'S WRONG WITH WIRELESS?: AN ARGUMENT FOR A LIABILITY APPROACH TO ELECTROMAGNETIC SPECTRUM REGULATION. 41 Ga. L. Rev. 671. "In 2002, the FCC announced the creation of the Spectrum Policy Task Force (SPTF), a body charged with analyzing the existing regulation scheme and evaluating new possibilities."

[16] 郭明瑞. 中华人民共和国物权法释义 [M]. 2版. 北京：中国法制出版社，2007：97.

源管理模式设计频谱管理制度[17]；有人为无线电频谱使用权设计了详细的用益物权制度[18]。然而，频谱用益物权无法回避以下三个问题。其一，频谱本质上不具有"物"的特征，其是无线电波的一种物理属性——频率的集合，在实现其使用权过程中没有物的交付、流转、占有和消耗，基于物的实际控制的用益物权理论是否适用？其二，在频谱拍卖制度发达的欧美国家，整个制度设计围绕着"权利"（right）[19]，而非"物"（object）、"财产"（property）或者"资源"（resource），为频谱权利建构的是"命令-控制"（command-and-control）型法律关系，而非民事合同关系。这是否已经超越了传统用益物权理论可接受的限度？其三，频谱共享是无线电技术发展的趋势，虽然其不能彻底解决稀缺问题，但可以解决频谱独占导致的借频交易成本畸高[20]。在技术不允许频率复用的时代，以用益物权理论构建频谱使用权独占制度，并未表现出明显弊端，尤其是在我国频谱使用权流转制度空白的国情下[21]。面对技术挑战和国际频谱制度转型，频谱用益物权遇到了无法逾越的障碍，比如面对不特定的使用人，"一频率一权利"如何体现？如果采用共同占有模式，频率占用费是资格费还是出租费？当前，我国刚刚启动频谱的竞争分配制度[22]，尚未建立频谱流转制度，在此背景下，更应当深切认识频谱的本质和规制模式。[随着无线电技术的发展，频谱共享成为趋势，"只有独占才可防止干扰"的前提已被颠覆，使用权共享让频谱用益物权理论显得捉襟见肘；]另外，建立频谱使用权流转制度一直是学界关注的重点：作为财产权利，其应当被

批注：With the development of radio technology, spectrum sharing is becoming a tendency, because the premise of "only monopoly could prevent interference" has been overthrew, and the sharing of "the right of use" makes "the right of usufruct theory" have too many problems to deal with.

---

[17] 许小亚. 无线电频率资源应以自然资源规划方法合理配置[J]. 通信世界：2008（33）：25.
薛永刚，姚禹. 做好科学规划，提高频率资源管理成效[J]. 数字通信世界：2008（9）：12.
朱三保. 频率资源的性质和地位及其有效利用[J]. 中国无线电管理：1994（3）：15.
高远. 无线电频率资源的常规使用与管理[J]. 上海计量测试. 2008（2）：32.

[18] 李建. 无线电频谱资源法律问题研究——无线电频谱资源利用的法律完善[D]. 成都：四川大学，2004.

[19] David Porter, Vernon Smith. FCC LICENSE AUCTION DESIGN: A 12-YEAR EXPERIMENT[J]. Journal of Law Economies and Policy, 2006, 3（1）：63.

[20] JOHN S. LEIBOVITZ. The Great Spectrum Debate: A Commentary on the FCC Spectrum Policy Task Force's Report on Spectrum Rights and Responsibilities[R]. Yale J. L. & Tech. 2003 (6): 390. "The exclusive rights approach provides more flexibility, but the transaction costs associated with negotiating spectrum access with existing license holders--even for unused frequencies--would be prohibitively high in relation to the small time-frequency slices of spectrum used by open spectrum technologies. ... The chief theoretical criticism of the spectrum commons approach stems from skepticism about the central claim that technology can eliminate spectrum scarcity. ..."

[21] 我国目前尚未建立频率使用权流转制度。从经济学角度看，为发挥物的最大效益，除非危害物（枪支、毒品、淫秽读物），应允许流转。关键是建立可操作性的流转制度。由于无线电管制的需要，频率使用权流转制度应当类似于自然资源流转制度，如土地流转制度，流转合同经批准生效。

[22] 国家频率资源分配方式实行重大改革[N]. 人民日报，2003-03-03，国民经济版。"2003年2月27日信息产业部无线电管理局公布的9家电信企业获得的3.5 GHz频率使用权，以招投标方式获得。"

允许用于任何可行性用途[23]，而建立二级市场所凸显的流转标的到底是物还是权利的问题，指向了频谱用益物权理论的要害。

频谱技术的发展是解决其稀缺性的根本手段。目前最有潜力的技术是动态频谱分配（DSA）技术。"动态频谱分配策略……根据无线电系统的实际通信量，动态地分配频谱资源给该无线电系统。……包括连续的动态频谱分配和分块的动态频谱分配两种方式，前者是将连续的频谱块分配给不同的无线接入网络，而后者是任何无线接入网络可能被分配到在时空上不连续的频谱块[24]。"[动态频谱分配(DSA)技术可以使用户在特定时空共享频率，比固定频谱分配（FSA）下的频谱使用效率有了质的飞跃。]2003年美国联邦通信委员会（FCC）给出了更加宽泛的认知无线电（Cognitive Radio）定义，"能够通过与工作环境交互，改变发射机参数的无线电设备"。认知无线电具有认知能力和重构能力，前者可以感知特定时空的未使用频率资源（也称频谱空洞），后者可以重构参数，比如频率、调制方式、发射频率等，在不对频谱授权用户产生有害干扰前提下，利用授权系统的空闲频谱提供可靠的通信服务。一旦该频段被授权用户使用，认知无线电要么切换到其他空闲频段工作，要么改变发射频率或调制方案以避免干扰授权用户[25]。由此可见，[未来的频谱制度发展方向不是独占，而是协调各频谱使用人的频谱共享[26]。]

[频谱共享技术向频谱用益物权提出了挑战：如果仍援用用益物权理论设计频谱制度，频谱共享技术下的分配就要设计成同时共同占有[27]，各共同占有人在不

批注：The technology of Dynamic Spectrum Allocation (DSA) makes users to share radio frequency in specific space-time. This technology increases the spectrum utilization efficiency on a substantial leap over Fixed Spectrum Allocation (FSA).

批注：In the future, the tendency of spectrum system development is not exclusive, but spectrum sharing in the coordination of various users thereof.

批注：The technology of sharing spectrum challenged the theory of usufructuary. In the condition of the technology of spectrum sharing, the allocation of spectrum should be designed as simultaneous joint tenure, which

---

[23] Harold Hallikainen. SPECTRUM FOR SALE OR RENT COMMENTS ON US SPECTRUM AUCTIONS[J]. Int'l J. Comm. L. & Pol'y 1. 2000 (5)."The lessee would be free to sublease or transfer the unexpired portion of the lease. The lessee would be able to use the spectrum in whatever manner it sees fit…".

[24] 夏金祥，范平志．无线电频谱利用面临的问题、机遇与对策 [J]．中国无线电，2006（6）：7．

[25] 工业和信息化波无线电管理局．无线电频谱知识百问百答 [M]．北京：人民邮电出版社．2008：16．

[26] Thomas W. Hazlett. RESPONSE & REPLY: A REJOINDER TO WEISER AND HATFIELD ON SPECTRUM RIGHTS[J]. Geo. Mason L. Rev. 2008 (15):1031."The challenge ahead is to expand the scope of market spectrum allocations, developing the property institutions that guide entrepreneurs, inventors, lawyers, and regulators as to how rival frequency uses can be efficiently coordinated."

[27] 梁慧星，陈华彬．物权法 [M]．北京：法律出版社，1997：412．共同占有之一种形式，又称通常共同占有，与统一共同占有相对．

妨害他共同占有人的情形下，可以共享多个频段。(1) 频率占用费如何收取？(2) 干扰冲突规范如何？(3) 退出和加入"频谱共同体"的法律关系如何设计？(4) 对于多个"频谱共同体"之间的法律关系，是设计成各自"外部独占、内部共同占有"，还是将全频谱设计成共同占有，从而为将来"频谱共同体"间的动态频道借用留足制度空间？这些都是用益物权制度难以解决的。用益物权理论不仅难以涵盖本质上不属于"物"的频谱，而且无法给技术发展留出制度空间。] 用用益物权设计频谱制度，是口号式"保护国家自然资源"的后果: 在没有认真研究频谱本质的情况下，盲目迎合由于稀缺而将频率"准资源化"的经济学便利。

allows every joint tenant to share more than one frequency band in the condition of not interfering with other joint tenures. However, if we still cites the theory of usufructuary to design the system of spectrum, the following questions are hard to be solved: (1) how to collect frequency occupation fee; (2) what is the conflict rules when interference occurring; (3) how to design the relationship about joint in and withdraw from the "spectrum community"? (4) concerning the legal relationship among a number of "spectrum communities", should it be designed as "outside of the community, it is monopoly; inside of the community, it is joint tenure", or full-band is for joint tenure so as to leave enough institutional margin for dynamic channel borrowing among "spectrum communities" in the future. Not only could the theory of usufructuary hardly cover the spectrum that does not substantially belong to "property", but also it could not leave institutional margin for technology development.

第三节　频谱使用权制度构建

Section 3　The Structure of Spectrum Right

1. 频谱使用权的准物权特征

[德国法将财产权（对物权）的客体分为有形物、狭义无体物（精神产品）和财产性权利，并为其分别确立了物权、知识产权和准物权。"德国民法中的物权，仅为对有体物的支配权[28]"。为财产性权利设立的对物权为准物权。]"财产性权利在作为支配权的客体时，也具有稀

批注: In Germany Civil Code, the object of property right (right in rem) can be classified into 3 groups, which are tangibles, intangibles (intellectual product) in narrow sense, property rights, and the law established the respective rights for each of them: property right, intellectual property right, quasi-property right. The "property rights" in Germany Civil Codes limited the control right to tangibles. The right in rem established for property right is quasi-property right.

---

[28] 孙宪忠. 德国当代物权法 [M]. 北京: 法律出版社，1997: 21-22.

缺性和效用性，但其价值乃制度拟制的结果，也不能脱离法律的主观拟制而独立存在[29]。"因而，准物权设定于财产性权利之上，因其客体非有形物，故不是物权[30]。有学者用"权利物权"称谓，并将其界定为权利抵押权和权利质权[31]；也有学者持相反观点，认为准物权具有物权的绝对性、支配力、对抗效力等特性，故仍属物权，因其"含有使用、收益的内容，符合用益物权的规格[32]"，故是一组性质有别的权利的总称，包括矿业权、取水权、渔业权、狩猎权[33]。我们不去探讨准物权是否属于物权，仅论证频谱使用权的准物权特征。但如前所述，频谱使用权不具物权特征，因而，起码从频谱使用权角度看，可以说，准物权非物权。

"客体是否具有特定性、权利构成是否具有复合性、权利是否具有排他性、权利的追及力如何、权利的优先性是否具有特色等因素，均为判断某种权利是否属于准物权的标准[34]。"按照这个标准，可以判定[无线电频谱使用权属于准物权，而非用益物权：其客体是"发射特定频谱的无线电波的行为权利"，具有行政特许权利特点；其排他性不能靠权利人自力实现，而需依赖公权的震慑和救济；由于初始获得需通过行政许可、行使权利过程受到严格管制，其具有浓重的公权力色彩；其不具有追及力，不存在返还原物请求权，只有停止侵害和排除妨碍的救济方式；权利的优先性决定于频谱分配规则和自由频段冲突规则；其"一频率一权利"的特点源于技术限制，技术发展后，一个频率可以设定多个使用权，甚至可以将行为许可改为入门资格许可，所有入门成员有权根据各频段的空闲状态，动态使用全部频段。]

从频谱的非物、非精神产品特征看，

批注：The radio spectrum right belongs to quasi-property right, rather than usufructuary, the object of which is "behavior right of emission of specific radio frequency spectrum", with the trait of administrative franchise, whose exclusiveness could not be realized by obligee independently, but relay on deterrent and relieve offered by public authority. On account of authorization in initial acquisition and being strictly controlled in the process of enforcement of right, the right of use of radio spectrum possess the feature of public right, which is lack of the force of recourse, and whose relief does not include the claim for return of original property, but only the claim for cessation of infringement and removal of obstacle, and whose priority of right depends on allocation rules and conflicting rules within the joint community, and whose feature of "one frequency, one right" stems from technology restriction. After the technology development, more than one right of use could be established on a single frequency, and the behavior permission could even be changed to

---

[29] 徐涤宇.物权法体系构造之若干问题探讨[J].法治与社会发展.2002：（4）：145.
[30] 徐涤宇.物权法体系构造之若干问题探讨[J].法治与社会发展.2002（4）：144-145.
[31] 王泽鉴.王泽鉴法学全集·第十五卷，民法物权·通则、所有权[M].北京：中国政法大学出版社，2003：55.
[32] 崔建远，等.物权法[M].北京：清华大学出版社，2008：260-261.
[33] 崔建远.准物权研究[M].北京：法律出版社，2003：21.
[34] 崔建远，等.物权法[M].北京：清华大学出版社，2008：258-259.

对其控制权既不是物权，也不是知识产权，而是准物权。虽然在上文分析频谱使用权与物权的区别时，发现这种准物权表现出了很多知识产权特征，但由于[频谱使用权本质上不是知识产品，不能归入知识产权。其与知识产权的相似，源于二者都是法律拟制的权利，权利的产生、流转和消灭完全依赖法律规定，而和有形物的控制、使用和消耗无关。]我国《物权法》第五十条之所以将频谱所有权纳入到物权范围，是由于考虑到频谱的效用性和稀缺性与"物"类似，为节省立法成本，在物权法中对这种准物权做原则性规定，其具体制度留待以后专门制定特别法。这应当属于崔建远教授呼吁的：从实用主义的角度看，由于现行立法体系缺失准物权制度，在物权法定主义制度下，物权法应明文列举准物权类型，承认其物权效力[35]。

批注：entry qualification permission, that is to say, once acquiring admission, all members have the right to dynamically use full-band subject to its idle state.

批注：The spectrum right is substantially not intellectual product, could not be ascribed into intellectual property right. The similarity between them derives from that they both are legal artificial right, whose generation, transmission, elimination are completely relied on legal stipulation, and have nothing to do with tangible property's control, using and consumption.

2. 频谱使用权制度构建

随着技术的发展，更高效的频谱使用方式不断被发明出来[36]。虽然现在技术上可利用的频率上限是 3 000 GHz，但人类超越这一极限只是时间问题。从发展角度看，[理论上说，技术可以使频率资源变得无限。技术是解决频谱稀缺的最终方法[37]，法律只是在现有技术条件下应对频谱稀缺的临时措施。]

批注：Theoretically, technology would make the frequency resource infinite. Technology is the ultimate method to solve the scarcity of spectrum, on the other hand, law is merely the temporary measure to deal with the scarcity of spectrum in the existing technology condition.

频谱具备有用和稀缺的自然资源特征，物权法第五十条将其认定为资源并确立了国家所有，但该法并未认定其为自然资源。作为准物权，频谱使用权应当有别于自然

---

[35] 崔建远. 我国物权立法难点问题研究[M]. 北京：清华大学出版社，2005: 358-359.

[36] Charles Jackson, etc. Spread Spectrum Is Good -- But it Does Not Obsolete NBC v. U.S.![J]. Fed. Comm. L.J. 2006 (58): 245 ."we conclude by noting that there is substantial cause for optimism regarding future use of the radio spectrum. Emerging technologies, such as Multiple-Input Multiple-Output ("MIMO") and Multi-User Detection ("MUD"), will expand spectrum capacity several times over."

[37] Daniel Sineway. WHAT'S WRONG WITH WIRELESS?: AN ARGUMENT FOR A LIABILITY APPROACH TO ELECTROMAGNETIC SPECTRUM REGULATION[J]. 41 Ga. L. Rev. 671."spectrum scarcity, the basic ground on which both the Act of 1927 and the exclusive rights approach are based, is no longer an issue thanks to newer technologies."

资源使用权。自然资源具备物的属性，用物权制度保护恰当且充分，但频谱资源并非自然物，不具有物的消耗性和直接控制性，不适用基于对物的直接控制建构的物权制度。[既然不是物，频率不应当成为出租和流转的标的，有关频率的全部法律制度应当所在。]

[频率使用权和码号使用权一样，都归国家所有，而不能进行私有化。原因在于，随着技术的进步，频率和码号用途的不可知性越来越大，国家必须保留不断调整其用途的权利，也就是说，这些资源永远不会到达一个稳定的、不再需要改变用途的状态。][随着技术发展、使用人数的变化、特定行业预留，国家对它们的宏观调控会一直进行下去。私有化将不利于国家保留随技术进步和使用人数变化而随时调整这些资源的用途的权利，比如码号7位升8位；][又如2009年2月，工业和信息化部下发了《关于1 900—1 920 MHz频率无线接入系统相关事宜的通知》要求所有频段在1 900到1 920 MHz内的无线接入系统必须在2011年底前完成清频退网工作（小灵通正在这个频段），确保不对1 880—1 900 MHz频段的TD-SCDMA系统产生干扰。]

从经济学角度看，稀缺且有用的，就是资源，需要建立分配制度。[频谱使用权属于行政特许权，国家授权某主体有偿"使用"频率，不应认定为国家向该主体出租频率，而是国家对其独家许可——允许其排他地从事发射某频率无

批注：Now that frequency is not property, it should not be regarded as the object of rent and circulation, and all institutions concerning frequency should center on right (the frequency right), which is the manifestation of quasi-property thereof, other than object of right (frequency resource).

批注：The frequency right, similar to phone number right, is owned by the nation, and could not be privatized, the reason is that, with the development of technology, the unpredictablity of the usage of frequency and phone number is wider and wider, thus, the nation has to reserve the right of adjusting their usage constantly, that is to say, these resource would never reach a stable and unchangeable state.

批注：With the development of technology, variation of users population, reservation for specific industry sector, the nation would always go on macro-controlling to them. Privatization is not in favor of the nation to reserve the right to adjust at any time the usage of these resource, with the development of technology and the variation of user population, taking an example of the phone number upgrading from 7 digits to 8 digits.

批注：Taking another example, February 2009, Ministry of Industry and Information issued "Notification of the matter of frequency 1 900-1 920MHz radio access system", which required all radio access systems working between frequency 1 900 to 1 920MHz (Personal Handphone System is within this band) are obliged to finish the job of turning over the frequency and withdrawing from the network before the end of 2011, so as to protect the TD_SCDMA system working between 1 880 to 1 990 MHz from interference.

线电波的行为。]这种行政许可类似于知识产权制度中的独占许可，整个过程中没有物的交付、占有、消耗、归还，[频率所有人——国家收取的频率占用费并非基于物的消耗而获得的租金，而是特许费。]无线电频谱使用权与知识产权使用权的来源不同，前者源于国家所有人的行政许可授权，后者是私人权利人授权，但二者都源于授权。因而，[比照知识产权中的独占许可制度设计无线电频谱资源制度，不仅解脱了借用用益物权时必须证明的"频率占有""一频率一权利"属于物权特征的牵强附会，还为其流转规范以及技术发展留下了足够的制度空间。]

> **批注**：The spectrum right belongs to administrative franchise, that is the nation authorizes some entity to paid-use specific spectrum, and could not be regarded as the nation rent the spectrum to the user but exclusively franchising the right of use. That is to say, the user is exclusively permitted to exercise the behavior of emitting the specific frequency.

> **批注**：The nation, the owner of frequency, charges frequency occupation fee, which is not the rent based on property consuming but royalty charge.

> **批注**：To design the radio spectrum resource system in light of exclusive license of intellectual property right, does not only get rid of the necessity to demonstrate far-fetched "frequency occupation" and "one frequency, one right" conforming to usufruct trait, when referring to the theory of usufruct, but also leave enough institution margin for circulation system and technology development.

　　在技术无法克服同频干扰的背景下，为频率资源设计的制度只能是"一频率一权利"的独占许可。动态频谱分配技术的发展，可以做到自动地根据特定环境的实际通信量动态地分配频谱资源，这使得多人可以共用一个频率而不干扰。相应地，频率资源制度就应将独占授权改为普通授权，国家保留赋予其他人该频率使用权的权利，这就从根本上解决了用益物权制度下的"一频率一权利"无法克服的频率共享问题[38]。另外，频率使用权流转制度，如转让频谱使用权或以其投资，重点在于规范频率使用人和所有人（国家或其代表，如无线电管理委员会）之间的使用权出让合同，应当在颁发行政许可时签订许可证合同，而非按照物的流转设计制度；在频率使用权侵权救济制度中，频率使用人可以要求所有人（国家或其代表）查处，也可以侵权人为被告提起民事诉讼，但其只能主张停止侵害、排除妨碍，这也可以比照知识产权许可的侵权救济设计制度，而非物权请求权。总之，[为频率资源设计的法律制度应当围绕作为准物权的频谱权利进行，并可以借鉴知识产权中的多项制度。]

> **批注**：The legal system designed for frequency resource should concentrate on the right of spectrum as quasi-property right, which could reference on a number of institutions about intellectual property right.

[38] Jerry Brito. The Spectrum Commons in Theory and Practice[J]. Stan. Tech. L. Rev. 1. 2007. "A new school of scholars, …. propose to make spectrum a commons. They claim that new spectrum sharing technologies allow a virtually unlimited number of persons to use the same spectrum without causing each other interference and that this eliminates the need for either property rights in, or government control of, spectrum."

生词和词组

第七章

1. 频率管制 frequency control
2. 电话码号 phone number
3. 静地卫星轨道 Static satellite orbit
4. 通信管道：Communication pipeline, Communication channels
5. 物权法 property law, real right law
6. 无线电管理条例 radio management regulations
7. 无线电频谱 radio-frequency spectrum
8. 法学界 Law community, legal circle
9. 势在必行 evitable, be deadly certainty, imperative
10. 有偿使用 paid use, compensated use, rewarding use
11. 统一规划 unified planning, integrated planning
12. 频段 frequency band
13. 变相出租 in disguised form of rent
14. 规定（名词）stipulation, provision, regulations, rules
15. 国家安全 national security
16. 强制性 coerciveness, mandatory, enforceability, obligatory
17. 电磁干扰 electromagnetic interference
18. 跨地域的 transregional
19. 在一定时空下 under a certain space-time
20. 物权 real rights
21. 技术瓶颈 technology bottleneck
22. 独占许可：Exclusive License
23. 动态频谱分配 dynamic spectrum allocation(DSA)

24. 频谱独占权 the exclusive right of spectrum

25. 用益物权 usufructuary right, the right of usufruct

26. 共同占有 joint tenure, joint possession, commonly-possessed

27. 共同占有人 joint tenant, joint possessor

28. 频率占用费 frequency occupation fee

29. 冲突规范 rule of conflict, conflict rules

30. 制度空间 institutional margin, systems spatial, system, institutional elastic space

31. 动态频道借用 dynamic channel borrowing

32. 财产权 property right （财产权也叫"对物权"）

33. 对物权 right in rem, in rem

34. 有形物 things corporeal, tangibles （"有形物"对应的权利为：property right）

35. 无体物 incorporales, bodiless substance, intangible（"无形物"也叫精神产品，对应权利为 intellectual property right）

36. 精神产品 intellectual products

37. 财产性权利 Property rights （也叫"准物权"）

38. 准物权 quasi-property right

39. 支配权 eminent domain, right to control, desposition, right of dominion

40. 行为权利 behavior right

41. 权利人 obligee, creditor, right holders

42. 债务人 debtor, obligor

43. 公权力 public power, public authority

44. 行使权利 exercise right, enforcement of right

45. 追及力 force of recourse

46. 追索权 recourse

47. 返还原物请求权 the right of claim to the return of the original property

48. 停止侵害 cessation of infringement, ceasing the infringing act

49. 排除妨碍 removal of obstacles, exclusion of hindrance, elimination of obstruction

50. 权利优先性 right priority

51. 入门资格许可 entry qualification permission
52. 空闲状态 idle state, idle condition
53. 拟制权利 Artificial right
54. 有偿使用 paid-use, compensational use
55. 许可费 license fee, royalty fee, permission charge
56. 独占许可 exclusive license
57. 流转制度 circulation system, transferring system
58. 权利客体 object of right
59. 私有化 privatization (n.), privatize (v.)
60. 保留权力 reserve the right to
61. 清频退网 turn over the frequency and withdraw from the network

第八章
Chapter 8

电信资费
Telecom Service Price

第一节 我国当前电话资费模式及法理依据
Section 1　Our Country's Current Telecom Tariff Mode and Legal Basis

[我国当前的电话资费模式可以概括为"三个二元"。其一，资费构成二元：由月租费和通话费两部分构成，这个资费模式源自美国，在全球已沿用了100多年。其中月租费用来补偿建设成本[1]，通话费用来补偿运营成本[2]。其二，资费类型二元：包括市话和长途（包括国内长途和国际长途）。其三，资费依据二元：即按照通话时间和通话距离（市话还是长途）来确定资费数额。]

[这种资费模式自电话产生之日就开始使用，有些国家一直沿用至今。在电信发展早期，电信资源稀缺、电信技术落后，运营商计算电话资费、管制机构进行价格管制，都依据了这种计费模

批注：At present, the telecom charges mode of our country could be summarized as "3 binary patterns", that is: (1) tariff constitution is binary, constituting of monthly rental and call fee. This mode, came from USA, has been used more than 100 years in global, in which monthly rental covers construction cost, and call fee covers operation cost. (2) tariff type is binary, constituting of local fee and long-distance fee (including domestic long-distance fee and international long-distance fee). (3) tariff basis is binary, which decides the price amount on the basis of call duration and distance (local or long-distance).

批注：This tariff mode began to be used since the invention of telephone, and has still been

---

[1] 月租费基于以下经济学原因产生：具有自然垄断性的电信网络，建设投资巨大。然而，由于通信权利涉及公民基本权利，通信服务带有公益属性，资费受到国家管制，不可能过高，故收回电信网络建设的投资需要相当长时间。因此，电信网络建设投资实际上是一块巨大的沉没成本。在电信业发展早期，基础运营商无法承受如此巨大的沉淀资本，就将其转嫁给用户，通过初装费、月租费形式让用户买单。

[2] 高仰止. 电信资费改革探究 [J]. 中国新通信. 2007（12）：45.

式。即便在电信业发展迅猛的今天，该资费模式在世界部分国家和地区依旧盛行。]

[按照通话时间和距离收费，是由于在电信技术发展初期，必须在通信者之间，建立一条物理连接（物理信道），且在整个通话过程中只能由这二者独占使用。这类似于房屋租赁，房屋被一个房客租赁期间是不能让其他人使用的。因此，在当时技术条件下，电信网络适用租赁物权理论，租金与租期（通话时长）和租赁物的数量（通信距离越长占有的网络数量越多）成正比。这种资费模式适应了电信网络的稀缺特征：网络传输距离与传输容量都非常有限，用户接入并独占使用电信网络则意味着在通话时长内租赁电信网络资源。][因而，用户对电信网络的使用权源自对物的租赁：用户在通话过程中对电信网络的使用既符合物权的一物一权原则，也体现了用户对电信网络使用权的相对排他性特征。用户对电信网络设施占用的多少及占用的时间长短，决定了电信资费。]

基于通话距离和通话时间的资费模式，在传统民法的物权理论及租赁合同理论上找到了依据。[这种模式下的电话资费即为对物的使用之对价，而用户与电信网络所有人之间的关系，则为基于用益物权的租赁合同关系。]在今天的某些发展中国家和地区，这种资费方式被广泛应用。然而，近三、四十年以来，尤其是近二十年，通信技术取得了巨大

used up to now. In the early time of telecom development, telecom resource was scarcity and technology was undeveloped, when telecom operators charging telecom service price and regulators carrying out price control, both had relayed on this mode. Even in the present when telecom technology developed rapidly, this charging mode has been still popular in most countries and regions in the world.

批注：The reason for charging on the basis of call duration and distance is that, in the incipient stage of technology development, there was a physical connection (physical channel) existing between two users and exclusively occupied by them in the whole process of communication. This is similar to house leasing, in which the house could not be occupied by others in the leasing period.

批注：Therefore, in the condition of technology at that time, the theory of leasing usufruct could apply to the telecom network, that is to say, rental is in direct proportion to lease term (call duration) and quantity of leased item (the much the call distance, the more the network occupied). This tariff mode is suitable to the scarcity feature of telecom network, that means, transmission distance and capacity of the network were limited, and the face of customer accessing into and excessively occupying the network meant leasing the network resource during the call duration.

批注：Therefore, the customers' right of use of telecom network comes from leasing the property thereof, which means that, the customers' use of telecom network during call duration complying with the principle "one property, one right" of real right, and manifesting the relative exclusiveness feature of the right of use of telecom network.

进步[3]。二十年前还严重匮乏的网络容量，现在已经变得严重过剩[4]，通信网络资源已不再是一种稀缺资源[5]。以电信技术发展初期建立的"时间－距离"资费模式作为计价的依据，已经显得不合时宜[6]。电信技术的发展动摇了电信网络的物权基础，原有的租赁合同关系在新形势下面临着前所未有的挑战。

第二节　电信技术发展引发的电信网络使用权的准物权特征

Section 2　The Quasi-right Characteristic of Telecommunications Network Caused by the Development of Technology

1. 电信技术的发展

早期的电信传输主要依靠电缆、微波等，传输距离和容量都非常有限；而光纤传输带来了电信传输的巨大变革。光纤通信是以光作为信息传送载体，以光纤作为传输媒介的通信方式[7]。光纤通信技术是近30年迅猛发展起来的新型通信传输技术，其给信息传输带来了巨大的进步[8]。与传统的电缆或微波等通信方式相比，光纤通信具有传输频带极宽、通信容量极大、速率极高等优点[9]。因而，被各国广泛应用，由此带来了传输距离和传输容量上的飞跃，甚至出现了网络资源的严重过剩。[光纤传输、波分复用、多路调制技术使得一路光纤上可以同时传输200万个双向话路，并且"距离死亡"使得长途和本地的区分不再重要[10]，网络资源可以被无以计数的人同时使用而互不干扰。]

批注：The technology of optical fiber transmission, wavelength division multiplex (WDM), and multiple modulation, enables a single optical fiber to support simultaneously 2 million bi-direction telephone channels, furthermore, "distance died" makes the distinction between long-distance and local no more important, and network resource could be used simultaneously by countless users without interference.

---

[3] 张耀寰.通信技术演进中的市场模式变革研究[D].北京：北京邮电大学，2006.
[4] 同上，第1页.
[5] 同上，第64页.
[6] 林致远.电信资费由何而定——垄断还是技术进步[J].北京观察.2001（7）：40.
[7] B. Desthieux. Optical Fiber Technology[M]. San Diego: Elsevier Inc, 2009: 333-406.
[8] Rees, John. TECHNOLOGICAL CHANGE AND REGIONAL SHIFTS IN AMERICAN MANUFACTURING[J]. The Professional Geographer，1979, 31（1）：46.
[9] 张耀寰.通信技术演进中的市场模式变革研究[D].北京：北京邮电大学，2006.
[10] ［美］罗伯特·W·克兰德尔.竞争与混沌——1996年电信法出台以来的美国电信业[M].匡斌，译.北京：北京邮电大学出版社，2006：67.

以传输速率和容量为例，近十年来，随着大容量智能节点的出现，光电子的传输速率由 1.6 Tbit/s 增长到了 10 Tbit/s~100 Tbit/s。而相对于技术的飞速发展，电信业市场的需求增长并非如此迅猛，这就造成了供给能力严重过剩。有数据显示，1998 年到 2001 年，地下埋设的光缆数量增加了 5 倍，同时由于技术的进步，每根光缆的传输能力增加了 100 倍，因此，光缆的总传输能力增加了 500 倍。但是，在此期间的需求只增加了 3 倍。因而，电信技术的飞速发展使得三四十年甚至一二十年前还严重不足的网络容量，现在严重过剩。根据美国联邦通信委员会（FCC）公布的数据，美国电信运营商有 90% 左右的光缆容量在闲置，其光纤过剩在 15 年内不会改变。我国几大电信运营企业的光缆线路总长度已超过 400 万千米，而目前我国的光纤利用率仅约 10%[11]。由此可见，电信技术进步带来的资源过剩是个普遍现象。

电信技术革命以及光缆的普遍应用使电信网的传输容量取之不尽、用之不竭；光缆严重过剩的传输容量使构成电信成本的"距离－时间"因素消失了[12]。[从理论上讲，随着容量的急剧扩大，与距离相关的传输成本已趋近于零[13]，由此产生了"距离－时间死亡"现象。] 早在 1998 年就曾有来自国际电信联盟（ITU）的数据显示，每话路分钟的光缆传输成本最多也不应超过 0.000 8 元，即不到人民币 1 厘。光缆传输的单位成本在长途业务的总成本中所占的比例小到可以忽略不计[14]。[在现有的电信技术条件下，电信网络的用户数量、传输距离、使用时间对电信成本的影响可以忽略不计。]

批注：Theoretically, with the capacity increased sharply, the transmission cost relating to distance approaches zero. Therefore, the phenomenon of "distance-time died" is emerging.

批注：Under the present condition of telecom technology, the impact to telecom cost from the quantity of customers of telecom network, transmission distance and service time could be ignored.

2. 电信技术发展带来的社会经济效应

电信技术的迅速发展及由此带来的资源过剩，引发了一定的社会经济效应。具体表现为电信技术进步和社会福利之间的矛盾，也就是，电信成本急剧降低与电话

---

[11] 张耀寰．通信技术演进中的市场模式变革研究 [D]．北京：北京邮电大学，2006．
[12] 阚凯力．中国电信向何处去？[M] // 阚凯力．对电信业的思考与挑战．北京：北京邮电大学出版社，2005：60-61．
[13] 阚凯力．中国电信向何处去？[M] // 阚凯力．对电信业的思考与挑战．北京：北京邮电大学出版社，2005：60-61．
[14] 阚凯力．谈电信传输的"距离死亡" [M] // 阚凯力．对电信业的思考与挑战．北京：北京邮电大学出版社，2005：57-58．

资费降速过缓之间的矛盾。这种矛盾长期得不到解决，公众无法分享电信技术进步带来的社会效益，技术福祉被运营商独占。

　　我国同大多数发展中国家一样，电话资费降低的幅度远没有赶上技术进步产生的电信成本的降低幅度。原因就在于电话资费模式没有改变，距离和时间仍然是决定电话资费的主要因素。在大多数发展中国家的电话资费模式中，电信成本的波动不能反映到电话资费的变动中，并且缺乏透明的电信成本核算及独立的监督管理机制[15]。在这种资费模式下，电信运营商有垄断定价的空间[16]。正如有些学者所言，电信运营商宁肯让大量光缆黑在地下，也要盘剥消费者，不给消费者打便宜一些的电话。这与资本家把牛奶倒进大海有什么区别[17]？如此一来，"消费者和国民经济的其他行业不能充分享受到电信技术进步带来的利益，电信技术的发展不能有效地转化为社会福利，却成为电信运营商获取暴利的重要手段，整个社会为此付出着沉重的代价[18]。"技术只有真正转化成社会福利才算完成了最终的技术革命之使命。因而，电话资费模式应适应技术的发展而适时调整。

3. 电信技术发展对电话资费法律关系的影响

[电信技术的发展深刻地改变着电信资费法律关系。随着单一光纤上同时使用的用户数的无限累加（理论上有上限，事实上超过几个数量级的冗余，可以视为无限，下同），电信网络的物权特征由用益物权，变为信道的使用许可权——可以被无限人同时使用的权利物权，即准物权。用户对电信网络的使用权不是基于物的租赁，而是准物权（权利物权）的许可。]因而，用户与电信网络所有者之间的合同关系，由租赁变为使用许可。

批注：The development of telecom technology has changed profoundly the legal relationship around phone tariff. With the quantity of users on a single optical fiber simultaneously accumulating infinitely (theoretically, there is a upper limit, but when considering that the redundant margin is several orders of magnitude, it could be deemed infinite), the feature of telecom network changes from usufruct into permitting license to admission of the communication channel, which, being a kind of right in rem in right, i.e. quasi-right in rem, could be simultaneously used by countless users, whose right of use of the telecom network does not base on leasing property, but permission license of quasi-right in rem (right in rem in right).

---

[15] Carsten Fink, Aaditya Mattoo, Randeep Rathindran. An Assessment of Telecommunications Reform in Developing Countries[J]. Information Economics and Policy,Elsevier. 2003, 15(4): 443-466.
[16] 何志新．从美英两国的电话资费管制看我国先行电话资费管制的不足 [J]．长沙通信职业技术学院学报，2004 3(4)：59-60．
[17] 阚凯力．信息社会与电信业的未来 [M]// 阚凯力．对电信业的思考与挑战．北京：北京邮电大学出版社，2005：9．
[18] 阚凯力．以传输网络与电信业务的分离为起点进行我国电信企业的改革 [M]// 阚凯力．对电信业的思考与挑战．北京：北京邮电大学出版社，2005：21．

可以说，电信技术的发展改变了网络资源的物权属性。[在电信技术的强大支撑下，网络，表面上的有形物，越来越具有了无形财产的法律属性：无限多用户同时使用同一有形物，而不降低其使用价值和使用效率。这种使用不是基于对物的控制和占有，而是接入许可；获得接入权的用户产生的使用成本，与其对物的占有时间、占有数量和同时使用人数无关。因而，电信技术引发的电信网络的准物权特征，要求作为电话网接入对价的电话资费，顺应技术发展潮流，由租赁费变为接入许可费，即不限次数、距离和时间的包月制。]这也是电信技术福祉被社会分享的大势所趋。

电信网络物权属性的弱化和准物权属性的凸显，必对电话资费法律关系的各主体产生影响。伴随电信技术的进步，一方面，电信网络资源由稀缺转为过剩，在法律层面，电信网络的物权属性淡化，其使用权凸现出准物权特征；另一方面，电信技术进步使得电信业传输容量和距离大幅提升而成本降低，带来一定的社会经济效应。[电信网络使用权准物权特征的凸显应当引起电话资费模式的变革。确立基于电信网络使用许可制度的用户接入权，将是电话资费改革的方向，]其将带来电话资费降低，将电信技术进步转化为社会福利。

批注：In the strong support of telecom technology, although being apparently tangible, network possess more and more attribute of intangible property, because infinite users could use a single tangible network simultaneously without decreasing use value and efficiency. This kind of use does not base on control and possession of the tangible network itself, but access grant, of which once the users acquire, their cost is independent of occupying duration, quantity and the population on it simultaneously. Therefore, the feature of quasi-right in rem deriving from telecom technology, requires the phone tariff, which is the consideration of access to phone network, to comply with the trend of technology development and be changed from rental fee into access grant fee, which is a fixed rate plan no matter times, distance and call duration.

批注：Concerning the telecom network right, the appearance of the attribution of quasi-right in rem should cause the transformation of phone tariff mode, whose trend would be establishing access right of customers based on the system of access to telecom network.

第三节 电信网络使用权的准物权特征及用户的电信网络接入权

Section 3　The Attribution of Quasi-right in Rem of Telecom Network and Users' Access Right to Telecom Network

电信技术的发展使电信网络传输能力大幅提升，传输距离和时间对电信成本的影响可以忽略不计，网络传输容量在理论上趋近于无穷大，世界各国普遍存在着网络传输容量过剩。[电信技术的发展使得同一电信网络上同时可以设定无限多使用权，电信网络基于实物占有和控制的物权特征已经消失，而具有了基于使用许可的准物权特征。因而，应当修正用户与电信网络所有者之间的围绕电信网络物权设定的租赁合同关系，变更为围绕用户许可接入权的许可关系，进而确立起用户的网络接入权。原有的所谓的"基于电信网络物权的租赁合同关系"是电信运营商攫取垄断暴利的借口，应当建立基于电信网络使用权许可制度的电话资费包月制，资费本质上是使用许可费。在缴纳了该使用许可费后，用户即获得了电信网络接入权，可以不限次数、不计时长和距离地使用电信网络。]这种法律关系的重塑不仅回应了电信技术发展带来的电信网络使用权准物权特征的凸显，在经济上更能发挥网络资源的使用效率，并且能将电信技术发展带来的福祉分享于全社会。

批注：The development of telecom technology enabled people to establish infinity right of use simultaneously on a single network, thus the trait of right in rem of telecom network based on occupying and controlling thereof has disappeared, meanwhile, it possesses the trait of quasi-right in rem based on the right of access to thereof. Therefore, we should adjust the relationship between users and the owner of telecom network, from contract relationship around the right in rem, into permission relationship around access, furthermore, establishing the users' right of access to the network. The original so-called "leasing contract relationship based on the right in rem of network" is pretext of operators who intent to seek excessive profit from monopoly. We should establish fixed rate system based on the right of access to telecom network, the rate substantially being the access fee for accessing to the network. After paying the fixed rate, users would acquire the right of access to the network, regardless of times, duration and distance.

1. 电信网络物权特征的淡化

电话资费没有随着电信技术的进步而降低，社会无法分享技术进步带来的福祉，原因在于电话资费模式没有随技术革新而改变。电话资费模式改革的前提是，重新认定电信网络的法律特征，并由此重塑电话资费法律关系，确立用户的电信网络接入权。

在电信技术发展初期，电信网络作为稀缺资源，同一时间允许接入通话的用户数量相当有限，用户对电信网的占有与使用具有相对的排他性，符合物权理论中用益物权特征。我国"三个二元"的电话资费模式确立了用户与电信网络所有者之间基于物的使用量（通话距离）和使用时间（通话时长）的租赁合同关系。

随着技术的发展，电信网络物权特征淡化，一物一权的特征消失了。物权理论认为，在同一物上，不能同时设定两个以上互相冲突的权利。而事实上，随着电信技术的发展，同一电信网络上同时存在的使用权数量逐渐增加，到今天，理论带宽超过实际用量的几十倍，而且带宽冗余越来越大。电信技术从来就没有停止过在一个电信网络上设定无穷多使用权的努力，而且每日都在向这个目标靠近，越来越多的用户不需要对网络实现有形控制和占有，就可以同时使用同一物。

当电信网络的物权特征开始动摇，租赁合同关系自然站不住脚。面对技术发展，我国以租赁合同关系为基础的"三个二元"的电话资费模式不仅与法理违背，也阻碍了将电信技术发展的福祉回报给社会。

2. 电信网络使用权的准物权特征

单纯讨论作为实在物的电信网络的物权特征，就如同讨论存储计算机软件的光盘的物权特征一样，没有实在意义。光盘所"承载"的权利，是软件的许可使用权，而非光盘本身的物权；同样，电信网络所"承载"的权利，是电信网络的许可使用权，而非网络本身的物权。与知识产权相似，作为有形物的电信网络（光纤网），如果可以供无限多用户同时使用而互不影响，就褪去了其基于占有、控制的物权特征，而具有了基于使用许可的准物权（权利物权）特征。

为财产性权利设立的对物权为准物权。"财产性权利在作为支配权的客体时，也具有稀缺性和效用性，但其价值乃制度拟制的结果，也不能脱离法律的主观拟制而独立存在[19]。"因而，准物权设定于财产性权利之上，因其客体非有形物，故不是物权[20]。有学者用"权利物权"称谓[21]。准物权中的"准"字，其汉语含义为"程度上不完全够，但可以作为某类事物看待[22]。"在传统准物权理论界，准物权的外延主要包括与自然资源相关的权利，如渔业权、矿业权、水权等，而极少涉及其他资源，如电信网络资源。

以光缆为基础的电信网络容量既然已经严重超出了社会需求，就应当作为公共

---

[19] 徐涤宇. 物权法体系构造之若干问题探讨 [J]. 法制与社会发展. 2002（4）：145.
[20] 徐涤宇. 物权法体系构造之若干问题探讨 [J]. 法治与社会发展. 2002（4）：144-145.
[21] 王泽鉴. 王泽鉴法学全集·第十五卷，民法物权·通则、所有权 [M]. 北京：中国政法大学出版社，2003：55.
[22] 谭柏平. 自然资源物权质疑 [J]. 首都师范大学学报（社会科学版），2009（3）：3.

资源被全社会以低价所共享[23]。因为电信网络是信息社会正常运转不可或缺的基本资源,其与传统自然资源在稀缺性、社会依赖程度上并无差异。因而,建立类似于自然资源准物权制度的电信网络资源的准物权制度,不仅保证了这种基础资源的社会获得性和可持续性,还可以通过降低许可费,充分发挥冗余网络资源的效能,让全社会分享科技发展带来的福祉,而不是让垄断基础运营商独享电信技术发展的成果。

著名民法学者崔建远先生认为,判断某种权利是否属于准物权的标准包括:客体是否具有特定性、权利构成是否具有复合性、权利是否具有排他性、权利是否具有追及力、权利的优先性是否具有特色等因素[24]。根据此标准,我们来判断电信网络使用权是否具有准物权属性。

在客体的特定性方面:与物权客体的严格特定有别,准物权不具备或不严格具备客体特定性。比如采矿权、水权的客体无特定性;渔业权、狩猎权的客体特定性不严格。对于电信网络使用权,用户接入电信网络后既有可能使用本地电信网络,也有可能使用本地以外甚至本国领土外的电信网络(国内长途和国际长途),因而这种权利呈现出对客体特定性要求不严格的特征。

在权利构成方面:准物权具有复合性,比如,渔业权包含占有一定水域并养殖和捕捞水生动植物之权、水体使用权、保有水体适宜水生动植物生存和成长标准之权。再如,矿业权包含在特定矿区或者工作区内勘探和开采矿产资源之权、特定矿区或者工作区内的地下使用权等。电信网络使用权也具有复合性,用户既享有接入本地电信网络的权利、在其他电信服务商处互联互通的权利(漫游或国际长途等)、自身码号或频率的使用权、指定接受人的码号解析权、紧急呼叫、查号等辅助性权利,也包括通过电信网络传输语音、数据过程中的信息安全和通信自由等权利。因而,电信网络使用权也具有复合性。

在权利的排他性及优先性方面:物权属于对世权,对物的占有和使用享有绝对排他的权利,这也是"一物一权"原则的体现,此外物权还有优先性,主要表现为物权优先于债权。准物权则不具备该种完全的排他性、优先性特征,在同一个客体上往往可以同时存在多个权利主体和内容,且各主体行使权利互不影响,也无先后关系,权利的排他性及优先性并不明显。由于电信技术的发展,同一时间在同一电信网络上存在着多个电信网络使用权,用户本身并不对电信网络实施有形的占有,而且各用户之间同时行使权利也互不影响。随着网络容量的与日俱增,同一电信网

---

[23] 阚凯力.中国电信向何处去? [M] // 阚凯力.对电信业的思考与挑战.北京:北京邮电大学出版社,2005: 60-61.
[24] 崔建远.准物权的理论问题 [J].中国法学,2003(3): 76.

络上可以同时设立的权利逐渐趋向无穷多。因而用户的电信网络使用权并不具备排他性及优先性。

在权利的追及力方面：物权属于对世权、绝对权，因而权利人对其物所享有的权利具有追及力；而如矿业权、水权、渔业权、狩猎权等自然资源的准物权仅仅在极少数特殊情况下产生追及力。电信网络用户由于对电信网的权利不具排他性及优先性特征，而且更重要的是，其并不实际占有和控制电信网络本身，故其所享有的权利也非绝对权，因而无追及力。

综上所述，电信网络使用权的准物权特征显而易见，其决定了用户与电信网络所有者之间的法律关系，不是物的租赁合同关系，而是使用权许可关系。

第四节　确立用户的电信网络接入权及电话资费改革

Section 4　Establishing Users' Right of Access to Telecom Network and Phone Tariff Reform

1. 通过电信网络使用权许可赋予用户接入权

用户与电信网络所有人的法律关系的重塑，不仅反映了电信技术发展带来的网络使用权的准物权特征，而且能充分发挥网络资源的使用效率，将技术发展带来的福祉分享于全社会。[租赁合同关系与接入许可关系的区别在于：租赁是通过"客体排他"间接地完成"利益排他"，而接入中的"客体共享"意味着不是通过配置客体本身，而是通过赋予权利人以特殊的"入门资格"（电信网络接入权）来赋予使用客体的权力[25]。]

批注：The distinction between leasing contract relationship and access grant relationship is that the former indirectly achieves "exclusive interest" through "exclusively control of the leased object"; on the other hand, "object sharing" in the latter, authorizes the right of using the object through empowering the obligee specific "entry qualification" (the right of access to telecom network), rather than allocating the object itself.

---

[25] 邓卓. 兄妹一样——物权与知识产权 [EB/OL]. 民商法网刊，2007（9）：6. http://www.civillaw.com.cn/wangkan.

在确立了用户与电信网络所有人之间的使用许可法律关系后,用户通过缴纳使用许可费,可以获得一定时期(通常为一个月或一年)的不限次数、时间、距离的网络使用权。用户缴纳的使用许可费,就是通常所说的包月费或包年费。[通过缴纳使用许可费,用户获得的电信网络使用权实际上是一种"接入权",是用户将自己的电信终端设备接入电信网络并获得基于网络的服务的权利。]

[在这里,不妨将传统电信法上的"接入"做扩大解释,涵盖用户接入电信网的情形,从而确立"用户网络接入权"。传统电信法上的"接入"概念,仅指电信运营商之间接入对方的电信网络,而不包括最终用户的接入,]即电信网络所有者"根据规定的条件,在排他性或非排他性基础上向其他企业提供设施和/或业务。它包括:接入网络元素和相关设施与业务;进入包括建筑物、管道、电视塔在内的设施;……[26]" [相关立法中的"接入"也仅限于运营商之间的接入,不包括最终用户接入。比如,美国电信法规定,"在位运营商有义务向任何提出接入请求的运营商在任何技术可行点上、在非捆绑的基础上提供非歧视性的网络元素接入,其资费、条款和条件必须是公正的、合理的和非歧视性的[27]。"]

法律之所以专门规定运营商之间的

批注:By paying access fee, users acquire the right of access to telecom network, which is substantially a kind of access grant, permitting the users to access their telecom terminal equipment (TTE) into telecom network and acquire service based on the network.

批注:We might expand the interpretation of "access" in traditional telecom law so as to cover the situation of users accessing into telecom network, thus to establish users' "the right of access to network". The concept of "access" in traditional telecom law refers only to operators accessing to each other's network, excluding the situation of users' access.

批注:The concept of "access" in relevant legislations refers only to operators thereof, excluding the end users' access, such as Act of Telecommunications of USA Sec. 251(c) 3.

SEC. 251. [47 U.S.C. 251] INTERCONNECTION

(c) ADDITIONAL OBLIGATIONS OF INCUMBENT LOCAL EXCHANGE

(3) UNBUNDLED ACCESS.—The duty to provide, to any requesting telecommunications carrier for the provision of a telecommunications service, nondiscriminatory access to network elements on an unbundled basis at any technically feasible point on rates, terms, and conditions that are just, reasonable, and nondiscriminatory in accordance with the terms and conditions of the agreement and the requirements of this section and section 252. An incumbent local exchange carrier shall provide such unbundled network elements in a manner that allows requesting carriers to combine such elements in order to provide such telecommunications service.

---

[26]　[加] Hank Intven,等. 电信规制手册 [M]. 管云翔,译. 北京:北京邮电大学出版社,2001:74.
[27]　美国电信法 .251(c): 3.

接入关系，目的是为了在自然垄断领域增加竞争者数量，使没有电信网络的运营商也能够利用竞争对手的网络资源开展竞争业务。通过法律设定新进入电信市场的运营商的接入权，使其不需拥有网络就可以开展一切电信业务，"进入者仍应能够从其竞争者即在位运营商那里以受规制的批发价格，实际上获得在位运营商的所有设施[28]"，包括交换设施、传输设施、码号资源、运营系统等。如果运营商的接入权没有法定，电信网络所有者为了保持竞争优势，就会拒绝竞争对手接入自己的网络和自己竞争[29]。换句话说，运营商的接入权不可能靠合同约定，只能通过法律规定。

[传统电信法上的"接入"概念排除用户接入，源于用户接入权属于用户和电信运营商之间的合同权利，法律没有必要专门设定。]为了出售电信业务，电信运营商必须允许用户接入网络。用户缴纳了电话资费，依据电信服务合同，就获得了接入电信网并享受电信服务的权利。

批注：The reason for traditional telecom law excluding user's access from definition of "access" is that user's right of access belongs to the right of contract signed between user and telecom operator, so law has no need to establish that right.

西方国家不需要将"接入"的外延扩大至用户接入，其依赖完全开放的电信市场、充足的竞争者数量、严格监管下的有效竞争，已经实现了电信资费模式的转变，适应技术发展的包月制资费模式已经成为惯例。然而，与西方完全开放的电信市场不同，我国还无法依赖电信运营商之间的有效竞争，自发地形成电话资费的包月制，我国电信寡头垄断严重，电话资费模式无法依赖市场实现转型，必须依赖政府的强制推进。因此，为适应电信技术引发的电信网络使用权的准物权特征，我国有必要在即将出台的电信法中明确规定用户的电信网络接入权，从而确立以电信网络使用许可费（接入费）为对价的资费模式，并严格规制电信网络使用许可费数额（接入包月额）。比如，可以规定"电信用户在缴纳了电信网络使用许可费后，获得一定时期的电信网络接入权，有权利在该时间段内不限次数、距离、时长地接入电信网络和获得电信服务。国家价格主管部门制定和调整电信网络使用许可费的指导价"。

2. 国外电信资费改革经验和对我国的启示

如何平衡放松资费管制与加强以成本为基础的资费监管这对矛盾，反映了各国电信资费改革的理念。在美国，20世纪80年代之前，FCC实行"合理报酬率"管制，以成本为基础，规定总资产报酬率上限；20世纪80年代之后，采取资费上限和不对

---

[28] [美] 罗伯特·W.克兰德尔.竞争与混沌——1996年电信法出台以来的美国电信业[M].匡斌，译.北京：北京邮电大学出版社，2006：9.

[29] 法定的接入义务可以获得三赢：对于网络资源所有人（接入被申请人），盘活了网络闲置资源，避免了网络资源浪费；网络资源租用人（接入申请人），绕开了大规模投入网络建设的沉淀成本瓶颈，可以快速进入电信市场，提供竞争业务；对于消费者，竞争带来的价格下降、质量提高。

称管制相结合的方式[30]。1996年电信法修改后，市场完全开放，价格管制逐渐放开。[1999年11月，美国联邦通信委员会（FCC）除保留了在电信运营商进行不正当竞争的时候进行干预的权力外，取消了对所有电信业务的资费限制，各电信运营商可以在向FCC备案后，自行制定和调整电信业务资费[31]。] 而在英国，自1998年开始，其全面开放了电信市场，采用了价格上限规制模型，有效抑制了恶性价格战，避免了非规制引起的市场成本。其2003年《通信法》加强了对资费成本的监控，确保资费正确反映成本，与价格上限相吻合[32]。OFTEL（英国电信管理局）给予BT（英国电信）极高的电信资费自主权，其只注重各组电信业务的上限而并不需要审定各项电信业务的成本[33]。

批注：Since November 1999, except for reserving the power of intervention on occasion of telecom operator carrying out unfair competition, FCC abolished all restrictions to tariff of every telecom business, that means, all operators have the right to fix and adjust their business's price after reporting to FCC.

在资费以成本为基础的理念下，国外的套餐或包月制电话资费模式应运而生，已经存在了很长时间，有着成功的经验可供借鉴。比如，澳大利亚在促进市场竞争、技术创新和及时对居民需求作出回应的资费管制目标下，竞争和消费者委员会（ACCCC）强制澳大利亚电信（Telstra）提供低收入套餐[34]。又如，美国和我国香港地区按月以一个固定金额（包月额）收取电话资费。美国自20世纪80年代AT&T解体并引入本地电信竞争以来，就开始实施固定电话包月资费模式。到今天，美国电信市场占主导地位的十大电信运营商如AT&T和Verizon等都采取了包月制资费方式[35]，例如AT&T公司推出的Call Vantage、Call Vantage Small Office Plan，南方贝尔公司的数字电话服务也采用了包月制资费模式[36]。在这种模式下，美国的固定电话用户只需交纳定额费，就可以任意拨打国内电话，若每月再多缴10美元就可以随意拨打美国与加拿大的任何地区。IP电话也有固定收费计划，如Vonage公司的IP电话费为每月24.99美元，允许拨打500分钟的被叫方为美国和加拿大任何地方的电话。再如香港的本地电话服务很早就采用了包月制模式，并根据电话的性质区

---

[30] 刘凤元.全球电信资费管制的经验和借鉴[J].中国物价，2008（3）：26.
[31] 何志新.从美、英两国的电信资费管制看我国现行电信资费管制的不足[J].长沙通信职业技术学院学报，2004（4）：18.
[32] 曾剑秋，陈婧俐.从英国《通信法》谈中国电信资费改革[J].当代通信，2006（12）：74.
[33] 何志新.从美、英两国的电信资费管制看我国现行电信资费管制的不足[J].长沙通信职业技术学院学报，2004（4）：18.
[34] 张冬生.澳大利亚、韩国电信资费管制考察报告[J].中国物价，2005（11）：52.
[35] Marc Lifsher. AT&T to raise monthly fee for basic service by 23%[J]. Los Angeles Times, 2008（10）：24.
[36] 信息产业部电信资费考察团.借鉴国外经验，建立有中国特色的电信资费管理体系[J].通信世界，2000（2）：18.

分住宅电话和商业电话。1999年前，住宅电话包月费为68.9港元/月，商业电话包月费为108.8港元/月。到1999年9月香港电讯将住宅电话月租费提高到90港元/月，商业电话包月费没有调整[37]。香港电讯盈科（PCCW）目前的商业电话和住宅电话最低包月额分别可为137.8港元/月和110港元/月[38]。

我国现有的电信资费体制缺乏透明的成本核算、资费结构和计算方式不合理、缺乏完善的价格监管法规[39]。要想与世界先进国家的电信资费体制接轨，应当在推进竞争、鼓励科技投入并使其成果尽快变为社会福利的宗旨下，既要放松电信资费管制，又要建立以成本为基础的资费监管体系。"电信资费问题在促进社会福利最大化方面具有关键与瓶颈作用"，因而，电信资费管制的首要目标是社会福利最大化，其次是电信企业能够正常运营[40]。[建立以成本为基础的资费监管体系，要求电信资费必须反应成本随科技发展的降低，将电信科技发展带来的实惠分享于全社会。]

批注：We should establish telecom tariff supervision system on the basis of cost, and make the tariff reflecting the cost reduction with technology development, so as to share the benefit brought by telecom technology development with the whole society.

我国电信资费改革的方向应当是确立电信网络使用许可制度。这种制度既适应了电信科技发展带来的管网物权属性的变化，又反映了还科技实惠于民的社会需求，其本质特征在于资费与通话时长和距离无关。设定用户接入权是该制度中最重要的一个环节。通过设定用户接入权实现的电信网络使用许可制度，要求电信资费模式为包月（包年）的使用许可费。包月费其实就是一个月的使用许可费，包年费则是一年的使用许可费。许可费数额（包月额或包年额）属经济学问题，由价格主管部门负责召集电信管制机构、电信运营商、公众通过听证等法定程序，依据电信业成本进行定价。使用权许可制度的核心在于控制权利行使的资格，而不关注权利人行使权利的行为。获得许可的权利人，在一定的时空范围内可以自由地行使权利。这正好符合了电信技术发展带来的"时间和距离死亡"的特征，既然电信成本不依赖于通话距离和时间，电话资费也应当与通话时间和距离无关。用户只要支付了受到价格管制的使用许可费，就获得了电信网络接入权，可以任意使用电信网络资源。电话资费包月制剥离了通话距离、时长与资费的关联，势必促使用户大量使用网络资源，实现网络冗余资源的有效利用。从社会经济性角度看，包月制电话资费模式能有效地将电信技术进步转化为社会福利。

---

[37] 何霞.国外电话资费管制政策的演进与发展[J].世界电信，2004（12）：37.
[38] 香港电讯盈科（http://www.pccw.com），最后登录2009年10月6日.
[39] 刘凤元.全球电信资费管制的经验和借鉴[J].中国物价，2008（3）：43.
[40] 彭云飞，马超群.中国电信资费管制问题与方法研究[J].北京邮电大学学报（社会科学版），2006，8（2）：24.

生词和词组

第八章

1. 电信资费 telecoms tariffs, telecom charges, telecommunication pricing, telecommunication tariff
2. 二元模式 binary pattern, dual pattern
3. 自费构成 tariff constitute
4. 月租费 monthly fee, monthly rental
5. 通话费 call charge, call fee
6. 补偿 compensate, make up for, cover
7. 资费依据 tariff basis
8. 成正（反）比 be in direct(inverse) proportion to
9. 租期 lease term, tenancy term
10. 通话时长 call duration
11. 通话距离 call distance
12. 租赁物 leased item, leased property
13. 物权 real right
14. 用益物权 usufruct, usufructuary right
15. 波分复用 wavelength division multiplexing (WDM)
16. 多路调制 multiple modulation
17. 双向话路 two-way telephone channel, bi-direction telephone channel
18. 可以忽略不计 can be ignored, can be neglected
19. 大几个数量级 is several orders of magnitude larger than
20. 信道 communication channel
21. 权利物权 right in rem in right
22. 物权（对物权） right in rem, real right, in rem（拉丁语，against a thing）
23. 准物权 quasi-right of property, quasi-right in rem

24. 法律属性 legal attribute, legal nature
25. 使用价值 use value
26. 接入许可 access grant
27. 接入权 access right, the right of access
28. 电信网络接入权 the right of access to telecom network
29. 通话时长 call duration
30. 包月制 flat rate plan, fixed rate plan
31. 使用许可制度 utilization permission system
32. 攫取暴利 seek excessive profits
33. 入门资格 entry qualifications
34. 电信终端设备 telecommunication terminal equipment (TTE)
35. 扩大解释 expanding interpretation
36. 进行不正当竞争 carry out unfair competition
37. 进行干预 intervene, make intervention
38. 定价 fix price

Chapter 9

电信转售
Telecom Service Resale

[通俗地说，转售就是整买零卖，是自然垄断行业促进竞争的重要手段。转售使没有电信网络资源的转售商（申请人）也可以进入电信市场参与竞争，它从基础电信业务经营者（被申请人）那里趸购电信业务，再包装后卖给最终消费者[1]。转售涉及两个价格，被申请人卖给申请人的趸售价是受规制的批发价，申请人卖给最终消费者的零售价是自由定价的零售价。批发价受规制的原因是，只有该价格低到申请人在加入适当利润后仍可以对抗被申请人直接向最终消费者提供的零售价，转售才是可行的。如果批发价过高，申请人将无利可图。批发价应在被申请人的零售价基础上，剥

批注：In layman's terms, resale is buy wholesale and sell retail, which is an important measure to facilitate competition in natural monopoly business. Resale enables the reseller (applicant) to enter telecom market for competition. The reseller, who does not possess telecom network resource, buys service in wholesale from basic telecom business operator (respondent) and repackage, then sell in retail to the end consumers. Resale relates to two sets of price, the wholesale price of respondent selling to applicant which is regulated, the retail price of applicant selling to the end consumer is free set. The reason for wholesale being regulated is that, only when it lower than the level that, after being added appropriate profit it could still compete with the retail price of respondent selling directly to end consumer, the resale is feasible. If the wholesale price is too high, applicant would be unprofitable. So the wholesale price should be

---

[1] 为了方便引用，下文中将使用如下定义。
　　基础电信业务经营者：也叫被申请人，其是拥有基础电信网络的电信基础电信业务经营者，其将自己提供的电信服务打包出售给转售商或者最终用户。
　　转售商：也叫申请人，无自己的基础电信网络设备，通过向基础电信业务经营者购买电信服务，然后包装成自有品牌进行出售。
　　用户：接受电信服务的最终用户。

离被申请人"可避免成本",即营销、计费等成本。如何认定"可避免成本"是转售实施的关键,但这仍是一个经济学问题,而非法律问题。]

1. 电信转售的定义

[转售业务是指一家企业以向最终用户直接或者捆绑销售某种服务为目的,而以批发的形式购买该服务的一种商业行为,这造成了其与服务实际提供者之间的直接竞争[2]。[美国联邦通信委员会(Federal Communications Commission, FCC)将电信转售定义为:一个实体订购另一家实体的电信服务和设施,进而以盈利为目的向公众提供该服务和设施[3]。][美国电信法 Sections 251(c)(4) 和 Section 252(d)(3),分别对转售义务及其批发价的定价原则进行了详细规定。]

2013 年 5 月 17 日,我国工业和信息化部发布了《移动通信转售业务试点方案》,其中将"移动通信转售业务"及其特点概括为"移动通信转售业务是指从拥有移动网络的基础电信业务经营者购买移动通信服务,重新包装成自有品牌并销售给最终用户的移动通信服务。

on the basis of respondent's retail price, peeled off respondent's avoidable cost, i.e. marketing, billing cost etc. How to identify "avoidable cost" is hinge of implementing resale, which is a question of economy other than law.

批注:Resale is a kind of commercial behavior, by which an enterprise buys services in wholesale price in order to directly sell or in-bundled sell the same service to end customers, which causes direct competition between the reseller and the actual provider of the service.

批注:FCC of USA defined the concept "resale" as an activity wherein one entity subscribes to the communications services and facilities of another entity and then reoffers communications services and facilities to the public (with or without 'adding value') for profit.

批注:Act of Telecommunications USA stipulates the resale duty in sections 251(c)(4) and its wholesale price regulated principle Section 252(d)(3).

sections 251(c)(4) RESALE.--The duty
(A) to offer for resale at wholesale rates any telecommunications service that the carrier provides at retail to subscribers who are not

---

[2] Alexander C. Larson. Resale Issues In Telecommunications Regulation: An Economic Perspective[J]. 2 Mich. Telecomm. Tech. L. Rev, 1996, 2(1) : 57.
"Resale is the ability of a firm to purchase a service on a wholesale basis, for the purpose of reselling that same service, either alone or in combination with other services or features, to end users in direct competition with the original service provider."

[3] "an activity wherein one entity subscribes to the communications services and facilities of another entity and then reoffers communications services and facilities to the public (with or without 'adding value') for profit."
In re Regulatory Policies Concerning Resale and Shared Use of Common Carrier Services and Facilities, 60 F.C.C.2d 261 (1976), modified 62 F.C.C.R. 2d 588 (1977), aff'd sub nom. AT&T Co. v. FCC, 572 F.2d 17 (2d Cir.), cert. denied, 439 U.S. 875 (1978) (involving private line resale).

telecommunications carriers; and

(B) not to prohibit, and not to impose unreasonable or discriminatory conditions or limitations on, the resale of such telecommunications service, except that a State commission may, consistent with regulations prescribed by the Commission under this section, prohibit a reseller that obtains at wholesale rates a telecommunications service that is available at retail only to a category of subscribers from offering such service to a different category of subscribers.

Section 252(d)(3) WHOLESALE PRICES FOR TELECOMMUNICATIONS SERVICES.--For the purposes of section 251(c)(4), a State commission shall determine wholesale rates on the basis of retail rates charged to subscribers for the telecommunications service requested, excluding the portion thereof attributable to any marketing, billing, collection, and other costs that will be avoided by the local exchange carrier.

[在电信转售业务中，转售企业不自建无线网、核心网、传输网等通信网络基础设施，避免了电信设施的重复建设，但必须建立客服系统，可依需建立业务管理平台、计费、营账等业务支撑系统。"]

批注：In the mode of resale, the reseller need not build by itself communication network infrastructure such as wireless network, core network, transmission network, avoiding the repeated construction of telecom facilities. The reseller should build customer service system, and if needed, built business management platform, billing and collecting supporting system.

2. 电信转售的目的

[基础电信业务经营者更倾向于通过发展分销商来扩大市场份额，而不愿意增加竞争对手。但从政府的角度出发，转售是培育市场竞争的一种简单有效的手段。]移动通信出现后，由于对电信管网的依赖减弱，转售的需求更加强烈。早在20世纪90年代，就出现了全球第一个移动转售商——移动虚拟网络运营商（mobile virtual network operator，MVNO），名叫Sense Communications公司，但是基础电信业务经营者出于抵制竞争的需要，不愿与之合作，导致Sense通信公司未能建立起运营体系。不过这一尝试也让人们看到了移动转售商的价值，出现了更多的MVNO。经过二十年的发展，全球共有1 100多家MVNO，据Informa Telecoms & Media 的研究显示，2011年全球共有MVNO用户数1.05亿，占全球移动电话用户数的1.8%；未来还会继续向上增长，因为虚拟运营的市场空间还有很大潜力[4]。根据国外电信市场经验，在成熟

批注：Basic telecom business operator tends to enlarge market shares by developing distributors, rather than increasing competitors. However, from the regulator perspective, resale is an easy and effective method to cultivate market competition.

---

[4] 刘涛. 从海外经验上看资源比较优势下的MVNO发展模式[EB/OL].（2013-10-17）http://bbs2.c114.net/thread-735127-1-1.html.

的电信市场中，转售市场的用户渗透率将维持在 7% 左右 [5]，这对美国 2 亿电信用户、中国 10 亿电信用户来说，都是一个巨大的绝对用户量。

[电信业务转售是电信市场打破垄断、促进竞争的重要手段之一，其在三方面对电信竞争起到促进作用。

（1）促使基础电信业务经营者，面对转售商的正面竞争，提高服务质量和企业效率。

（2）转售商从基础电信业务经营者那里购买服务，不需要自行投资铺设自己的电信管网，有利于提高已有电信网络设施的利用率，避免重复建设。

（3）转售商的引入有利于细分电信市场。转售商的出现，一方面会使基础电信业务经营者更加专注于核心业务，避免丧失竞争优势；同时，将相对边缘的业务剥离给转售商，这样，推进边缘电信业务，催生电信服务的多样化。] 从国外的经验看，由于转售商服务的专门化和一门心思做市场，往往会建立强大的分销渠道，其开拓、渗透细分市场的能力要高于基础电信业务经营者 [6]。这样的分工能使原有的电信市场更大、更细，给电信业带来更多的电信用户与业务收入。

> 批注：Telecom resale business is one of the most important method to break monopoly and facilitate competition, in the following three aspects, resale promotes telecom competition:
> (1) To facilitate the basic telecom business operator to improve service quality and efficiency when facing reseller's positive competition.
> (2) To be beneficial for the existing telecom network facilities to increase utilization rate, and avoid repeated construction, when reseller buying in wholesale service from basic telecom business operator with no need for investing in building telecom network.
> (3) To expedite market segment after reseller entering the market, which makes basic telecom business operator focus more on key business to avoid losing competition advantage, meanwhile, spin off edge business into reseller, thus boost edge business and hasten telecom service diversity.

3. 电信转售的归责原则

转售商从基础电信业务经营者处打包买来电信服务，包装后提供给最终用户，这就产生了一个问题：[电信服务的实际提供者是基础电信业务经营者，而其又未与最终用户建立法律关系，与最

> 批注：The actual telecom service provider is basic telecom business operator, but it does not establish legal relationship with the service customer, with whom the reseller has established legal relationship but are lack of service ability. Therefore, once telecom service has problem, the customer's interest could not be secured.

---

[5] 刘多. 移动通信转售市场前景几何？[N]. 人民邮电，2014-01-21（007）.
[6] 如 Lebara Mobile 是一家在欧洲多个国家运营的通信公司，其通过转售 VoDafone（英国）的国际长途业务进入移动虚拟市场。Lebara Mobile 聚焦在移民群体，主要包括外国学生、外籍工作者、移民、游客及旅行者。这类人群本地通话需求很少，主要是海外通话，因而 Lebara Mobile 根据用户的特点，提供价格低廉的话音业务，成为全球最大的面向移民的虚拟运营商。

终用户建立法律关系的转售商又缺乏实际服务能力[7]，因此，一旦电信服务出现问题，用户的权益无法得到保障。］［这个问题的实质是，经过产品或服务的多级销售，转售商或分销商隔离了生产者和消费者，为保护消费者利益，如何让产品的生产者或服务的实际提供者承担产品或服务的瑕疵担保义务？即消费者是否有追索权，可以直接向未与其建立合同关系的缺陷产品的生产者或缺陷服务的提供者主张赔偿？］［我们知道，产品的瑕疵担保问题已经解决，那就是通过《产品质量法》建立了产品质量的严格责任制度[8]，无论产品经过了多少道销售，产品生产者都要向最终用户承担产品质量责任。那么，服务是否也可以比照产品，设定严格责任制度呢？这就是服务的归责原则问题。］

［国际上对于服务责任的归责并不统一，主要有三种归责方式。］

［（1）以英国、美国为代表的国家采取过错责任原则。英国1982年制定的《商品与服务供给法》规定，任何提供服务的契约，服务提供人对于其营业均默示地约定其将以"合理之注意与技术"提供服务，此处的服务提供人"以合理之注意与技术"提供服务，即是过错责任[9]。美国法院对服务提供者与产品生产者加

> 批注：That's the real issue, after multiple levels of sale of product or service, reseller or distributor segregates customer apart from manufacturer or provider. In order to secure the consumer's interest, how to make the manufacturer or the service's actual provider undertake the obligation of defect warranty for the product or service? That is to say, whether the consumer has the right of recourse to claim directly for compensation toward the manufacturer of defect product or provider of defect service, who does not established contract relationship with the claimer?

> 批注：As we know, the warranty for defect product is solved, by "Product Quality Law" which established strict liability system for product. No matter how many distribution channels the product is sold through, the manufacturer should undertake liability for its defect product to the end consumer. Then, could service reference to the product, and establish strict liability criterion for defect service? This question relates to attribution principle of defect service.

> 批注：In the worldwide, the attribution principle for liability of defect service is not the same, mainly divided into three ascriptions:

> 批注：(1) The fault liability principle represented by UK and USA. The "Commodity and Service Supply Law" of UK enacted in 1982 stipulates that, in any service supply contract, it is presumed that the service provider impliedly promise that the service would be provided with reasonable diligence

---

[7] 一个完整的电信服务通过以下环节实现：网络建设覆盖、网络维护优化、渠道建设、宣传推广、促销销售、安装/开通、业务支撑、计费支撑、营账支撑、知识库、客服热线/渠道等11个主要环节。从这些环节来看，转售商缺少网络建设覆盖、网络维护优化、安装/开通、业务支撑等实际电信服务能力。

[8] 《产品质量法》第二十六条 生产者应当对其生产的产品质量负责。第四十三条 因产品存在缺陷造成人身、他人财产损害的，受害人可以向产品的生产者要求赔偿，也可以向产品的销售者要求赔偿。

[9] 金福海.论服务责任的性质和归责原则［J］.法学论坛，2001（05）：43-47.

以区别，不仅对服务提供者不适用严格责任，而且对结合产品和服务的混合合同也不适用严格责任[10]。]

[（2）欧盟采取过错推定原则。过错推定原则，仍是过错原则，只不过举证责任倒置，如果服务提供者不能证明服务过程中无过错，则推定过错，将举证责任由消费者转移给了基础电信业务经营者。上述情况反映了服务责任的立法趋势，是从过失责任到过失推定，最终向着无过错责任发展的趋向[11]。]欧盟曾经也试图对服务侵权采用无过错原则，最初的《委员会关于服务提供业者责任的理事会指令议案》对于服务，也和产品一样，对侵权规定了严格责任，但它受到了学者的诸多批评和欧洲议会相关委员会的反对，最终被撤回。不过，其最终建议稿采用过错推定原则。

[（3）少数国家或地区采用严格责任。比如，1990年巴西《消费者保护法》第十四条规定："服务的提供者，不论是否具有过错，对由于提供有缺陷的服务造成消费者损失的，以及对于使用和风险未能提供足够和恰当信息而造成消费者损失的，应承担赔偿责任。"]又如，1994年我国台湾地区《消费者保护法》第七条，"从事设计、生产、制造产品或提供服务之企业经营者应确保其提供之产品或服务无安全或卫生上之危险。产品或服务具有危害消费者生命、身体、健康、财产之可能性者，应于明显处为警告标示及紧急处理危险之方法。企业经营者违反前二项规定，致使损害于消费者或第三人时，应负连带赔偿责任。但企业经营者能证明其无过失者，法院得减轻其赔偿责任。"

and skill. Here, the provider offering service in reasonable diligence and skill is fault liability doctrine. US courts differentiate the service provider and commodity producer, and neither applies strict liability to service provider, nor to the performer of mix contract of product and service.

批注：(2) EU adopts fault presumption doctrine, which is also fault doctrine, but reversing the proof burden, in which doctrine, the proof burden shifts from consumer to basic telecom business operator, which means, if the latter (proof burden undertaker) could not prove innocent in the service, then it is presumed fault. This doctrine reflects the legislation trend about service liability, which is from fault liability to fault presumption liability, at last, converging into no-fault liability.

批注：(3) Minor countries or regions adopt strict liability for service. For example, in Brazil's "Consumers Protection Law" enacted in 1990, the 14th clause stipulates that service provider, no matter whether has fault or not, should undertake the compensation liability, if the service was defect and caused consumers' loss, as well as the supplier had not offered enough and appropriate information about usage and risk.

---

[10] See Talor. Applicability of Strict Lability Warranty Theories to Service Transactions[J]. 47S. C. L. Rev, 1996: 232-233.
[11] 孙颖. 服务侵权的无过错责任 [J]. 法学, 2008（11）: 107-115.

同时确立了产品和服务的严格责任，虽不如巴西《消费者保护法》明确，但台湾学界通常认为该条确立了服务的无过错责任[12]。

[对服务采取更加严格的归责原则是国际上共同的立法趋势[13]。随着第三产业的兴起，服务和产品更多地交织在一起，许多产品中掺杂着服务。][从消费者保护的角度考虑，人为地区分服务和产品并规定不同的归责原则，违背了保护消费者权益的初衷。具体到电信转售服务，相对于其他传统服务，由于其具有"类产品性"，更应该首先确立严格责任制度。]

[电信服务的"类产品性"表现在：

（1）电信服务的客体清晰。电信转售的客体包括基础语音通话、短信、数据业务，无论是基础电信业务经营者还是转售商，都是通过出售此三种客体或其组合来提供服务，这种清晰的服务客体类似于产品买卖中的客体一样明确、客观、具体。]

[（2）电信服务具有可储存性。当月没有使用完的电信服务套餐余量留到下一个月使用，这与产品的可储存类似。]

[（3）电信服务的生产和消费具有分离性。传统服务的产生和消费往往是共存的，而电信服务中的带宽往往先产生（租用或自有），即使无人消费也持续

批注：To apply more strict liability ascription to service is a legislation trend in the world. With the emerging of the service sector, service and commodity are more and more overlapped, many products being mixed with service.

批注：From the perspective of protecting consumer, the method to artificially distinguish between service and product, then stipulate different ascription liability doctrine, violates the legislation motive of protect consumer. As for telecom business resale, comparing with other traditional services, in sake of possessing "quasi-product" feature, telecom service should introduce the strict liability doctrine firstly.

批注：The manifestation of "quasi-product" feature of telecom service is as following:
(1) its object is distinct. The object of telecom resale consists: basic voice communication, short message, data business. Either basic telecom business operator or reseller, provides telecom service by offering the 3 above objects or their combinations, which are distinct, definite, specific, similar to the object in selling and buying product contract.

批注：It possesses the feature of storability. The packet margin of current month could be accumulated into next month's, similar to storability of product.

批注：Its manufacture and consume could be separated. The manufacture and consume of traditional service usually coexist, however, the bandwidth of telecom service exists in advance (leased or owned), even if nobody consumes it, it still exists. We can find that, its separability of manufacture and consume resembles product.

---

[12] 朱柏松.消费者保护法论[M].增订版.台湾：翰芦图书出版有限公司，2004：87.
[13] 美国对服务课以无过错责任有增多的趋势，如在飞机零件安装、幼儿照顾、电梯维修、电力供给等领域出现了相关的判例。参见谢哲胜.无过失医疗责任：医生的梦魇？病人的救星？[M]//苏永钦.民法七十年之回顾与展望纪念文集（一）.北京：中国政法大学出版社，2002：239.

存在，生产和消费的可分离性与产品类似。]

[因此，对于具有"类产品性"的电信服务，应该采用与产品责任一致的归责原则。根据这一原则，在用户和转售商签订电信服务合同时，转售商有义务向消费者披露基础电信业务经营者，使得消费者具有更大的选择权，在电信服务瑕疵出现后，可以直接起诉基础电信业务经营者，更好地保护自身权利。]

4. 转售的要求

[转售是一种法定义务，确切地说，是一种法定的要求基础电信业务经营者与转售商建立趸售合同关系的义务。在法律要求强制性建立合同关系这一点上，类似于互联或接入的强制性合同关系。法律对转售的要求，分为对转售商和对基础电信业务经营者的要求。][前者较简单，主要是出于保护消费者权益而赋予转售商的义务，比如，我国台湾地区要求转售商，在获得许可后，需就其服务条件制定营业规章，在实施前向监管机构报备，并在各营业场所及网站公开[14]，侵害用户权益事件发生后，这些规定为判定转售商责任提供了明确的标准。]

[对基础电信业务经营者的要求，出发点是限制其滥用垄断地位。转售商购买基础电信业务经营者的业务，并与后

批注：Therefore, as for telecom service with the feature of "quasi-product", we should adopt the same liability ascribing principle as product, according to which, when signing contract with consumers, the telecom reseller has obligation to disclose the basic telecom business operator to consumers, so that, when consumers find telecom service defect, they have right to alternatively choose the reseller or actual service provider to sue in a litigation for protecting their rights.

批注：Resale is a mandatory duty, or rather, an obligation for basic telecom business operators to establish wholesale contract relationship with reseller. From the prospective of mandatory duty of establishing contract relationship, resale is similar to enforced contract relationship of interconnection or access. The legal requirement of resale could be classified into two kinds, one is for reseller, the other is for basic telecom business operator.

批注：The former is simpler, mainly to impose duty to reseller to protect consumer's interest, for example, in Taiwan region of China, the reseller is required to do the following things after acquiring license:

(1) To formulate business rules stipulating service conditions;

(2) To report and register to regulatory agency before implementing the above;

(3) To make public announcement in every business place and website.

If the consumer's interest is infringed, those rules would provide definite criterions for identifying reseller's liability.

---

[14] 杨筱敏. 我国台湾地区MVNO历经十年发展监管政策设计较为成熟 [J]. 世界电信, 2013（6）：29-33. 营业规章中应包括以下内容：营业项目；各项服务收费标准及调整费用的条件；用户基本数据利用的限制及条件；经营者经受废止许可，或暂停或终止其营业以致对用户权益产生损害时，对用户的赔偿或补偿方式；对用户申诉的处理及其他与使用者权益有关的项目；虚拟移动网络服务经营者经受废止许可、暂停或终止其营业或变更合作的移动网络业务经营者时，对既有用户号码的处理方式及其权益的保护措施等事项。

者竞争，这就注定了其处于竞争劣势。为保证公平竞争，监管部门必须对处于优势地位的基础电信业务经营者实行管制，以防止其滥用支配地位。]

批注：The requirement to basic telecom business operators aims to constrain it from abusing monopoly position. The reseller competes with basic telecom business operator from which the reseller bought service in wholesale beforehand. This dooms the reseller's inferiority in competition. To protect the fair competition, regulation agency must regulate the basic telecom business operators in superior position to prevent them from abusing dominated position.

[转售价格规制，是保护转售商利润空间和竞争可持续的最有利手段。转售商支付给基础电信业务经营者的趸购成本，是要转嫁给消费者的，而其收取的消费者的零售价又不能高于基础电信业务经营者的零售价，否则没有竞争力。]

批注：The regulation to resale price is a most effective method to protect the profit margin for reseller and the persistence of competition. The cost of wholesale paid to basic telecom business operator by reseller would be transplanted to consumers, meanwhile, the retail price collected from consumers by the reseller should not higher than that of basic telecom business operator, or the reseller would lost competition potency.

[转售商支付给基础电信业务经营者的趸购价越高，盈利空间就越小。当转售价高到一定程度，转售商将无利可图，最终会被逐出电信市场。只有政府规制转售价格，才能保证转售商的盈利空间和竞争的持续。][各国对此都有相关规定，美国《电信法》第251（c）（4）规定[15]，基础电信业务经营者必须以批发价格向转售商提供任何最终用户可以买到的服务。另外，根据252（d）（3）的规定[16]，州委员会有权根据零售价格决定转售中执行的批发价，以保障251（c）（4）条的实施。] 韩国通信委员会（KCC）要求三

批注：The higher the wholesale price paid to basic telecom business operator by reseller, the less is their profit margin. When the wholesale price climbs to a certain level, reseller would be no profit to gain, at last expelled out of market. Only if the wholesale price is regulated by government, the profit margin of the reseller and the persistence of competition could be guaranteed.

批注：Various countries have regulations about resale price. Taking Act of Telecommunications of USA for example, Section 251(c)(4) stipulates basic telecom business operator has obligation to offer what service the end users could buy in market to the reseller in wholesale price. Furthermore, Section 252(d)(3) stipulates every state committee has the right to set the wholesale price according to retail price so as to protect Section (c)(4) implementing.

---

[15] 美国电信法 SEC.251(c) "to offer for resale at wholesale rates any telecommunications service …".

[16] 美国电信法 SEC.252(d)(3) requires a state commission to "determine wholesale rates on the basis of retail rates charged to subscribers for the telecommunications service requested."

家基础电信业务经营者以批发价格给转售商批发业务,并要求批发价格比零售价低31%~44%。另外,丹麦监管机构要求运营商给虚拟运营商的批发定价必须客观、透明、非歧视[17]。[同样,在我国此次电信转售试点中,试点文件也明确规定了转售价格必须低于公众市场上同类业务的最优惠零售价格水平[18]。]

[除价格数额管制外,价格透明化也是保护转售商盈利空间的重要手段。价格透明化要求基础电信业务经营者披露其同类业务的零售价,在美国CMC电信公司诉密歇根州贝尔公司一案中得以体现[19],在该案中,CMC认为其转售业务受到了无理由的阻碍,密歇根州贝尔公司有义务公开其零售价以使其可以判断什么是合理的批发价,密歇根地方法院支持了CMC公司的诉求。]

[出售标的的非捆绑,是保护转售商交易自由的主要手段,它要求基础电信业务经营者趸售给转售商的业务不得捆绑销售,由转售商自主选择趸购业务。美国电信法Sections 251(c)(4)规定的电信转售业务范围为"任何最终用户可以买到的电信服务",在大西洋贝尔诉佛蒙特州一案中,法院对应遵守转售业务的"电信服务"做出了界定,认为电信服务包括"任何交互式双向通信,包括

批注:In our country's pilot project of telecom resale, the documents definitely stipulate that the resale price should mandatorily less than the most favor retail price in public market.

批注:Except for price regulation, price transparency is another method to protect reseller's profit margin. Price transparency requires the basic telecom business operator to disclose the retail price of the similar business, which is manifested in the case of CMC Telecom. Vs. Michigan Bell Tel. Co., in which case the plaintiff complained its resale business was impeded without any reasonable cause, so the defendant was obliged to disclose its retail price so that the plaintiff could decide what the reasonable wholesale price should be.

批注:To make the target business unbundled is the main method to protect reseller's transaction freedom, that requires the business sold to the reseller by basic telecom business operator to be unbundled, so that the reseller could freely choose the business in wholesale. Act of Telecommunications of USA Sections 251(c)(4) stipulates the scope of resale, which is "any telecommunications service that the carrier provides at retail to subscribers who are not telecommunications carriers". In the case of Bell Atlantic Vs. Vermont, the court defined the "telecommunication service" which should be resold as ""the transmission of any interactive two-way electromagnetic communications including voice, image, data, and information."

---

[17] 杨筱敏. 评论:"有形之手"如何助MVNO一臂之力[N].人民邮电报,2013-04-15(007).
[18] 移动通信转售业务试点方案第四条(四):"基础电信业务经营者给予转售企业的批发价格水平应低于其当地公众市场上同类业务的最优惠零售价格水平"
[19] Volume Discounts ATT'S RESTRICTIONS VIOLATE LAW, RESELLERS SAY CMC Telecom. v. Michigan Bell Tel. Co.,10 No. 24 Andrews Telecomm. Indus. Litig. Rep. 12;April 18, 2007.

语音、图像、数据和信息[20]"。][在AT&T诉西南贝尔公司一案中[21]，AT&T试图进入西南贝尔公司所在的俄克拉何马州开展转售业务，但是西南贝尔公司趸售给AT&T的业务是一项套餐，不可拆分销售，AT&T认为这构成了不正当的阻碍，后经第10巡回法院审理认为，AT&T有权单独购买西南贝尔公司提供的基础电信服务，重新包装后变成与西南贝尔公司不同的套餐销售。][我国这次移动转售业务试点中并未规定基础电信业务经营者的非捆绑义务，这给了基础电信业务经营者限制趸售标的权力，对转售商不利。例如，在此次试点中，中国电信给予虚拟运营商企业的移动套餐的转售价格最低，但限制条款是不允许进行套餐拆包销售。]

批注：In the case of AT & T Vs. SBC，the plaintiff intend to enter the Oklahoma state to launch resale business where the defendant had dominant position. The business being resold in wholesale to the plaintiff by the defendant was a package, which could been split and sold. The plaintiff complained this constituted unfair impediment. The 10th Circuit Court held that, the plaintiff has the right to buy in wholesale the basic telecom service separately, repackages it before reselling it as different package to that of the defendant.

批注：This mobile service resale pilot project of our country did not set "unbundled selling" as an obligation to basic telecom business operator, who reserved the right of restraining the target business for wholesale, which is unfavorable to reseller. For example, in this pilot project, although China Telecom sells package service to Mobile Virtual Network Operator (MVNO) at the minimum price, the restriction condition is the package, could not be split to sell.

---

[20] In re PETITION OF VERIZON NEW ENGLAND INC.2002 WL 32153875，Supreme Court of Vermont.，Appellate Petition, Motion and Filing (Approx. 10 pages), "[T]he transmission of any interactive two-way electromagnetic communications including voice, image, data, and information.", site: https://international.westlaw.com/result/previewcontroller.aspx?TF=756 & TC=4 & mt=314 & findtype=Y & tc=-1 & rp=%2ffind%2fdefault.wl & spa=naloc-0000 & ordoc=0288046353 & serialnum=2002886151 & vr=2.0 & fn=_top & sv=Split & tf=-1 & pbc=CE0D7725 & rs=WLIN14.04 & RP=/find/default.wl & bLinkViewer=true [2014.06.25]

[21] Resale: 10TH CIR. REVERSES ORDER ON END-USER LIMITATION，6 No. 11 Andrews Telecomm. Indus. Litig. Rep. 14，November 5, 2002

生词和词组

第九章

1. 基础电信业务经营者 Basic telecommunication business operators
2. 通俗地说 generally speaking, in layman's terms
3. 整买零卖 buy wholesale and sell retail
4. 转售商 reseller
5. 被申请人 respondent, defending party to the application
6. 重新包装 repackage
7. 可避免成本 avoidable cost
8. 计费 billing, charging
8. 分销商 distributor
10. 正面竞争 positive competition
11. 利用率 utilization rate
12. 细分市场 market segment
13. 核心业务 core business
14. 将业务剥离给 strip business to, spin off business into
15. 边缘业务 edge business
16. 瑕疵担保义务 Defect warranty obligations
17. 承担义务 undertake an obligation, assume an obligation, lay an obligation on sb.
18. 追索权 right of recourse
19. 严格责任 strict liability, strict responsibility
20. 销售渠道 distribution channel
21. 归责原则 attribution principles
22. 过错责任原则 fault liability doctrine
23. 无过错责任原则 No-fault liability doctrine, liability without fault doctrine
24. 默示合同 implied contract

25. 合理注意 reasonable care, due care, reasonable attention, reasonable diligence, due diligence

26. 推定事实 presumed fact, presumed facts, presumption of facts

27. 过错推定 presumption of fault

28. 举证责任 burden of proof

29. 举证责任倒置 inverted evidential burden, reverse burden of proof

30. 第三产业 tertiary industry, service sector

31. 套餐余量 packet margin

32. 赋予义务 impose obligation

33. 制定营业规章 formulate business rules

34. 公示 publicity, announcement, proclamation; public announcement; public notification

35. 营业场所 business place

36. 竞争劣势 competitive weakness, competitive inferiority, competitive disadvantage

37. 试点 pilot project

38. 价格透明化 price transparency

39. （法院）审理认为 held that

40. 虚拟运营商 Virtual Network Operator (VNO)

41. 移动虚拟运营商 Mobile Virtual Network Operator (MVNO)

第十章
Chapter 10

电信建设和通路权
Telecom Construction and Right of Way

［电信建设是在他人具有使用权的土地之下或之上，通过土地使用权出让合同的形式使用土地，进行电信基础设施建设的行为。无论是埋设电信管线、架设电信杆路、搭建电信线路、设置基站，还是建设电信塔台，电信建设者必须征得产权人同意，并支付一定对价，从而获得他人土地或建筑物的穿越权或使用权。］［电信建设中的争议，通常是由于电信管网要穿越的土地或架设于其上的房屋的物权人（以下称"被用物权人"）与电信建设者之间就补偿达不成一致而引起。为解决此争议，需要确定电信建设者的电信通路权。在我国未来的电信法中，准确界定电信通路权的法律属性，是确立该权利并划定其边界，进而平衡电信建设者和被用物权利人利益的基础。］

批注：Telecom construction refers to that, under or above the land owned by others, by the means of signing contract for granting land use right, a constructor uses the land and constructs telecom infrastructure. Either burying duct or cable, erecting pole line, building circuit, installing base station, or constructing tower, the telecom constructer should acquire the land owner's consent and pay a certain remuneration, thus obtaining the land right of penetrating and using.

批注：The dispute in telecom construction usually arises from disagreement concerning compensation between telecom constructer and the owner or real right holder of land penetrated or building installed. To solve the above dispute, we should establish the right of way for telecom constructer. In the prospective Telecommunication Law of our country, accurately defining the legal attribution of right of way is the base of establishing that right and demarcating its bounder, thus balancing the interest of telecom constructer and real right holder.

第一节 电信建设争议
Section 1　Dispute of Telecom Construction

[我国近年来电信建设争议时有发生，被用物权利人与电信建设者就是否可以穿越土地或搭建基站以及补偿数额难以达成一致；尤其是在搭建无线基站发射装置时，无论电信建设者支付多少补偿金和如何证明辐射远小于国家标准[1]，被用物权利人仍然以辐射有害健康为由拒绝电信建设者使用其不动产。][由于我国没有行政仲裁机构可以快速、低成本地裁决此类纠纷，此类纠纷只能诉至法院，而法院的诉讼效率又难以满足电信建设的进度要求。于是当纠纷发生后，电信网络建设者往往只能放弃此路由，改用成本高出许多的其他不动产穿越或搭建电信设施。]

[产生上述问题的原因在于我国目前尚未建立电信通路权制度，无法清晰界定电信建设者和被用物权利人的权利边界，也没有建立纠纷产生后的行政救济制度；而现有的有关电信建设的规范不能从根本上解决此问题。][不仅如此，我国现有的《物业管理条例》与《电信条例》相关规定间还存在着冲突[2]。《物业管理条例》规定穿越或使用不动产须经业主同意[3]，而《电信管理条例》仅要求通知并补偿即可。]按照《物业管理

批注：Telecom dispute relating to construction occurs constantly in our country, because it's difficult for the real right holder and telecom constructer to reach consent of the compensation for penetrating land or setting up base station. Especially, in the process of installing emission equipment in wireless base station, no matter how much the compensation is paid, and how to prove the radiation is far less than national standard, the real right holders still refuse the telecom constructer to use their real estate.

批注：In sake of lack of administrative arbitration body to rule this dispute expediently and low costly, this kind of dispute could only be sued to court where the litigation efficiency could hardly satisfy the schedule requirement of telecom construction. So when dispute occurring, telecom constructer usually has nothing to do but abandon the disputing route and find other real estate to penetrate or set up telecom equipment whose cost is much higher.

批注：The reason for this problem is our country has neither established telecom access right system to demarcate the bounder of telecom constructer and real right holder, nor established administrative relief system after telecom dispute occurred. On the other hand, the existing regulations concerning telecom construction could not solve the problem radically.

批注：Furthermore, the existing "Real Estate Management Regulations" and "Telecommunications Regulations" conflict somewhere,

---

[1] 关于电信设施辐射量的国家标准，请参见信息产业部、国家环保总局于2007年7月31日发布的《移动通信基站电磁辐射环境监测方法（试行）》。
[2] 马志刚.电信通路权法定化问题之研究 [J].通信世界，2004（7）：28.
[3] 即便如此，在实践中，召开业主大会也是一件十分困难的事情，更不要说由业主大会来做出决议。

条例》第十一条第五项、第十二条规定，涉及"物业管理区域内物业共用部位和共用设施设备的使用"，须得到二分之一以上有投票权的业主参加才能召开业

which is, according to the former, penetrating or using real estate has to acquire the owner's consent, but according to the latter, notification and compensation is enough.

主大会，只有与会二分之一以上有投票权业主的同意，业主大会才能作出决议。而《电信条例》第四十七条规定："基础电信业务经营者可以在民用建筑物上设置小型天线、移动通信基站等公用电信设施，但需要事先通知建筑物产权人或者使用人，并按照省、自治区、直辖市人民政府规定的标准向该建筑物的产权人或者其他权利人支付使用费。"同时该条例第五十二条规定"任何组织或者个人不得阻止或者妨碍基础电信业务经营者依法从事电信设施建设和向电信用户提供公共电信服务"。

第二节　电信通路权

Section 2　Telecom Access Right

[电信建设中出现的被用物权利人和电信建设者之间的纠纷，都可以归结为电信通路权问题。电信通路权，也叫电信线路通行权，是指电信网络建设者在埋设电信管线、架设电信杆路、搭建电信线路、建设电信塔台等过程中，穿越或使用他人所有的土地、房屋等不动产的权利。电信通路权是电信法律规范[4]赋予电信网络建设者的一项重要权利。]只有其界定清晰，才可避免纠纷，既保证了被用物权利人的利益，又利于电信网络建设的顺利进行。[如何平衡被用物权利人利益和电信网络建设者的利益，是电信通路权的重要内容。如果过分保护被用物权利人利益，将导致电信建设的谈判成本畸高、效率低下；如果过分

批注：All of the disputes between real right holders and telecom constructors could be ascribed into the question of telecom access right, which, also called penetrating right for telecom line layer, refers to the right of penetrating or using real estate such as land, buildings, etc. owned by others in the process of telecom constructor engaging in the following behaviors: burying duct and line; erecting pole line; setting up circuit; installing tower. The Telecom access right is an important right that telecom law and regulation endues telecom network constructor.

批注：How to balance the interest of real right holder and telecom constructor is the main content of telecom access right. To protect real right holder excessively would cause abnormally high cost and low efficiency of telecom construction negotiation. On the other hand, to protect telecom constructor excessively, would make it hard to protect the private right of real right holder.

---

[4]　《电信条例》第四十七、五十二条。

保护电信网络建设者利益,被用物权利人的私权利将难以保证。]因而,有必要探讨在我国尚未出台的电信法中如何建立这种权利制度。

[电信建设者代表了准公共利益,即使不涉及普遍服务,也代表了接受电信服务的广大客户的通信权利,应该予以保护。准公共利益,是指一个人背后的多数人利益。准公共利益的主体并非以集体名义出现并代表多数人利益的自律组织,如记者协会、律师协会、工会,而是"一个人背后的多数",是以一个人(或法人)的名义出现,但代表了多数人利益,通常指特定的职业者,如记者(代表了大家听的权利)、电信公司(代表了被服务者的多数人权利,尤其是普遍服务)、教师(代表了广大被教育者)。保护一个人就是保护其后面的多数人。]

[法律需要权衡的两端是电信建设者的建设权和被用物权利人的物权,前者代表了广大电信用户的"听"的权利(宪法权利言论自由的起点),后者是一个人的经济利益,权衡的结果自然不言自明——电信建设者比被用物权人具有优先权。保护电信建设者的方法就是授予其电信通路权,该权利介乎公权力和私权利之间,其保护程度达不到公共利益需求的市政施工权,如诉讼和复议不影响强迁;但高于被用物权利人的物权。例如,对于地理唯一通道的电信建设,经相关程序后,可以剥夺被用物权利人的物权,并以经济利益进行补偿。]

批注:The telecom constructor represents quasi-public interest, which should be protected in sake of delegating the communicating right of vast clients accepting telecom service, even excluding universal service. Quasi-public interest refers to as majority interest behind a single person, whose subject is not self-regulation organization (SRO) which is in the name of collective and represents majority such as journalist's association, bar association, labor's union, but "majority behind a single person", which is in the name of a single person (or legal person) and represents majority, usually referring to specific professionals such as journal (who represents the right of hearing of majority), telecom operator (who represents the interest of majority being served, especially in universal service), teacher (who represents the vast educated) . To protect the single person is to protect the majority behind him.

批注:Two ends the law should weigh are the construction right of telecom constructor and the real right of its holder, the former representing the "hearing" right (which is the start point of speech freedom right established in the Constitution) of the vast clients accepting telecom service, the latter representing a single person's interest. The result of weighing is self-evidenced, that is the telecom constructor has the priority to the real right holder. The method to protect the telecom constructors is authorizing them the right of way, which is in the middle between public right and private right, so the protection degree for telecom constructors could not reach that of municipal construction right supported by public interest, such as litigation and administration reconsideration could not become reasons for delaying forced demolishing; but it is higher than the real right, for example, concerning telecom construction at the only access in geography, after the relating procedure and telecom constructor paying the compensation, the real right could be deprived.

解决电信建设争议的关键是划清电信通路权的边界，平衡电信建设者和被用物权利人利益，而澄清该权利属性又是确立电信通路权的最重要的一步。我国有学者将电信通路权归入地役权范畴，试图利用《物权法》第一百五十六条规定的地役权来保证电信通路权的实现。其理由是，电信网络建设属于一个不动产产权人（电信网络建设者）依据合同使用另一个不动产产权人（被穿越或使用土地的所有权人）土地的行为，而这正好符合《物权法》第一百五十六条规定的地役权范畴，即"按照合同约定，利用他人的不动产，以提高自己的不动产的效益"[5]。还有学者专门撰文论证运营商的发射塔座基地的使用权属于地役权，而非租赁权[6]。

以地役权或相邻权[7]理论解决电信通路权注定是行不通的。电信管网包含多种电信线路或设备，如电信信道、无线发射天线、电信基站，广义的还包括交换机房。电信管网中的交换机房、电信基站属于不动产；电信网络、无线发射天线属于动产，其移动并不改变物的价值，比如，电信网络可以由地下埋设变为高空架设或者绕道穿越，并不影响其功能；无线发射天线在小范围内变动也不会影响其效用。无论是属于不动产的交换机房和电信基站，还是属于动产的电信网络、无线发射天线，它们都不是"需役地"。由于不存在需役地，电信网络建设者穿越或使用他人不动产的权利不应当属于地役权。

为铺设电信管网而穿越或使用他人土地，本质上属于租赁他人土地进行电信建设，属于《物权法》第一百三十五条规定的建设用地使用权，即"建设用地使用权人依法对国家所有的土地享有占有、使用和收益的权利，有权利用该土地建造建筑物、构筑物及其附属设施。"故而，[电信通路权本质上属于建设用地使用权，而建设用地使用权属于不动产租赁权之一种，因此，电信通路权就属于不动产租赁权。]这符合"建设用地使用权可以在土地的地表、地上或者地下分别设立"[8]的《物

批注：Telecom access right substantially belongs to the usufruct of construction land, which belongs to leasehold of real estate. Therefore, telecom access right belongs to leasehold of real estate.

---

[5] 王春辉.电信竞争的法律规制——电信竞争中的热点法律问题透析[M].北京：北京邮电大学出版社，2008：277.

[6] 宁全洲.浅谈《物权法》对电信类公司物权关系的可能性影响及对策[J].决策与信息（财经观察），2008（12）：34.

[7] 根据物权通说，相邻关系理论旨在谋求不动产相邻各方的关系衡平，其重点在于不动产权利人一方的忍耐，而非对方的支配权，故"相邻关系"的称谓比"相邻权"更准确。然而，为了和地役权、电信通路权等"权"后缀并列，将"相邻关系"称为"相邻权"并无不妥。"相邻关系又称相邻权。"梁慧星.物权法.北京：法律出版社，1997：164."相邻关系……因此也成为'相邻权'。"崔建远，等.物权法[M].北京：清华大学出版社，2008：130.

[8] 参见《物权法》第一百三十六条.

权法》规定。另外，在被用物权利人房屋上设置小型无线基站，则属于租用被用物权利人的房屋使用权。可以看出，电信通路权本质上不属于地役权，而是不动产法定强制租赁权。

"土地使用权出让合同实质上也是一种财产租赁合同，只是它同一般财产租赁合同相比，它的'租期长'，支付'租金'集中"[9]。[电信建设者和被用物权利人之间建立的是土地使用权出让合同关系。将电信通路权归为不动产租赁权并不能从根本上解决电信建设者与物权人的冲突。因为租赁权属于依合同生成的债权，合同的合意性（意思自治原则）无法保证电信建设的效率。]

[电信建设的效率可以通过将上述租赁权法定化保证。将电信通路权认定为租赁权，虽然其债权特点（合意性）妨碍了电信建设的效率，但租赁权的法定化为被用物权利人设立了强制出租义务，实现了债权的物权化——祛除债权的意定性而采用物权的法定性，保证合同的意思自治不至于过分妨碍电信建设效率。如果双方达不成租赁合同，电信建设者可以启动行政或司法救济，由行政或司法机关判定法定补偿金及其他合同内容。这种法定强制租赁制度类似于电信网络接入制度，合同仍然建立在合意基础上，只不过法律规定了双方善意谈判的义务。电信通路权的设置可以仿照电信接入权，具体权利内容是权利人和被用物权利人合

批注：The relationship between telecom constructor and real right holder is land usufruct leasehold contract. To ascribe the telecom right of way into real estate leasehold right could not solve the conflict between telecom constructor and real right holder radically, because leasehold right belongs to creditor's right generated by contract whose consensual feature (autonomy of will) could not guarantee the telecom construct efficiency.

批注：The telecom constructing efficiency could be guaranteed by legalization of the above leasehold right. To regard telecom access right as leasehold right, notwithstanding whose feature of creditor's right (consensual will) impedes the telecom constructing efficiency, but the legalization of leasehold right would impose mandatory lease duty to real right holder and achieve the effect of creditor's right being legalized as real right, which means, the trait of its consensual would be eliminated and possess the legality of real right so as to guarantee the autonomy of will existing in contract relationship not to impede excessively the telecom constructing efficiency. If the two parties could not reach consent about leasing contract, the telecom constructor might initiate administrative or judicial relief, so that the compensation and other contract content could be judged by administrative or judicial body. This kind of mandatory leasehold system is similar to telecom network access system, that is the contract is still based on the consent in bargain, but the law stipulates both parties' duty of bargain in good faith. The system of telecom right of way could simulate the right of access, whose content is the result of bargain between telecom right holder and the real right holder, and the duty of bargain in good faith is legalized, if the negotiation could not reach consent, the administrative or judicial relief could be initiated.

---

[9] 郑立，王作堂. 民法学[M]. 北京：北京大学出版社，1995: 384.

意的结果，而他们善意谈判的义务又是法定的，谈判不成将启动行政和司法救济。]

第三节　各国立法

Section 3　Legislation of Other Countries

[大多数发达国家的电信法都规定了电信通路权，内容主要为：权利本身法定、权利实施依约定、达不成合意提供行政和司法救济。]

[欧盟《电信框架指令》赋予电信运营商权利，可以申请管制当局对运营商在公共或私人领地穿行或建筑电信设施权利进行裁决[10]。]

[美国《电信法》SEC. 621(a)（2）规定，产权人是国家的，即穿越公共基础设施的，只需要政府批准即可，因为政府可以代表公共利益行使权利；产权人是私人的，必须经过产权人同意，如果产权人不同意或者补偿数额无法达成一致，任何一方可以启动行政仲裁或法

批注：Most developed countries' telecom law stipulates the right of way, whose main content is that, the right is legalized, but the realizing of that right is depended on contract, and administrative and judicial relief could be initiated in case of no consent after a fixed period.

批注：EU "Framework Directive" (2002/21/EC) Article 11 endues telecom operator with right, according to which the operator could claim to regulator for verdict on penetrating through or building telecom facilities in public or private property.

批注：USA "Act of Telecommunications" Section 621 (a) (2) stipulate that, when telecom line penetrating infrastructure owned by state, it's only need to be ratified by state, which could execute right representing public interest. If the infrastructure is owned by private, the constructor should obtain the owner's

---

[10] 欧盟电信框架指令【Directive 2002/21/EC】Article 11 Rights of way Rights of way
1. Member States shall ensure that when a competent authority considers:
- an application for the granting of rights to install facilities on, over or under public or private property to an undertaking authorised to provide public communications networks, or
- an application for the granting of rights to install facilities on, over or under public property to an undertaking authorised to provide electronic communications networks other than to the public, the competent authority:
- acts on the basis of transparent and publicly available procedures, applied without discrimination and without delay, and
- follows the principles of transparency and non-discrimination in attaching conditions to any such rights.
The abovementioned procedures can differ depending on whether the applicant is providing public communications networks or not.
2. Member States shall ensure that where public or local authorities retain ownership or control of undertakings operating electronic communications networks and/or services, there is effective structural separation of the function responsible for granting the rights referred to in paragraph 1 from activities associated with ownership or control.
3. Member States shall ensure that effective mechanisms exist to allow undertakings to appeal against decisions on the granting of rights to install facilities to a body that is independent of the parties involved.

consent; if the owner disagree, or they could not reach consent on compensation, either party could initiate administrative arbitration or lawsuit.

SEC. 621. [47 U.S.C. 541] GENERAL FRANCHISE REQUIREMENTS.

(2) Any franchise shall be construed to authorize the construction of a cable system over public rights-of-way, and through easements, which is within the area to be served by the cable system and which have been dedicated for compatible uses, except that in using such easements the cable operator shall ensure--

(A) that the safety, functioning, and appearance of the property and the convenience and the safety of other persons not be adversely affected by the installation or construction of facilities necessary for a cable system;

(B) that the cost of the installation, construction, operation, or removal of such facilities be borne by the cable operator or subscriber, or a combination of both; and

(C) that the owner of the property be justly compensated by the cable operator for any damages caused by the installation, construction, operation, or removal of such facilities by the cable operator.

律诉讼[11]。］[在平衡公用事业和电信建设者的权利时，美国电信法 SEC.224(f)(1) 规定，"公用事业公司，包括本地电话公司，必须向有线电视系统或电信运营商无歧视地提供其所有或控制的对杆、路由、信道、路权的接入（共享）。"]

我国电信建设者和被用物权利人之间矛盾的彻底解决寄希望于我国即将出台的《电信法》，如何规定电信通路权，是一个关系到保证电信建设效率和不动产物权人利益的重要议题。[借鉴先进国家的电信法，在我国尚未出台的电信法中设定电信通路权，应持有以下原则：]

批注：In balancing the rights of public utilities and telecom constructor, USA "Act of Telecommunications" Sec 224 (f) 1 stipulates that, "A utility shall provide a cable television system or any telecommunications carrier with nondiscriminatory access to any pole, duct, conduit, or right-of-way owned or controlled by it."

批注：Through reference to advanced countries' telecom law, the telecom right of way in our prospective telecom law, should consist the following principles:

---

[11] 美国电信法 SEC. 621. [47 U.S.C. 541] GENERAL FRANCHISE REQUIREMENTS.
(2) Any franchise shall be construed to authorize the construction of a cable system over public rights-of-way, and through easements, which is within the area to be served by the cable system and which have been dedicated for compatible uses, except that in using such easements the cable operator shall ensure--
(A) that the safety, functioning, and appearance of the property and the convenience and the safety of other persons not be adversely affected by the installation or construction of facilities necessary for a cable system;
(B) that the cost of the installation, construction, operation, or removal of such facilities be borne by the cable operator or subscriber, or a combination of both; and
(C) that the owner of the property be justly compensated by the cable operator for any damages caused by the installation, construction, operation, or removal of such facilities by the cable operator.

[（1）既然现行物权法中有关地役权范畴没有涵盖电信通路权，根据物权法定原则，不应当将电信通路权认定为地役权；]

[（2）我国电信法中应当明确定义电信通路权，并将其设定为类似接入权的法定权利，该权利本质上属于强制租赁权；]

[（3）电信通路权的基本内容法定，比如电信建设者经行政许可有权进行电信建设活动即获得了电信通路权、实施该权利需要对途经的公共和民用不动产进行补偿、使用公共不动产备案即可、使用民用不动产需获得被用物权利人同意等；]

[（4）电信通路权的细节内容依赖于电信通路权人和被用物权利人之间的意定；双方达不成合意时，任何一方可以启动行政和司法救济，以保证这两个权利的平衡。]

批注：Now that the "easement" concept in our existing Real Right Law does not include telecom access right, according to the Numerus Clauses Principle, i.e. "real right generated by legalization", we should not ascribe it into easement.

批注：In our prospective telecom law, the telecom access right should be definitely defined, and established as a legal right similar to the right of access, which in essence belongs to enforced leasing right.

批注：The basic content of telecom right of way should be legalized, such as:

(1) since the telecom constructor obtaining administrative permission to carry out construction, the telecom access right is generated and authorized to the constructor;

(2) when the constructor implements the access right, it should compensate the owner or the holder of public or private real estate being penetrated;

(3) if public real estate being penetrated, the constructor's duty is to register to the regulator; if private real estate being penetrated, the constructor should gain consent of the real right holder, etc.

批注：The detail content of the telecom access right depends on the negotiation and consent of the telecom right owner and the real right owner. In case of disagreement after a fixed time, either could initiate the administrative and legal relief, so as to maintain the balance of both rights.

生词和词组

第十章

1. 土地使用权 land use right, land usufruct
2. 土地使用权出让合同 Grant Contract of Land Use Right, land usufruct leasehold contract
3. 埋设电缆、直埋电缆 buried cable
4. 架空电缆 arial cable
5. 架设杆路 erect pole line
6. 搭建线路 set up circuit
7. 建设塔台 built tower
8. 设置基站 install base station
9. 自律组织 self-regulation organization (SRO)
10. 以集体名义 in the name of the collective
11. 律师协会 bar association
12. 私权利 private right
13. 隐私权 privacy right
14. 民事权利 civil right
15. 市政施工 municipal construction
16. 行政复议 administrative review, administrative reconsideration
17. 强制拆迁 forced demolition, forced relocation, obliging removing
18. 剥夺权利 disfranchise, deprival of rights, disentitle, proscription
19. 唯一地理通道 the only access in geography
20. 使用权、用益权 usufruct
21. 建设用地使用权 usufruct of construction land
22. 租约 lease
23. 租赁权 leasehold

24. 不动产租赁权 the leasehold of real estate
25. 债权 creditor's rights, obligatory right
26. 债务 debt, liability
27. 合意性 desirability, acceptability, consensual will
28. 意思自治 autonomy of will, party autonomy, meaning autonomous, autonomy
29. 债权的物权化 creditor's right legalized as real right.
30. 善意谈判 bargain in good faith
31. 行使权力 execution of power, exercise of rights
32. 公用事业 public utilities
33. 尚未出台的电信法 prospective telecom law
34. 地役权 easement, right of way, servitude
35. 物权法定原则 Numerus Clauses Principle

第 11 章
Chapter 11

电信设施共享
Telecom Infrastructure Sharing

[如果任由所有运营商各自建立基础设施网络，则会造成重复投资、资源闲置和市容破坏。电信设施共享要解决的问题是如何确立电信资源的强制使用权，以增加竞争；尤其在特殊地段，由于自然环境的限制，只能允许建设一个电信设备（如在地势较为狭窄的区域只能建设一个铁塔），如何将有限的电信设备对竞争的限制降到最小。] [克服物的有限性对竞争的限制的有效方法，就是建立物的国家专有或者国家严格监管的物的私人所有制度，以及在此之上的强制性物的出租制度，租价受到政府管制。] [这类似于，机场、火电网、铁路独家所有，各个航空公司、发电厂、铁路运营公司可以租赁这些"有限物"开展运营竞争，租价受到政府严格规制。对于电信基础设施共享问题，法律可以确立一种制度，由一家运营商获得电信设施的建设权，以及建成后的电信设施所有权，其他运

批注：If all operators are allowed to construct infrastructure network by themselves, then the result would be overlapping investment, resource idle, destroying city appearance. The aim of telecom infrastructure sharing is to solve the problem of how to establish the enforced usufruct right for telecom infrastructure, so as to facilitate competition; especially at the extraordinary place where could support only one telecom construction on account of geographic constrain, for example only one telecom tower could be erected at the geographic narrow place, how to minimize the impact of limited telecom infrastructure to telecom competition?

批注：The effective method of overcoming the restriction from resource limitation on competition, is on establish the system of state owning exclusively or private owning under the strict supervision of government, as well as on the base thereof, enforced resource leasehold system, by which government controlling the rent price.

营商有权以受规制的价格共享该电信设施的使用权（强制租赁权）。]

1. 概念

[电信设施共享制度是指电信运营商对其控制的用于支撑电信业务的电信基础设施，允许竞争对手以基于成本的价格按照非歧视的条款与条件，共同使用其中的部分或全部电信基础设施。需要共享的电信基础设施一般包括：电信管道、涵洞、电缆井、铁塔、电线杆、天线、建筑物及其附属设施、安置电信设备或设施的空间、陆地或海底光缆及其使用权等[1]。]

[电信基础设施共建共享，具有以下四个特征：（1）共建共享责任的承担者为从事基础电信业务的电信运营商；（2）共建共享物为支撑电信业务的电信基础设施，如用户接入设施等；（3）设施的共享费用，须是基于成本的价格；（4）共建共享的非歧视性，即提供电信基础设施共享的运营商，应平等对待所有提出共享要求的电信运营商，其子公司、控股公司、附属公司或其他关联机构在设施共享方面所享受的待遇，不能优于其他无关联关系的电信运营商所享受的待遇[2]。]

[电信设施共享与接入的区别在于，前者共享的标的不包括电信网络本身，只是网络的附属设施，而接入专指共享

批注：This is similar to the system, by which airport, power grid and railway are owed excessively, and every airline company, power plant and railway operation company have the right to lease these limited resource to conduct operation competition on the price regulated strictly by the government. As for the telecom infrastructure sharing, a system could be established, in which one operator is granted the telecom infrastructure constructing right and the ownership of the infrastructure when finished, other operators have the right to share its usufruct right, namely enforced leasehold right, at the regulated price.

批注：Telecom infrastructure sharing system refers to that, telecom operator allows its competitors to share a portion of or all of its infrastructure supporting telecom business, on the price based on its cost in the terms and condition of indiscrimination. Generally, the system requires the following infrastructure to be shared: telecom duce, tunnel, well, tower, pole ,antenna, construction and its attachment, space for installing telecom equipment or facilities, land or submarine optical fiber cable and its usufruct right etc.

批注：Telecom infrastructure co-building and sharing system possesses the four features:

(1) the undertakers of co-building and sharing responsibility are telecom operators engaging in basic telecom business;

(2) the infrastructure to be co-built or shared is the supporting telecom business, such as customer's access facilities;

(3) the price for sharing infrastructure should be on the base of cost;

(4) the indiscrimination requirement in co-building and sharing, refers to that, the operator, whose infrastructure would be

---

[1] 白永忠.新加坡电信基础设施共享制度简介.中华全国律师协会信息网络与高新技术委员会.信息网络与高新技术法律前沿——中华全国律师协会信息网络与高新技术专业委员会成立大会论文集[C], 2001: 6.
[2] 高照.推进电信基础设施共建共享政策的研究[D].北京：北京邮电大学经济管理学院，2010.

他人的电信网络。举一个简单的例子，如果共享的是电信管道，则属于电信设施共享；如果共享的是管道里面的光缆，则属于接入，因为共享者已经接入了网络所有人的电信网中了。有关驻地网问题（小区最后一千米），本质上属于接入问题，而非电信设施共享问题。]

2. 起因

电信设施共享的起因在于，电信基础设施建设投资成本较高，单一运营商无法完成全领域的投资建设，而已建成的网络利用率较低；同时，随着电信竞争的激烈化，电信竞争的内容逐步由网络覆盖范围、信号强度等向服务质量、业务形式转变，共建共享使得运营商可以把关注点放在拓展服务项目和业务创新方面。另外，在唯一地理通道地段，由于自然环境限制，只能允许建设一个电信设施，共享是引入多家运营商的前提。

[并非任何电信基础设施都应该被强制租用（共享），应当区分瓶颈设施和非瓶颈设施，只有瓶颈设施才有必要强制租用，以降低市场进入门槛。"但如果对非瓶颈设施也实行非绑定，基础建设将变为公共地建设"[3]。电信法并不干涉自愿共享电信设施，其重点是对于瓶颈设施，必须建立强制共享制度，即用益物权。][这些需要建立用益物权的设施应该具有地理环境的唯一性，或者对竞争构成实质影响且不适于重复建设，必要时，可以由政府建立强制租赁的网

shared, should treat equally to all operators applying for sharing, the same as its own subsidiaries, holding companies, affiliate companies or other related bodies, which could not gain more favor in sharing the infrastructure than other irrelative operators.

批注：The distinction between telecom infrastructure sharing and access is that, the former does not include the network itself, but attachment or subsidiary facilities thereof; on the other hand, the latter specifically refers to sharing others' network itself. For example, if sharing telecom pipe and duct, it belongs to telecom infrastructure sharing; if sharing the optical fiber inside the pipe or duct, it belongs to access, because the sharer has already accessed into the other's network. As for customer's premises network problem, also called "the last one kilometer problem", it belongs to access problem in essence, rather than telecom infrastructure sharing problem.

批注：Not every telecom infrastructure should be leased compulsorily (be shared), we should distinct bottleneck one and non-bottleneck one, and only bottleneck one is necessary to be leased compulsorily, so as to lower barriers to market entry. However, if we enforce the non-bottleneck infrastructure leased, that would become public construction. Telecom law does not interfere with sharing telecom infrastructure volunteered, but its emphasis should be bottleneck infrastructure, for which we should establish the enforced sharing system, i.e. usufruct right.

批注：Those infrastructure requiring to establish usufruct right system should possess the feature of unique geographic, or would cause substantia impact on competition and not suitable to reconstruct. If necessary, the government could establish the checklist to

---

[3] 温丹辉. 电信业的过度竞争、串谋与资源共享 [D]. 北京：北京邮电大学经济管理学院，2006.

络设施清单[4]。][这样做有一个风险，就是会影响电信设施建设者的投资热情和科技升级努力，正如美国1996年电信法的失败一样，鼓励共享势必削弱了建设者的竞争优势，这将挫败建设者的投资热情，使得无网可供共享。][政府需要平衡的就是共享费用（受规制的强制租金），既不能高到对共享申请者构成竞争障碍，也不能低到无人愿意建设电信设施。]

3. 形式

[电信设施共享的形式，从广义上说，包括转售、组建合资公司和以受规制的价格强制租赁。狭义的共享不包括转售，仅指组建合资公司和以受规制的价格强制租赁。转售之所以被排除于狭义的共享，是因为共享者并没有亲自使用"共享"设备提供电信服务，而是把被申请人提供的服务趸购了过来，包装后再次出售。狭义的共享，要求使用其他人的电信设备自己提供电信服务。][组建合资公司是比较简单的共享，双方或单方将电信设施作为出资投入到合资公司中，由合资公司再出租给各方使用，或者合资公司用其自己提供电信服务。]

4. 实例

[我国合资公司型电信设施共享的实例就是2014年7月18日挂牌成立的中国铁塔股份有限公司（俗称"铁塔公

批注：list all required enforced leased infrastructure.

批注：There is a risk of this method, it could weaken the telecom infrastructure constructor's investment enthusiasm and science and technology improvement efforts. Just like the failure of USA "Act of Telecommunications" (1996), to encourage sharing is bound to impair the constructor's advantage in competition, which would frustrate its investment passion and cause the result of no network to be shared.

批注：The government is needed to balance the price for sharing (regulated rent for enforced lease), which should not too high to become competition barrier for sharing applicant, and not too low to make nobody like to construct telecom infrastructure.

批注：The form of sharing telecom infrastructure, generally includes resale, establishing joint venture, and enforcing leasehold on regulated price. Narrowly the way of sharing does not include resale, and only refers to the latter two. The reason for resale being excluded from narrow meaning of sharing is that, the sharer does not use the shared infrastructure to provide service by itself, but only buy in wholesale the service from the respondent, then after repackaging, resale out. Sharing infrastructure, in narrow sense, means providing service by itself using the leased infrastructure.

批注：To set up a joint venture is an easy way to sharing infrastructure, in which way both parties or either party invest telecom infrastructure as contribution capital in the new company, and when the new company generated, the company would lease the infrastructure to either party, or use for supplying telecom service by itself.

---

[4] 张应中. 全球化背景下电信设施共用之政府监督与救济 [D]. 北京：中国政法大学，2005. 该论文提出了共用"电信设施"之认定与审验原则，即绝对必须共用、弹性共用、不得拒绝之共用、不得共用等诸情形。

司")[5],]它解决了电信行业重复建设的问题，避免了在相同或相近的地域内不同运营商都建设铁塔设施的现象；同时，铁塔的统一建设解决了运营商之间站址选择的难题，使得特殊地理位置的站址资源得到了充分的利用。它的共享模式为，收编现有存量铁塔，垄断新建铁塔业务，开展铁塔出租业务，需要使用铁塔设备的三大运营商必须向铁塔公司租赁。

批注：An example of the joint venture type of telecom infrastructure sharing of our country is China Tower co., LTD. (commonly known as Tower Company), established on 18th July, 2014.

5. 法律依据

[电信设施共享，属于《物权法》第一百一十七条规定的用益物权，"用益物权人对他人所有的不动产或者动产，依法享有占有、使用和收益的权利"，]是非所有人对他人之物所享有的占有、使用、收益的排他性的权利，这种权利保证了非所有权人有权使用他人的不动产或动产，因此，其实在他人之物上设定的使用权。然而，我国现有《物权法》仅规定了土地承包经营权、建设用地使用权、宅基地使用权、地役权、自然资源使用权（海域使用权、探矿权、采矿权、取水权和使用水域、滩涂从事养殖、捕捞的权利）等用益物权，而[根据"物权法定"的原则，没有法律规定就没有物权，我国现有《物权法》不包括电信设施的用益物权，这不能不说是我国立法上的缺陷。][电信设施的用益物权必须法定，除非电信法或物权法设定了此权利，其他下级法律规范，包括电信主管部门的部门规章都不能创设此权利、限制权利人的物权。][工业和信息化部、国务院国有资产监督管理委员会于2008年9月28日发布了《关于推

批注：Telecom infrastructure sharing belongs to usufruct right stipulated in Article 117 of "Property Law" of China, which is "A usufruct right holder shall enjoy the right to possess, use and seek proceeds from the real property or movable property owned by someone else according to legal provisions."

批注：According to Numerus Clausus Principle, usufruct right could not be generated without law establishment. "Property Law" of China does not include usufruct right of telecom infrastructure, we cannot help to say, it is one of the defections of that law.

批注：The usufruct right of telecom infrastructure must be established by law, therefore, unless "Telecommunication Law" or "Property Law" has established that right, all the lower level rules, including regulations of administrative organ in charge of telecom, have no power to create that right and constrain others' real right.

---

[5] 2014年7月18日，中国铁塔股份有限公司（俗称为"铁塔公司"）正式挂牌成立。铁塔公司由中国移动通信有限公司、中国电信股份有限公司和中国联合网络通信有限公司共同出资设立，三大运营商各持有40.0%、30.1%和29.9%的股权。公司成立之初名为中国通信设施服务股份有限公司，公司注册资本100亿元人民币，经营范围包括：通信铁塔建设、维护、运营；铁塔附属基站机房、电源、空调配套设施的建设维护、室分系统的运维及基站设备的维护。2014年9月11日，中国通信设施服务股份有限公司进行了工商变更登记手续，正式更名为"中国铁塔股份有限公司"。来源于《中国通信设施服务公司正式更名》，中国新闻网，网址http://finance.chinanews.com/cj/2014/09-12/6585040.shtml。

进电信基础设施共建共享的紧急通知》，这个规定只能针对国企，对民营企业的电信设施无约束力。由于部门规章无权设定用益物权，其限制他人电信设施的物权是无效的，换句话说，除非获得了法律授权，工信部的部门规章是无权设立电信设施的强制租赁权（共享使用权）的。]

[我国《电信条例》第五十一条规定了管道共享的机制，从事电信线路建设，需要使用已建电信管道的，应当与已建电信线路的产权人协商，并签订协议；经协商不能达成协议的，根据不同情况，由国务院信息产业主管部门或者省、自治区、直辖市电信管理机构协调解决。]

建立电信设施共享制度最直接的依据是，在我国电信设施共建共享主要包括几方面内容。第一，已有铁塔、杆路必须共享。第二，新建铁塔、杆路必须共建。拟新建铁塔、杆路的基础电信企业必须告知其他基础电信企业，实施共享或共建。其他基础电信企业未在规定期限内提出共建需求的，三年内不得在同地点、同路由新建。第三，其他基站设施和传输线路具备条件的应共建共享。第四，禁止租用第三方设施时签订排他性协议。

[美国电信法第259条（SEC259）规定了电信基础设施的共享，要求"在位本地网运营商"（ILEC）向申请人根据公平合理的条款和条件开放公共交换网络基础设施、技术、信息和通信设备和功能，并提供信息服务接入。美国《电信法》SEC. 224. [47 U.S.C. 224]规定了水、

批注：The Ministry of Industry and Information and the State Owned Assets Supervision and Administration Committee of State Council, jointly enacted "the urgent notification concerning of boosting telecom infrastructure co-building and sharing" on 28 November, 2008, which only constrains government owned enterprise, without binding for private enterprise. Because department regulations have no power to establish usufruct right, their constraints to the real right of others' telecom infrastructure are invalid. In other words, unless obtaining the authorization from laws, the regulations of Ministry of Industry and Information have no power to create enforced leasehold right (sharing usufruct right) of telecom infrastructure.

批注：The Telecommunication Regulations of China Article 51 stipulates the mechanism of duct sharing, that is, in the process of telecom construction, when existing duct is needed, the constructor should negotiate with the owner thereof and reach agreement. In case of not reaching consent after a fixed period, depending on different situations, the information administrative agency of state council or the telecom regulation agency of province, autonomous region, municipality is in charge of coordination and settlement.

批注：Act of Telecommunications of USA SEC. 259 stipulates the telecom infrastructure's sharing, which "require incumbent local exchange carriers (as defined in section 251(h)) to make available to any qualifying carrier such public switched network infrastructure, technology, information, and telecommunications facilities and functions as may be requested by such qualifying carrier for the purpose of enabling such qualifying carrier to provide telecommunications services, or to provide access to information services, in the service area in which such qualifying carrier has requested and obtained designation as an eligible telecommunications

电、气等公共市政设施和电杆、管道、路权等电信附属设施的共享,其中224(f)(1)规定,"公用事业公司,包括本地电话公司,必须向有线电视系统或电信运营商无歧视地提供其所有或控制的对杆、路由、信道、路权的接入(共享)。"]

carrier under section 214(e). "

  Act of Telecommunications of USA SEC. 224 stipulates the utilities sharing, including water, power, gas, etc., and telecom attachment sharing, including pole, duce, right of way. Sec. 224(f)(1) stipulates, "A utility shall provide a cable television system or any telecommunications carrier with nondiscriminatory access to any pole, duct, conduit, or right-of-way owned or controlled by it."

Act of Telecommunications of USA SEC. 259. [47 U.S.C. 259] INFRASTRUCTURE SHARING.

(a) Regulations Required.--The Commission shall prescribe, within one year after the date of enactment of the Telecommunications Act of 1996, regulations that require incumbent local exchange carriers (as defined in section 251(h)) to make available to any qualifying carrier such public switched network infrastructure, technology, information, and telecommunications facilities and functions as may be requested by such qualifying carrier for the purpose of enabling such qualifying carrier to provide telecommunications services, or to provide access to information services, in the service area in which such qualifying carrier has requested and obtained designation as an eligible telecommunications carrier under section 214(e).

(b) Terms and Conditions of Regulations.--The regulations prescribed by the Commission pursuant to this section shall--

(1) not require a local exchange carrier to which this section applies to take any action that is economically unreasonable or that is contrary to the public interest;

(2) permit, but shall not require, the joint ownership or operation of public switched network infrastructure and services by or among such local exchange carrier and a qualifying carrier;

(3) ensure that such local exchange carrier will not be treated by the Commission or any State as a common carrier for hire or as offering common carrier services with respect to any infrastructure, technology, information, facilities, or functions made available to a qualifying carrier in accordance with regulations issued pursuant to this section;

(4) ensure that such local exchange carrier makes such infrastructure, technology, information, facilities, or functions available to a qualifying carrier on just and reasonable terms and conditions that permit such qualifying carrier to fully benefit from the economies of scale and scope of such local exchange carrier, as determined in accordance with guidelines prescribed by the Commission in regulations issued pursuant to this section;

(5) establish conditions that promote cooperation between local exchange carriers to which this section applies and qualifying carriers;

(6) not require a local exchange carrier to which this section applies to engage in any infrastructure sharing agreement for any services or access which are to be provided or offered to consumers by the qualifying carrier in such local exchange carrier's telephone exchange area; and

(7) require that such local exchange carrier file with the Commission or State for public inspection, any tariffs, contracts, or other arrangements showing the rates, terms, and conditions under which such carrier is making available public switched network infrastructure and functions under this section.

(c) Information Concerning Deployment of New Services and Equipment.--A local exchange carrier to which this section applies that has entered into an infrastructure sharing agreement under this section shall provide to each party to such agreement timely information on the planned deployment of telecommunications *services and equipment, including any software or upgrades of software integral to the use or operation of such telecommunications equipment.*

(d) Definition.--For purposes of this section, the term "qualifying carrier" means a telecommunications carrier that--

(1) lacks economies of scale or scope, as determined in accordance with regulations prescribed by the Commission pursuant to this section; and

(2) offers telephone exchange service, exchange access, and any other service that is included in universal service, to all consumers without preference throughout the service area for which such carrier has been designated as an eligible telecommunications carrier under section 214(e).

SEC. 224. [47 U.S.C. 224] REGULATION OF POLE ATTACHMENTS.

(a) As used in this section:

(1) The term "utility" means any person who is a local exchange carrier or an electric, gas, water, steam, or other public utility, and who owns or controls poles, ducts, conduits, or rights-of-way used, in whole or in part, for any wire communications. Such term does not include any railroad, any person who is cooperatively organized, or any person owned by the Federal Government or any State.

(2) The term "Federal Government" means the Government of the United States or any agency or instrumentality thereof.

(3) The term "State" means any State, territory, or possession of the United States, the District of Columbia, or any political subdivision, agency, or instrumentality thereof.

(4) The term "pole attachment" means any attachment by a cable television system or provider of telecommunications service to a pole, duct, conduit, or right-of-way owned or controlled by a utility.

(5) For purposes of this section, the term "telecommunications carrier" (as defined in section 3 of this Act) does not include any incumbent local exchange carrier as defined in section 251(h).

(b) (1) Subject to the provisions of subsection (c) of this section, the Commission shall regulate the rates, terms, and conditions for pole attachments to provide that such rates, terms, and conditions are just and reasonable, and shall adopt procedures necessary and appropriate to hear and resolve complaints concerning such rates, terms, and conditions. For purposes of enforcing any determinations resulting from complaint procedures established pursuant to this subsection, the Commission shall take such action as it deems appropriate and necessary, including issuing cease and desist orders, as authorized by section 312(b) of title III of the Communications Act of 1934, as amended.

(2) The Commission shall prescribe by rule regulations to carry out the provisions of this section.

(c) (1) Nothing in this section shall be construed to apply to, or to give the Commission jurisdiction with respect to rates, terms, and conditions, or access to poles, ducts, conduits, and rights-of-way as provided in subsection (f), for pole attachments in any case where such matters are regulated by a State.

(2) Each State which regulates the rates, terms, and conditions for pole attachments shall certify to the Commission that--

(A) it regulates such rates, terms, and conditions; and

(B) in so regulating such rates, terms, and conditions, the State has the authority to consider and does consider the interests of the subscribers of the services offered via such attachments, as well as the interests of the consumers of the utility services.

(3) For purposes of this subsection, a State shall not be considered to regulate the rates, terms, and conditions for pole attachments--

(A) unless the State has issued and made effective rules and regulations implementing the State's regulatory authority over pole attachments; and

(B) with respect to any individual matter, unless the State takes final action on a complaint regarding such matter--

(i) within 180 days after the complaint is filed with the State, or

(ii) within the applicable period prescribed for such final action in such rules and regulations of the State, if the prescribed period does not extend beyond 360 days after the filing of such complaint.

(d) (1) For purposes of subsection (b) of this section, a rate is just and reasonable if it assures a utility the recovery of not less than the additional costs of providing pole attachments, nor more than an amount determined by multiplying the percentage of the total usable space, or the percentage of the total duct or conduit capacity, which is occupied by the pole attachment by the sum of the operating expenses and actual capital costs of the utility attributable to the entire pole, duct, conduit, or right-of-way.

(2) As used in this subsection, the term "usable space" means the space above the minimum grade level which can be used for the attachment of wires, cables, and associated equipment.

(3) This subsection shall apply to the rate for any pole attachment used by a cable television system solely to provide cable service. Until the effective date of the regulations required under subsection (e), this subsection shall also apply to the rate for any pole attachment used by a cable system or any telecommunications carrier (to the extent such carrier is not a party to a pole attachment agreement) to provide any telecommunications service.

(e) (1) The Commission shall, no later than 2 years after the date of enactment of the Telecommunications Act of 1996, prescribe regulations in accordance with this subsection to govern the charges for pole attachments used by telecommunications carriers to provide telecommunications services, when the parties fail to resolve a dispute over such charges. Such regulations shall ensure that a utility charges just, reasonable, and nondiscriminatory rates for pole attachments.

(2) A utility shall apportion the cost of providing space on a pole, duct, conduit, or right-of-way other than the usable space among entities so that such apportionment equals two-thirds of the costs of providing space other than the usable space that would be allocated to such entity under an equal apportionment of such costs among all attaching entities.

(3) A utility shall apportion the cost of providing usable space among all entities according to the percentage of usable space required for each entity.

(4) The regulations required under paragraph (1) shall become effective 5 years after the date of enactment of the Telecommunications Act of 1996. Any increase in the rates for pole attachments that result from the adoption of the regulations required by this subsection shall be phased in equal annual increments over a period of 5 years beginning on the effective date of such regulations.

(f)(1) A utility shall provide a cable television system or any telecommunications carrier with nondiscriminatory access to any pole, duct, conduit, or right-of-way owned or controlled by it.

(2) Notwithstanding paragraph (1), a utility providing electric service may deny a cable television system or any telecommunications carrier access to its poles, ducts, conduits, or rights-of-way, on a non-discriminatory basis where there is insufficient capacity and for reasons of safety, reliability and generally applicable engineering purposes.

(g) A utility that engages in the provision of telecommunications services or cable services shall impute to its costs of providing such services (and charge any affiliate, subsidiary, or associate company engaged in the provision of such services) an equal amount to the pole attachment rate for which such company would be liable under this section.

(h) Whenever the owner of a pole, duct, conduit, or right-of-way intends to modify or alter such pole, duct, conduit, or right-of-way, the owner shall provide written notification of such action to any entity that has obtained an attachment to such conduit or right-of-way so that such entity may have a reasonable opportunity to add to or modify its existing attachment. Any entity that adds to or modifies its existing attachment after receiving such notification shall bear a proportionate share of the costs incurred by the owner in making such pole, duct, conduit, or right-of-way accessible.

(i) An entity that obtains an attachment to a pole, conduit, or right-of-way shall not be required to bear any of the costs of rearranging or replacing its attachment, if such rearrangement or replacement is required as a result of an additional attachment or the modification of an existing attachment sought by any other entity (including the owner of such pole, duct, conduit, or right-of-way).

[欧盟《关于电子通信网及业务的共同管制框架（框架指令，Directive 2002/21/EC）》第 12 条规定，国内管制当局应该鼓励电信设施或地产的共享，成员国可以要求运营电子通信网的企业共享设施或地产（包括物理共址），共享协调安排包括按比例分摊设施成本。]

批注：EU "Framework Directive"(Directive 2002/21/EC) Article 12 stipulates Co-location and facility sharing, "Where an undertaking providing electronic communications networks has the right under national legislation to install facilities on, over or under public or private property, or may take advantage of a procedure for the expropriation or use of property, national regulatory authorities shall encourage the sharing of such facilities or property."

《on a common regulatory framework for electronic communications networks and services (Framework Directive)》（Directive 2002/21/EC）Article 12 Co-location and facility sharing

(1) Where an undertaking providing electronic communications networks has the right under national legislation to install facilities on, over or under public or private property, or may take advantage of a procedure for the expropriation or use of property, national regulatory authorities shall encourage the sharing of such facilities or property.

(2) In particular where undertakings are deprived of access to viable alternatives because of the need to protect the environment, public health, public security or to meet town and country planning objectives, Member States may impose the sharing of facilities or property (including physical co-location) on an undertaking operating an electronic communications network or take measures to facilitate the coordination of public works only after an appropriate period of public consultation during which all interested parties must be given an opportunity to express their views. Such sharing or coordination arrangements may include rules for apportioning the costs of facility or property sharing.

生词和词组

第十一章

1. 重复投资　overlapping investment
2. 资源闲置　resources idle, resource slack
3. 市容破坏　destroy city appearance, damage city amenity
4. 电网　power grid
5. 海底光缆　submarine optical fiber cable, undersea lightwave cable
6. 子公司　subsidiary company
7. 全资子公司　Wholly-owned subsidiaries
8. 租金　rent
9. 分公司，附属公司　affiliate
10. 控股公司　holding company, parent company, controlling company
11. 共享者　sharer
12. 驻地网　premises network
13. 降低市场准入门槛　lower barriers to market entry
14. 投资热情　investment enthusiasm, investment passion
15. 出资　contributive, contribution of capital
16. 物权法定　Numerus Clauses Principle
17. 民营企业　private enterprise, civilian-run enterprise
18. 无约束力　without binding for
19. 部门规章　regulation, departmental rules
20. 无效的　invalid, non-effective, void
21. 获得了法律授权　get legal authorization
22. 协调解决　coordinately solve, coordination and settlement